RECONSTRUCTING EDUCATION

International Educational Studies
General Editor: Dieter Lenzen

RECONSTRUCTING EDUCATION

East German Schools and Universities after Unification

Rosalind M.O. Pritchard

Berghahn Books
NEW YORK • OXFORD

Published in 1999 by
Berghahn Books

Editorial offices:
55 John Street, 3rd Floor, New York, NY 10038 USA
3, NewTec Place, Magdalen Road, Oxford, OX4 1RE, UK

Library of Congress Cataloging-in-Publication Data

Pritchard, Rosalind M. O.
    Reconstructing education : East German schools and universities after
unification / Rosalind Pritchard.
        p.   cm.
    Includes bibliographical references and index.
    ISBN 1-57181-954-1 (alk. paper)
    1. Education–Germany (East)   2. School management and
organization–Germany (East)   3. Education, Higher–Germany
(East)   4. Education, Higher–Germany (East)–Administration.
5. Education–Germany.   6. School management and organization–
Germany.   7. Education, Higher–Germany.   8. Education, Higher–
Germany–Administration.   I. Title.
LA772.P74   1998
370'.943'1–DC21   98-7436
                                                          CIP

British Library Cataloguing in Publication Data
A catalogue record for this book is available from
the British Library.

Printed in the United States on acid-free paper

Dieses Baumes Blatt, der von Osten
Meinem Garten anvertraut,
Gibt geheimen Sinn zu kosten,
Wie's den Wissenden erbaut.

Ist es *ein* lebendig Wesen,
Das sich in sich selbst getrennt?
Sind es zwei, die sich erlesen,
Daß man sie als *eines* kennt?

Solche Frage zu erwidern,
Fand ich wohl den rechten Sinn;
Fühlst du nicht an meinen Liedern,
Daß ich *eins* und doppelt bin.

— *Goethe*

CONTENTS

Contents

LIST OF TABLES

ACKNOWLEDGEMENTS

I n one way, the Federal Republic of Germany is a difficult country in which to conduct research; in another way it is easy. 'Difficult' because its federal structure results in diversity, and new facts have to be learned about each Bundesland. 'Easy' because of the warmth and helpfulness of its people. I am deeply grateful to those who befriended me by taking me into their homes: Hans-Ulrich Boas, Luise Dumrese, Renate Eichhorn, Andreas Eras, Christa Händle, Wolfgang Hörner, Burkhard Jung, Ruth Kundra, Birgit Mett, Christine Seyfarth and their spouses. A special thank you also to Friedrich Busch, Cornelia Condren, Roland Degen, Götz Doyé, Erich Geißler, Ulrich Heublein, Jan Hofmann, Adolf Kell, Friedrich Kuebart, Detlev Müller, Herbert Ochel, Christoph Scheilke, Klaus Schnitzer, Dorit Stenke, Rupert von Stülpnagel, Dietmar Waterkamp, Horst Weishaupt and Peter Zedler.

Without institutional support, the book could never have been completed. I acknowledge with gratitude a grant, number R000221395, from the Economic and Social Research Fund on the basis of which most of the research was carried out. I would like also to thank the German Academic Exchange Service for a grant which enabled me to deepen the research for chapter 4. Jürgen Baumert of the Max-Planck-Institut für Bildungsforschung (MPI) took an interest in the work, allowing me to study in the MPI library and doing everything he could to smooth my path. I am grateful to him, and to the MPI scholars and library staff. Hans Döbert of the Deutsches Institut für Internationale Pädagogische Forschung (DIPF) was consistently supportive, and opened the resources of the DIPF library to me. I would like to thank my friend Eberhard Jobst of the Bundesministerium für Bildung, Wissenschaft, Forschung und Technologie in Bonn for all his help and encouragement.

The following people who are experts in their fields have read some or all of the book: Gertraude Buck Bechler, Ian Connor, Ulrich Degen, John Field, Dietlind Fischer, Christa Händle, Heidrun Jahn, Jan Olbertz, Wolfgang

Mönikes, Kai Schnabel, Karen Schober and Heinrich Tüffers. Any mistakes or misinterpretations are of course my fault and not theirs, and I am deeply indebted to them for their help.

Last, but not least, I would like to thank my own University, especially in the person of Harry McMahon, Head of the School of Education, for using good auspices to facilitate completion of this book.

PREFACE

Personal Background to the Study

In 1993, I received a letter from the German Academic Exchange Service (DAAD) listing a number of short-term appointments for lecturers from abroad to assist in the reconstruction of education in the New Bundesländer after the fall of the Wall. One particular assignment seemed to match my interests and expertise so perfectly that I offered my services as a temporary lecturer. The Pädagogische Hochschule (College of Education) in Erfurt needed a modern language methodologist to work with its mature students who were learning English. Most of them had formerly been teachers of Russian and were retraining in the hope of being able to keep their jobs.

In the course of my stay in the beautiful city of Erfurt, I garnered many impressions – some aesthetic, some political and some human. My first view of Erfurt's famous Cathedral Square was on a snowy, starry night during a candlelit demonstration against racism. When it was finished, the demonstrators left their lighted candles on the steps leading up to the cathedral – a fiery plea rising up in the dark air. They carefully cleared away the wax next day, and some of them told me how good it felt to be able to demonstrate without fear of reprisals by the secret police. Though not all the demonstrators were churchgoers, I subsequently learned how the churches had suffered under socialism, and how important church music had been in maintaining a public profile and asserting protest of a sort.

My in-service students numbered 150, all but five of whom were women. They worked immensely hard. They taught during the day, studied during the night, travelled quite long distances to reach the Pädagogische Hochschule, and of course performed all the normal domestic duties such as looking after their families and homes. It seemed obvious that working women carried a particularly heavy burden during this post-unification period. Some of them invited me into their homes, and told me that in GDR times it would have taken days if not weeks of trouble and planning to put a comparable spread on the table. Yet although I knew that Thuringia has its own excellent, distinctive sausage and meat products, not much local produce was served. By then, shops were mostly in West German hands and had fixed contracts with suppliers from distant countries. At that time, even the Erfurters disdained their own produce and thought 'West was Best'. Though this was later to change, it seemed that the Easterners were going through a stage of self-rejection, both gastronomically and in some other respects.

It was clear from the Erfurt experience and from subsequent visits to other parts of East Germany that many Easterners felt vulnerable and insecure about the changes. They existed against a background of a great historical tradition which gave them a legacy of culture and beauty. Many of them were genuinely proud of their achievements under socialism. Yet these achievements seemed almost to be discounted in the new Germany, and some older people who had experienced Nazi rule, post-war Russian hegemony and now the accession to West Germany were bitter, confused or resigned – sometimes all three by turns.

INTRODUCTION

The Conduct of the Research

The question of how the unification of the two Germanys took place was one which I chose to address not just personally but also professionally in my particular sphere: education. Between March 1995 and June 1997, six research trips were undertaken in the course of which interviews were conducted in Bonn, Bochum, Münster, Hanover and in all the New Bundesländer, supplemented by a number of non-participant school observation sessions. The interviews and observation sessions, which numbered 141, were spread across universities, schools, Protestant and Catholic church authorities, the Federal Ministry of Education, Higher Education, Research and Technology in Bonn and Ministries of School and Higher Education in East Germany. The last two research trips were less intensively interview oriented so as to facilitate a deeper study of the scholarly literature. The Max Planck Institute in Berlin was particularly helpful in putting its library facilities at the service of the researcher.

The work is clearly qualitative rather than quantitative in nature. In a sense, it is a contemporary history of selected aspects of East German education after unification, as seen through the eyes of an outsider. Although it is angled predominantly towards schools, the text includes a substantial chapter on higher education with a particular interest in its significance for the teaching profession. Since space is limited in a book of this kind, there have been some deliberate exclusions, for example, pre-school education, distance education, further/continuing education and the education of the handicapped. Criteria applied to the evaluation of the reforms of East German education include the following:

- Their viability
- Their public acceptability and popularity
- Their potential for increasing freedom

- Their impact on women (in the spheres of teacher training and vocational education)
- Their possible impact on educational effectiveness

In terms of the historical development of East German education after the fall of the Wall, the period from 1995 to 1997 seemed the optimum one in which to undertake research. It was sufficiently removed from the turbulence of the Wende for the new laws and procedures to have been put in place, but not so distant from the German Democratic Republic for Easterners to have forgotten how things used to be. So far, researchers from the West have had limited access to empirical data bearing on everyday life in the former GDR schools and society. Consequently, formal decrees and organisational structures have received considerable attention, and rightly so since they are the bones of the education system – indeed, they receive due attention in the present volume. In addition, the interviews inform the research throughout. Mostly, this influence is implicit rather than explicit, but from time to time an occasional case study, exemplar of a happening, or description of an institution is included in the hope of giving a human feel to the book. This creates a perspective 'from below' which complements the emphasis on structures introduced 'from above'. It is recognised, however, that case studies can never be more than illustrative, and every attempt has therefore been made to frame each case study with concrete research findings that permit the reader to place the particular in a more general context.

The Structure of the Book

During the period of the division of Germany, the two parts of the country developed in different political directions. East Germany took 'equality' as its supreme guiding principle, and West Germany took 'freedom'. Of course, neither part of Germany was totally successful in living up to these great ideals, but they were the inspiration behind much law-making and institution-building. To understand the reform of the East German education system, it is necessary to ask what happened to eastern equality when the Wende came about, and what western freedom came to mean for the Easterners. In essence, the whole book is directed at exploring answers to these cardinal questions in the education sector. It will examine what, if anything, survived of GDR values and structures; what, if anything, deserved to survive from GDR days but did not; what Western institutions were introduced into the East and how they fared in a different education ecology. In cases where Western institutions appear to have been replicated in the East, the attempt to assess the success of the West German reforms will of necessity sometimes involve a critique of existing West German institutions.

The book demonstrates a recurring rhythmic pattern in the structure of its non-introductory material (from chapter 2 onwards). Initially, the situation in the former GDR is presented reasonably succinctly; it is followed by a description of the changes after unification and an attempt at some personal assessment of those changes. The rationale for structure of the various chapters is as follows:

CHAPTER 1: 'THE FALL OF THE WALL'. Education is a *politicum*, and needs to be seen in a macropolitical context. An aim of chapter 1 is to sketch that political context by describing the relationship between the two Germanys prior to unification, and to depict the German Democratic Republic's struggle for status and identity. The more rapidly the process of integration was introduced after the fall of the Wall, the less likely it was that time could be devoted to analysing East German institutions and working out what should be carried over into a united Germany. Chapter 1 therefore addresses the question of whether speed was really politically necessary in implementing unification, and if so, why. It outlines the legal basis for unification with special reference to education and ends with a discussion of how Easterners, particularly young people, felt in the early days of the Wende.

CHAPTER 2: 'REFORMING THE SCHOOL STRUCTURES'. In the GDR, equality had been interpreted as 'sameness'. After the Wende, the new rhetoric of 'freedom' implied freedom to be different. This was reflected in the introduction of a differentiated school system into East Germany at post-primary level. Chapter 2 gives a flavour of the debate among Easterners during the extraordinarily creative period between the fall of the Wall in autumn 1989 and the legal formalisation of unification in 1990. It describes how new schools were set up and how the differentiated structure soon came into a relationship of tension with demographic trends, and it gives examples of efforts to cope with this tension.

CHAPTER 3: 'SCHOOL LIFE AND LEARNING'. In a way, this chapter is the most down-to-earth in the whole book, but without it there would be a serious gap for anyone who really cares about education. Whereas chapter 2 deals with formal external structures of a 'freer' education system, chapter 3 sets out to look inside the schools and investigate the potential of internal reforms for promoting freedom in the minds and hearts of pupils and teachers. It addresses such issues as teaching materials, curriculum, syllabus and methodology, how these were devised and how they have gone down with those who use them. Since East German children's lives have been profoundly influenced by changes in the broader society, it also looks briefly at the youth policy of the federal government.

CHAPTER 4: 'RELIGIOUS EDUCATION, CHURCH SCHOOLS AND ETHICS'. Freedom is not an empty value. It is *about* something and needs a positive content if it is to be personally liberating and fulfilling. The discrediting of

Marxism-Leninism has for many New Bundesländer citizens left a moral deficit which cannot be easily filled because the new, democratic society is pluralistic and therefore does not espouse any single values system. Even if it did, the imposition of such a system would be undemocratic. In Western society, churches are an important repository of moral values, and chapter 4 thus examines some of the new approaches to Religious Education in the New Bundesländer where there is little mandate for Christianity. The role of the churches under socialism and their influence on young GDR people is analysed. The legal possibilities for church schools and Religious Education after the fall of the Wall are explored, and the use which the churches have made of them is discussed. Special attention is devoted to Ethics and to the endeavours in Brandenburg to find a form of moral education which will be acceptable in a largely atheist or agnostic society. The legal difficulties which this might cause and the conflict between Church and state are highlighted.

CHAPTER 5: 'TRAINING FOR THE WORLD OF WORK'. Economic forces exert strong mechanisms of control over freedom. In a society like the former GDR where people had been accustomed to state support from the cradle to the grave, the power of market forces and privatisation can be debilitating rather than invigorating. Chapter 5 examines the transfer of the West German Dual System to the inclement environment of East Germany where there is now so much unemployment that it is becoming difficult to find employers who will undertake the responsibility of training apprentices.

CHAPTER 6 'RENEWING THE TEACHING PROFESSION'. It is the teachers who must introduce the new freedoms in schools, yet the paradox of educational reform in the New Bundesländer is that the majority of existing teachers were trained and socialised under the GDR regime, and are likely to have internalised some of its norms. It is therefore important to evaluate the attempts made to restructure higher education and the teaching profession, and to 'cleanse' them of socialist influence. Chapter 6 examines different models of teacher training, both in the former GDR and in West Germany, and shows how teachers are being socialised into the new Germany, for example by learning to apply the law to specific circumstances. It ends by considering university lecturers', students' and teachers' reactions to change, and the extent to which the reforms have been successful.

CHAPTER 7: 'IN RETROSPECT'. This final section distils the findings of the previous chapters and attempts to relate them back to the initial questions: Was it necessary to introduce the reforms so quickly? What have been their most and least successful aspects? Why? What has been lost and what has been gained? What could or should have been done differently? How have freedom and equality fared in East German education? Does the reform of East German education have any implications for West Germany?

LIST OF ABBREVIATIONS

ABM	Arbeitsbeschaffungsmaßnahme
ABS	Außerbetriebliche Ausbildungsstätte
ADW	Akademie der Wissenschaften
AFM	Arbeitsförderungsmaßnahme
APR	Age Participation Rate
APW	Akademie der Pädagogischen Wissenschaften
AUT	Association of University Teachers
BAföG	Bundesausbildungsförderungsgesetz
BAK	Bundesarbeitskreis der Seminar- und Fachleiter/Innen
BB	Brandenburg
BBB	Berufsbildungsbericht
BBiG	Berufsbildungsgesetz
BFSFJ	Bundesministerium für Familie, Senioren, Frauen und Jugend
BLK	Bund-Länder-Kommission
BMBW	Bundesministerium für Bildung und Wissenschaft
BMFT/BWFT	Bundesministerium für Bildung, Wissenschaft, Forschung und Technologie (also abbreviated as BWFT)
BRD	Bundesrepublik Deutschland
CDU/CSU	Christlich-Demokratische Union/Christlich-Soziale Union
COMECON/ CMEA	Council for Mutual Economic Assistance (also referred to as CMEA)
DAAD	Deutscher Akademischer Austauschdienst
DDR	Deutsche Demokratische Republik
DFD	Demokratischer Frauenbund Deutschlands
DHV	Deutscher Hochschulverband
DJI	Deutsches Jugendinstitut
DLZ	Deutsche Lehrerzeitung

DM	Deutsche Mark (Anglicised as 'Deutschmark' in text)
DPZI	Deutsches Pädagogisches Zentralinstitut
DSF	Deutsch-Sowjetische Freundschaft
DSW	Deutsches Studentenwerk
DVV	Deutsche Verwaltung für Volksbildung
EC	European Community
EKD	Evangelische Kirche in Deutschland
EKiBB	Evangelische Kirche in Brandenburg
EOS	Erweiterte Oberschule
EV	Einigungsvertrag
F	Female
FDGB	Freier Deutscher Gewerkschaftsbund
FDJ	Freie Deutsche Jugend
FDP	Freie Demokratische Partei
FHS	Fachhochschule
FRG	Federal Republic of Germany
G7	The Group of 7 Industrialised Nations
GATT	General Agreement on Tariffs and Trade
GBl	Gesetzblatt
GCSE	General Certificate of Secondary Education
GDP	Gross Domestic Product
GDR	German Democratic Republic
GEW	Gewerkschaft Erziehung und Wissenschaft
GG	Grundgesetz
GST	Gesellschaft für Sport und Technik
HE	Higher Education
HEI	Higher Education Institution
HEP	Hochschulerneuerungsprogramm
HIS	HochschulInformationsSystem
HRK	Hochschulrektorenkonferenz
HS	Hauptschule
HSK	Hochschulstrukturkommission
HSP	Hochschulsonderprogramm
IAB	Institut für Arbeitsmarkt- und Berufsforschung der Bundesanstalt für Arbeit
IfL	Institut für Lehrerbildung
IFS	Institut für Schulentwicklungsforschung
IMF	International Monetary Fund
KITA	Kindertagesstätten
KMK	Kultusministerkonferenz
KoKo	Commercial Coordination Agency
LER	Lebensgestaltung – Ethik – Religion(skunde)

M	Male
MBJS des	Ministerium für Bildung, Jugend und Sport (des Landes Brandenburg)
MfS	Ministerium für Staatssicherheit (Stasi)
ML	Marxism-Leninismus
MPI	Max-Planck-Institut
MV	Mecklenburg-Vorpommern
NATO	North Atlantic Treaty Organisation
NBL	New Bundesländer
OBL	Old Bundesländer
PDS	Partei des Demokratischen Sozialismus
PH	Pädagogische Hochschule
PLIB	Pädagogisches Landesinstitut Brandenburg
POS	Polytechnische Oberschule
R & D	Research and Development
RC	Roman Catholic
RE	Religious Education
S	Sachsen
SA	Sachsen-Anhalt
SED	Sozialistische Einheitspartei Deutschlands
SPD	Sozialdemokratische Partei Deutschlands
StuRA	StudentenRat
TC	Training Centre
TH	Thüringen
THA	Treuhand
ÜBS	Überbetriebliche Ausbildungsstätte
USSR	Union of Soviet Socialist Republics
WIP	Wissenschaftler-Integrations-Programm
WR	Wissenschaftsrat
ZIJ	Zentralinstitut für Jugendforschung
ZHB	Zentralinstitut für Hochschulbildung

⊁ *Chapter 1* **⊀**

THE FALL OF THE WALL

The Berlin Wall

The closing of the East-West border and the erection of the Berlin Wall began at midnight on 13 August 1961. By 8 A.M. that morning, Berliners were staring at each other over barricades. On the first anniversary of the event, the East German newspaper *Neues Deutschland* published the following retrospective commentary:

On 13 August one year ago, the eyes of the world were on Berlin. Everyone was aware that a far-reaching decision had been made. On that day, only a few people understood its real meaning. It signified no more and no less than the rescue of peace. Let us remember what had happened in the summer of last year. The Bonn extremists in their blind delusions of power believed that the time had come to drive strong-arm politics forward to their full conclusion and roll up the German Democratic Republic. On 11 July, the leadership of the Adenauer CDU met and proclaimed in a declaration of principle that the German question must be solved and that the 'Zone' should be integrated into NATO. They turned on the heat against our Republic to the fullest extent. They spared no expense and no criminality in attempts to confuse the citizens of the GDR and unleash panic among the weaker brethren.... They considered military provocations and eventually open attack.... [W]ar threatened. Then the government of the GDR in collaboration with the other states of the Warsaw Pact introduced the necessary measures on 13 August. In one move the course of a diabolical programme hatched by the extremists was interrupted. Peace was saved, not just for our Worker and Peasant State but also for the West Berliners, for the West Germans, perhaps even for the whole world. Now that one year has elapsed, we can state: the protective Wall which we erected against the aggressors has proved durable and has guaranteed the security of peace.... Our state is stable, strong, invincible.... The measures of 13 August have consolidated the prestige and the sovereignty of the GDR. Even the Western powers have to admit the fact that two German states exist and the frontier of the GDR cannot be altered. (*Neues Deutschland*, 13 August 1962)

Over the period of its existence, the Wall was constantly renewed and perfected, reinforced with watch towers, barbed wire, concrete, steel, searchlights, land mines, electric fences, defoliant, dogs, automatic guns, and electronic surveillance devices like video cameras. In some places it was only the height of a man, whereas in others it was 4.5 metres high (Peto, 1997). By the time it had reached its fourth stage of technical evolution, it was supposed to be almost invincible, and in 1989, Erich Honecker claimed that it was going to last for another hundred years. In fact, it lasted twenty-eight years in all. During this time it is estimated that 191 people were killed actually trying to cross the Wall, and 350 deaths occurred amongst people attempting to escape from East to West (*Micropaedia*, 1992; *The Times*, 17 September 1993:11). From 1949 to 1961, 2,738,566 people, many of them well-educated professional people and about half under twenty-five years of age, fled from the GDR and the eastern sector of Berlin (Rühle and Holzweißig, 1981:154). The erection of the Wall reduced but did not staunch the haemorrhage: between 13 August 1961 and 1987, there were an additional 214,971 refugees.

Jens Reich (1990), founder of the New Forum political movement, describes how he felt about living behind the Wall. His words form a vivid contrast to the *Neues Deutschland* quotation above:

> 'Wall-sickness' was the eternal, lamenting analysis of our life blighted and circumscribed by *Die Mauer*. It came from being in a cage in the centre of Europe. Wall-sickness was boredom. We felt condemned to utter, excruciating dullness, sealed off from everything that happened in the world around us. Wall-sickness was loneliness, the feeling that you were condemned to die without having seen Naples, or Venice, or Paris, or London. Wall-sickness was the anguish of deprivation of a whole generation born between 1930 and 1950. We knew that we had lost. (pp. 76–77)

Erich Honecker hedged his claim about the Wall lasting a hundred years with the caveat '… as long as the conditions prevail that led to its construction'. The rest of this chapter will be devoted to showing how and why those conditions changed, and will indicate what the changed scenario meant for education.

The Process of German Unification

After the partition of Germany and the foundation of the German Democratic Republic (GDR) on 7 October 1949, the rhetoric on *both* sides of the

Iron Curtain was that Germany should at some stage be reunified. East Germany was regarded even by the Soviet Union as a provisional entity, and did not have a firmly established role in the Soviet's foreign policy. The USSR feared a united Germany, yet at the same time held out the prospect of reunification in the hope that this might impede or slow up West Germany's integration into the Western alliance. The desire for German reunification was deeply embedded in the German psyche and its achievement was the fruit of decades of careful diplomacy on the part of West German governments. Great skill was needed in order to minimise alarm and opposition among the Federal Republic of Germany's (FRG) allies and to mitigate the political handicaps which it suffered: its aggression in two world wars had caused it to forfeit both its sovereignty and the trust of the international community. Moves towards unification therefore had to be made in a way which would not threaten West Germany's European partners. To do so would have been self-defeating – if trust were ever to be recovered, then caution and constant reassurance were imperative.

It was clear to the Federal Republic's politicians that they could not succeed in their long-term aim simply by cultivating a series of bilateral relationships. Even those nations which had been victorious in the Second World War worked through international agencies such as the IMF, GATT, G7, the World Bank, NATO and the European Community; supranational cooperation was in keeping with the spirit of the age and congenial to the United States. Germany made such cooperation serve her own special purposes: successful policies had to be multilateral rather than bilateral, and needed to be pursued within a European matrix. Germany could achieve its own goals only by being pro-European and by winning the support of its allies. The division of Germany was a facet of the division of Europe, and the integration of Germany was thus intimately related to that of Europe. There was an acute consciousness that nothing could be achieved by confrontation with the Soviet Union, for without Moscow's agreement it would be impossible to develop closer links with the German Democratic Republic.

Timothy Garton Ash in his book *In Europe's Name* (1993) analyses the diplomacy of German unification in terms of a global concept of systematic horizontal and vertical synchronisation. A change in one international relationship brought about changes in other relationships and the principle of balance between the various world powers was all important. At a horizontal level lay relationships between the Federal Republic, the German Democratic Republic, the East European states and the USSR. At a vertical level stood the relationships between the FRG, West European states and the United States. The horizontal and the vertical relationships interacted with each other with the result that change in one entrained change in the other.

At the horizontal level, Bonn needed the Soviet Union's assent to develop closer ties with East Germany; better relations with the GDR made it desirable to have better relations with the USSR, which in turn had implications for other states behind the Iron Curtain. East Berlin, Warsaw and Prague all signed a friendship treaty with the Soviet Union and it was likely that a rapprochement between the two Germanys would be viewed with alarm by these 'friends'. Closer ties between the two Germanys therefore necessitated improvement in the relationships between the Federal Republic and various East European states.

At the vertical level, the FRG was firmly committed to economic and political integration into the West European community, to NATO and to the Western alliance. West Germany's key role in Europe's defence strategy greatly strained its relationship with East Germany, which accused it of betraying the commitment to a reunified Germany; yet the FRG persisted in that role because it knew that it had to preserve its Western ties if it wanted Western support. Since the division of Germany was a product of the division of Europe, answers to German questions had to be built into a framework in which answers were sought to European questions. There was, too, a sense in which Germany looked to Europe to save it from itself: from extreme nationalism, from warmongering and from the delinquencies of the past. In the event, the search for unity – a national interest discreetly pursued within a European framework – actually helped to enhance the political stature of the Federal Republic by giving it distinctiveness and international weight. In a similar way, West Germany's interest in the German Democratic Republic increased the GDR's diplomatic and political status.

FRG politicians were aware that unification policies would work only if no attempt were made to destabilise the GDR. To do so might cause loss of life in pursuit of a political goal, and this was obviously unacceptable. They therefore pursued the objective of liberalisation through stabilisation, reasoning that stability within the GDR would be conducive to stability in relationships between the two Germanys and that this in turn would contribute to stability in East-West relationships. Bonn hoped by its policy of stabilisation in East Germany to improve life for citizens on that side of the Iron Curtain: if the GDR government felt secure, then it would be less likely to treat its citizens ruthlessly and their lot would become more tolerable. There were, however, those who condemned this diplomacy as 'supping with the devil' or propping up an essentially tyrannical regime. The GDR was in fact more repressive than Hungary or Poland and had much tighter travel restrictions than either of those countries. Whatever the moral scruples surrounding 'liberalisation by stabilisation', the eventual outcome was that it did not actually pay off. Liberalisation when it came was achieved by *de*-stabilisation – but it is possible, indeed probable, that this would not have been efficacious without the intermediate stage of *détente* or what Egon Bahr called 'change through rapprochement' (*Wandel durch Annäherung*). Rapprochement was pursued by means of permanent negotiation, trade and recognition, often intertwined with each other.

It was perhaps paradoxical that the *Deutschlandpolitik* associated with Egon Bahr and Willy Brandt (who became Foreign Minister and later Chancellor) involved recognition of the very state whose existence they were in effect trying to abolish. It is curious to recall that when the Wall went up in August 1961, the Federal Republic was still at the stage of withholding recognition from the German Democratic Republic as a state. Internationally, the GDR suffered from a serious legitimacy deficit (as indeed did the Federal Republic whose Basic Law was merely a provisional Constitution). Following its creation, it had been recognised by few states and had been regarded as provisional by the Soviet Union and even by its own citizens. The Federal Republic had promulgated the 'Hallstein Doctrine' whereby it refused to accord full diplomatic recognition to any state which recognised the GDR. Yet recognition was a vitally important goal to the GDR because it meant 'statehood', acceptance into the international community and membership of the United Nations. The success of the Federal Republic in achieving sovereignty led the Soviet Union to react by giving the GDR partial sovereignty and diplomatic recognition. It became evident to the FRG that the status quo had to be recognised if there was ever to be any hope of changing that status, and it therefore granted a qualified form of recognition to the GDR in 1972.

The drive for recognition led East German politicians to maximise the contrast between the FRG and the GDR and to define them as sharply as possible in terms of their opposing values. The more different the two states could be shown to be, the greater the justification for their continuing separation; if they converged ideologically, there would be little hope of the GDR maintaining itself as a separate state. Whereas Willy Brandt pushed the idea of 'two states, one nation', Honecker emphasised the contrast between the socialist state and the capitalist state – a rhetoric conducive to separatism rather than the unification which the GDR had once espoused. The East German state attempted to consolidate its hard-won legitimacy by its policy of *Abgrenzung* – demarcating itself by avoiding contact with and exposure to West Germany and by profiling itself distinctively. This policy intensified in reaction to Brandt's *Ostpolitik* in the years 1969–71 but increasingly conflicted with the USSR's favourable response to West German efforts at *détente*. Goeckel (1990) points out that East Germany opposed any linkage between international *détente* and domestic liberalisation as an interference in its domestic sovereignty, and that by 1969 *détente* between the Soviet Union and the Federal Republic had blossomed at the expense of Walter Ulbricht, the GDR leader. The GDR's inability or un-willingness to adapt to the USSR's policy shift was a cause of Ulbricht's fall from power. The disjunction caused by the GDR's policy of Abgrenzung prefigured a later and much greater disjunction when Gorbachev's pere-stroika contrasted with Honecker's lack of reform. The East German Social-ist Unity Party (Sozialistische Einheitspartei Deutschlands (SED)) shielded itself from perestroika and glasnost by deploying repressive measures and by trying to ensure that its citizens enjoyed a reasonably comfortable standard of life. It hoped thereby to defuse discontent.

The improvement of the East German economy was a key to achieving stabilisation and the two Germanys were in constant negotiation about mat-ters pertaining to trade. The trading relationship was facilitated by the fact that East Germany was in effect an 'extra' member of the European Eco-nomic Community. This had come about through additions which the Fed-eral Republic had caused to be made to the 1957 Treaty of Rome. The FRG, through hard currency transfers, quick access to goods and services, tax con-cessions, interest-free overdraft facilities and government-guaranteed credits, sought to make life more tolerable for citizens in the other Germany. This action was humanitarian in its effects and intended to be so. It was, however, more than a mere palliative: in a deeper sense, it was intended to preserve some sort of de facto unity and to keep the nation together. Trading policy was thus political as well as economic in its objectives. The GDR, of course, realised this and, predictably enough, aimed to thwart the FRG's attempts to create bonds between the two peoples; it had a commercial coordinator whose purpose was to obtain as much hard currency income as possible whilst giving the least possible in return. After the demise of the GDR, it was discovered that only a small part of such payments had been used for their intended purpose (Garton Ash, 1993:155). Nevertheless, by the end of the 1980s, more than half of East Germany's Western trade was with the Federal Republic, and Karl Seidel, the head of the GDR Foreign Ministry department dealing with West Germany, stated that the need for the Deutschmark was the single most important driving force behind East Germany's negotiations with its West German neighbour (ibid.:158).

The principle of horizontal sychronisation was manifested *par excellence* in trading links. The Federal Republic cultivated its commercial relation-ships with the Soviet Union as well as with the GDR. The USSR depended extensively on West Germany for trade and technology; Helmut Schmidt reached a twenty-five-year economic agreement with Brezhnev in 1978, and by the end of the decade, West Germany had become the USSR's most important trading partner. By 1979, the total volume of German-Soviet trade was six times what it had been in 1967. It was a well-established prac-tice for bankers to accompany diplomats to Moscow, and when in March

1985 Gorbachev became the new party leader, he met J. Wilhelm Christians, the leader of the Deutsche Bank, within two weeks of taking office.

The power of money was used to buy freedom for some of those trapped in East Germany against their will. When the Wall was erected on 13 August 1961, West Berlin authorities paid for some wives and children to join relatives on the western side. Just over two years later in December 1963, a 'Permit Agreement' was concluded to allow West Berliners to visit their relatives over Christmas and the New Year. Such negotiations were the genesis of the Ostpolitik. From June 1962 onwards, the West German government began a systematic policy of 'buying free' (*Freikauf*) certain citizens from the East – for hard currency, of course. This human traffic continued for more than a quarter century; Garton Ash (1993:146) reports that by the early 1970s, the price for a 'normal' Freikauf was DM 40,000 and had reached DM 96,000 per head by the time of reunification. Over the period from 1963 until 1989, nearly 34,000 political prisoners were 'bought free', more than 2,000 children reunited with their parents and more than 250,000 cases of family reunification 'regulated' with government help. For these services, a total of DM 3.5 billion was paid. This ability of the East German government to rid itself of dissidents and malcontents naturally weakened the opposition, compared with Poland or Hungary or Czechoslovakia. Because of the departure of dissidents to the West, there were fewer opportunities for oppositional groups such as the Solidarity movement in Poland to build up.

Money was used to soften the effects of policies which were unpalatable to the Soviet Union and the GDR; it helped preserve *détente* and the fabric of horizontal synchronisation – in short, it was used to sustain Ostpolitik when it threatened to collapse. Oddly enough, these threats sometimes emanated from Bonn itself, which on occasion pursued policy objectives running contrary to German-German rapprochement. A firm believer in the Western alliance, the Bonn government deployed American missiles on German soil in autumn 1983. This was an unpopular act at home and abroad that threatened to upset the diplomatic balance of East-West German relationships. The government of the Federal Republic continued, however, to claim to the GDR that it desired cooperation and peace, and it demonstrated this continuing desire by granting a government-guaranteed billion Deutschmark credit for East Germany, negotiated by Franz-Josef Strauss. This gesture went far to appease the East German government, though it looked like buying oneself out of trouble.

West German payments did indeed make a crucial difference to the East German regime and certainly contributed towards stabilisation. The downside for the Easterners was that they became financially dependent. Moreover, the diminution of citizens' dissatisfaction took away any impetus for reform at home. Indeed, Honecker consciously used social benefits and consumer goods as a substitute for reform of the system; at the eleventh party conference he promised the people *Geborgenheit* (a safe, cosy haven). Ultimately, the lack of reform was very destructive because it engendered a contrast which made the GDR compare unfavourably with Hungary, Poland and above all with the Soviet Union after the advent of Gorbachev. Freer travel to the West – eventually permitted because of Honecker's misplaced confidence in the virtues of his own regime – only made that contrast seem all the more crass. Garton Ash (1993: 201) comments: 'The combination of direct experience of the West, change to the East and no change at home, turned the safety valve [of more liberal travel] into a steam-hammer.'

The decisive impetus for change in East Germany came from outside. Gorbachev wanted the Communist regimes to liberalise and to democratise, but more than anything his objective was to save the Soviet Union. The price of doing this was to relinquish the Soviet empire which was no longer economically sustainable. The defence costs alone of the USSR have been variously estimated between 12 per cent and 28 per cent of gross domestic product; Shevardnadze's estimate as Soviet foreign minister in 1990 was 25 per cent, which contrasted with the US's roughly 6 per cent (Roskin, 1994: 134). If Soviet forces in East Europe could be reduced and demobilised, there would be a substantial saving on expenditure. The GDR's old guard was outpaced by Gorbachev and was resistant to his reforms. When the Soviet leader came to attend the East German celebrations for the fortieth anniversary of the foundation of the state, he did not even attempt to conceal the fact that he was out of sympathy with Honecker. It was during this stay that he made the oracular statements: 'Those who come too late will be punished by history' and 'If you really want democracy, then take it and you will get it!' (Reich, 1990:85).

Other East European countries, especially Poland and Hungary, also sought change and their activities impacted on the GDR. The growth of Solidarity in Poland, which first pointed the way to change, has been called 'the first hole in the Berlin Wall'. The Poles had not enjoyed the same level of material well-being as the East Germans and there had been food riots and economic deprivation which fomented discontent in the population. Poland had not been able to rid itself of its dissidents in the way that the GDR had; their presence was conducive to the articulation of grievances and the formation of oppositional elites culminating in the introduction of a Solidarity-led coalition on 16 August 1989. Hungary was geopolitically in a special position due to its frontier with Austria. From May 1989 onwards, Hungary began to adopt an independent policy regarding this frontier, which nullified the GDR's travel restrictions and allowed German holiday-makers to travel

West to freedom, abandoning all that they possessed at home in East Germany. On 10 September, the Austro-Hungarian border was completely opened with the result that East Germans streamed over it by the thousands, entering the West German embassies in Prague and Poland. Despite the threatening nature of these events, the East German state failed to react effectively (Fulbrook, 1991:323). Crucially, Gorbachev did not use Russian force to stop the exodus of German people through Hungary; the Hungarian prime minister Miklos Nemeth had already assured himself of Gorbachev's position before his foreign minister, Gyula Horn, took the step of opening up the frontier. This action earned Horn the West German Grand Cross of the Federal Order of Merit, the highest honour which the country can bestow on a foreigner.

Meanwhile, the East Germans were observing these events on Western television (which they were not supposed to watch!) and were gathering courage to challenge their regime at home. New grassroots oppositional groups were founded which were intended to form the nucleus of an alternative government. In a sense, they were also a challenge to the Protestant Church which had traditionally acted simultaneously as both the carrier and container of dissent. With the rise of the new groups, the reform agenda was broadened and the Church lost exclusive control of it. The best-known such group was New Forum, but other groups also existed, such as Democracy Now, Left Platform and Democratic Awakening. Though the Church no longer had a monopoly of dissent, it still played a major role in the choreography of popular protest.

Leipzig rather than Berlin was the crucible in which the Peaceful Revolution was smelted. It owed this special position in some measure to the important fact that the dissidents resident in the GDR ('voice') made common cause with those who wished to leave or who had left the GDR ('exit'). Whereas in East Berlin, antagonism between voice and exit groups prevented exit from becoming an organised political force, in Leipzig – heartland of the GDR's depressed industrial South – a sharp consciousness of the decay of welfare socialism and a more 'action-oriented' voice opposition led the two constituencies to collaborate rather than to compete (Joppke, 1993:394). Since 1982, Peace Prayers had been taking place in Leipzig's Church of St. Nicholas almost every Monday. From the autumn of 1988 onwards, they began to be followed by political rallies under the influence of exit groups. The Protestant Church authorities eventually tried to exclude exit groups from the protests taking place under its aegis, but this actually helped forge increased solidarity between voice and exit groups and made the former more aggressive. Voice groups had traditionally wanted merely to change the existing regime, whereas exit groups rejected it to the extent of wishing to leave altogether and were thus more radical.

The first of the Monday demonstrations triggering the fall of the regime took place on 25 September 1989 and was attended by 5,000 people; it was followed by a second demonstration on 2 October at which 25,000 people were present. For the following Monday demonstration on 9 October, Erich Honecker issued a shoot-to-kill order, and a huge military presence looked set to confront the demonstrators, but to their amazement it refrained from using force and instead allowed the demonstration to finish peacefully. After this, the numbers of participants increased exponentially to over 100,000 on 16 October and more than a quarter of a million the following week (Fulbrook, 1993:329). On 18 October, Honecker resigned and was succeeded by Egon Krenz, who on 26 October conducted discussions between the SED and the New Forum. By now there were signs that the SED was divided as to how to deal with the crisis and was debating what line to take. On 30 October, more than 300,000 people took part in the Leipzig demonstrations and similar rallies were held elsewhere in East German towns and cities. On 4 November, there was a demonstration of up to a million people in East Berlin. On 6 November, another demonstration estimated at about 500,000 people took place in Leipzig. The demands of the protesters escalated from a concern with freedom to travel to calls for free elections, legalisation of New Forum and the disbanding of the Stasi (Fulbrook, 1993:330).

During the first nine days of November, it was as if the walls of Jericho had come tumbling down (for Jericho read 'Berlin'): the regime began to make huge concessions, such as the right to travel in the West, the establishment of a Constitutional Court and the introduction of democratic elections. Some of the most prominent figures resigned, such as Margot Honecker and Erich Mielke, chief of the Secret Police. The mass demonstrations continued, especially in Leipzig and Berlin, and East Germans poured out of the country. On 9 November, the Berlin Wall fell. In late November and early December, the change in the people's slogan from '*Wir sind das Volk*' to '*Wir sind ein Volk*' crystallised the demand for German unification. At first Chancellor Kohl was a little slow to accept that the opening of the Wall ineluctably meant unification, with all that this implied. The journalist David Marsh, then European Editor of the *Financial Times*, who was with Kohl when the dramatic events of the *Wende* took place, observed that he was taken aback and not overjoyed.

On 28 November, Kohl presented to the Bundestag a ten-point plan for unification of Germany and Europe which envisaged confederal structures rather than a dash for unity (Marsh, 1994:69). This coincided with the left-wing position espoused by Günter Grass (1990) who argued against a unitary, all-German political structure on the grounds that it would be dominated by 'the western ideology of capitalism which aims to wipe out every other kind of ideological "ism" and announces, as if holding a gun to the East Germans' head: "A market economy or else'" (ibid.:7). He believed that capitalism must be adapted to the GDR in a way that would not result in the total deformation and rejection of its culture, new social unrest and perhaps a shift to the right. Grass regarded confederation as an 'economically sound, politically and culturally flexible linkage of the provinces' and feared the consequences of a strong, united Germany: 'Germany has been unified under duress, and always to its own detriment' (ibid.:74). Annexing the GDR would leave the East Germans nothing of their painfully fought-for identity. One of the most important figures who also was convinced that it would have been better for the two Germanys to cooperate with each other as separate states was Karl Otto Pöhl, the president of the Central Bank up to 1991 (Marsh, 1994:84). His judgement was to be overruled by the power of events and circumstances.

Kohl's hand was forced by the threat of wholesale destabilisation of East Germany, which the USSR neither would nor could remedy, and by massive out-migration from the GDR – between 1,990 and 2,000 people a day after the Wende in the autumn of 1989. If this flow was to be staunched and the situation stabilised, then it was essential to give form to the new political entity. The need for speed of action was imperative. The major actors in the piece were West Germany and the USSR, with the United States playing a very positive role. Diplomacy was direct, personal and private with a closed style of decision-making which 'made the old roles of diplomats, embassies and bureaucracies both irrelevant and dysfunctional to political leaders intent on shaping their own agendas' (Szabo, 1992:118). The Germans wanted to avoid a large peace conference leading to a peace treaty which would entail reservations and conditions, reopen questions such as reparations and relegate Germany back into the role of the vanquished with the Allies as the victors. As Reich (1990:93) put it: 'The tactic during 1990 was to try to tie together both Germanys without violating international treaties by slipping under them.' It was the Americans who came up with the diplomatic formula of '2 + 4': the two Germanys and the four victorious powers of the Second World War; it was the Americans who insisted that the objective of the 2 + 4 negotiations was nothing less than German unity, and that all participants must accept this objective; it was the Americans too who were particularly committed to the policy objective of achieving a united Germany within NATO.

Agreement was needed on Soviet troop withdrawals from Germany and the future size of German armed forces. These agreements were reached in dramatic fashion by direct negotiation between Kohl and Gorbachev in the Caucasus during the days from 14–16 July 1990 which had the effect of completely upstaging the last two 2 + 4 meetings on 17 July and 11–12

September. Gorbachev agreed that Germany could remain within NATO; the Soviets were allowed four years to withdraw from Germany and were to receive compensatory financing (to allow for the effects of the introduction of the Deutschmark). The future number of German troops was fixed at 370,000. The four powers simultaneously gave up their rights in relation to Berlin and to Germany as a whole. The Unification Treaty between the GDR and the FRG was signed on 31 August 1990 and ratified by the GDR Volkskammer on 20 September and by the FRG Bundestag on 21 September. It came into force on 29 September, and on 3 October 1990, the GDR joined the Federal Republic.

These events were viewed differently by the various countries involved. The Americans were by far the most positive in their support for unification. In a geopolitical sense, unification was less of a threat to the US than to European countries because the US was a superpower that did not inhabit the same continental landspace and had no vested interest in keeping the Germanys divided. Also, hundreds of thousands of US military personnel and their families had gained positive, firsthand experience of Germany, and by 1989 the United States public was more supportive of German unity than any people in the West (Szabo, 1992:10). President Bush spelled out four principles regarding German unification (Szabo, 1992:42):

- that the principle of self-determination be respected;
- that the process occur as part of a broader process of European integration which included NATO and the EC;
- that it be gradual and peaceful and regard the interests of other Europeans;
- that it should occur with respect for the inviolability of borders as stated in the Helsinki Final Act, which opposed changing the status quo by force

The objective of keeping a unified Germany within NATO was the most difficult of these to accomplish. The United States did not want to see Germany moving towards a central European neutrality or, even worse, entering the Warsaw Pact, and it therefore took the lead in reformulating NATO's strategy and ensuring Germany's acceptance within NATO. Since this ran counter to Gorbachev's expressed wish to bring a united Germany within the Warsaw Pact, some Germans temporarily perceived the US's strategy as a deliberate attempt to block unity. The US, however, had taken a firm decision not to use its power to obstruct progress towards German unity, and looked to a post-national vision of Europe in which Germany would be the key power: a European Germany rather than a German Europe, to quote the words of Thomas Mann.

All of this was profoundly unpalatable to the French. The division of Germany had made the international role of France appear all the more important, and the French feared losing the Federal Republic as an ideological buffer against the East (Szabo, 1992:49). Mitterrand was angered by the American four-point plan and by Kohl's ten-point plan. In reaction, he actually tried to persuade Gorbachev to stop German unification, and paid a visit to East Germany (20–21 December 1989) which was openly provocative to Bonn (Cole, 1993). Suddenly the Franco-German alliance counted for nothing and relationships between Mitterrand and Genscher became very strained.

The momentum towards German unity was also troubling to the British. Before the Second World War, Britain had been able to hold the balance of power in Europe. Now the new relationship between Germany and the United States implied a downgrading of the former 'special relationship' between the United States and the United Kingdom. Margaret Thatcher feared the marginalisation of her country and the potential power of a united Germany. Her attempts to slow down the process were mitigated only by a concern not to alienate the Americans too much. The way in which the British newspapers handled the eventual achievement of German unity was almost grudging. On the day after the German unity ceremony (3 October 1990), *The Times's* most important headline dealt with a conference defeat suffered by Labour leader Neil Kinnock over the issue of defence policy. A lower level headline did give coverage to German unity, but the focus was on protest and violence associated with the event, featuring a photo of a burning Trabant car in Potsdamer Place. The British *Observer* at the end of that momentous week led with the death of Princess Caroline of Monaco's husband rather than with German unity. By contrast, the more Europhile *Irish Times* (4 October 1990) emphasised the happier aspects of Germany's great day: 'Germans Enjoy Their Hangover.' The fact was that both Britain and France were forced to take second place to direct negotiations amongst the Germans, the Soviets and the Americans, and they emerged weaker as a result of Germany's unification.

The sheer speed with which German unification had taken place left France and Britain outmanoeuvred. As we have seen, this speed was not originally what Chancellor Kohl had wanted. He would have preferred a gradualist approach such as that advocated by Günter Grass, but speed was forced upon him by events. Delay would have left the exodus of migrants from East Germany unchecked and would have jeopardised the ultimate success of the unity project by allowing leeway for other political powers to intervene and unravel the delicate negotiations. The grudging reaction of France and Britain to the successful achievement of unification leads one to suspect that, given more of a chance, they would certainly have obstructed or even derailed the process. Gorbachev did not remain in office for much longer (it can be argued that his political end was hastened by German unification), and it was necessary to use to the best advantage the unprecedented window of opportunity presented by his hostility towards the East German leadership. As a result of these factors, the legal basis for unification, including the broad parameters for education, had to be put into place quickly. This speed was at the cost of thorough, widespread consultation both in the FRG Parliament and in East Germany, where the transitional government passed independent legislation right up to the day before 3 October 1990, German Unity Day. The Easterners had hoped to bring more of their own values and outlook into the integrated framework than turned out in practice to be the case. The speed of unification was compelling in terms of *realpolitik*. However, it militated against gentle handling of East German identity which as we have seen was developed only with great difficulty over the forty years of the GDR's existence. Broadly speaking, for understandable reasons the East Germans were given the cultural and political framework which the West thought they ought to have, and this applied in the sphere of education, as elsewhere.

The Law and the New Länder

The legal apparatus which had given stability to the West Germans after the fall of the Third Reich was one of the institutions, together with the Bundesbank, in which the West Germans had the deepest confidence (Johnson, 1994:133), and it was to the law that people now turned for security and structure in uncharted waters. A favourable basis for unification already existed in law. In 1966, both German states ratified international pacts relating to economic, social and cultural rights[1] and to civil and political rights.[2] These pacts were important in helping to create a basis for common German law even if the commonalities were only of a formal nature and even if their interpretation and implementation took place within very different political contexts (Ramm, 1990:35). The existing constitutional basis of the Federal Republic was only provisional. Its 'Basic Law' (not 'Constitution') was drafted by the Herrenchiemsee Committee between 10 and 23 August 1948 and was regarded as a milestone on the way to a united Germany. It was a 'temporary political expedient' (Southern, 1992:36) which included two Articles (23 and 146), either of which could serve as

1. IPWSKR – Internationaler Pakt über wirtschaftliche, soziale und kulturelle Rechte, 19 December 1966.
2. IPBPR – Internationaler Pakt über bürgerliche und politische Rechte, 19 December 1966.

the basis of the eventual unity of Germany. Article 23 was actually intended to serve as the future peaceful basis of accession of the Saarland to the Federal Republic; this took place in December 1956. The text of the Articles is respectively as follows:

I. Article 23
This Basic Law is valid for the present time in the domains of the federal Länder Baden, Bavaria, Bremen, Greater-Berlin, Hamburg, Hesse, Lower Saxony, North Rhine-Westphalia, Rhineland-Palatinate, Schleswig-Holstein, Württemberg-Baden and Württemberg-Hohenzollern. In other parts of Germany, it is to come into force on their accession.

II. Article 146
This Basic Law ceases to be valid on the day on which a Constitution comes into force which has been decided upon freely by the German people.

Article 146 is more radical than Article 23 and would have required a referendum and a complete new Constitution for the whole of Germany. In the event, the decision was taken to base unification on Article 23 rather than on Article 146: the whole body of existing West German law was thus extended to the five new Bundesländer. This had certain advantages: it gave credence to the fiction that no new state was being created and made membership of the European Union entirely unproblematic for East Germany, whose external trade, as we have seen above, already functioned as European Community production; it also secured automatic international recognition for the merged entity (Goetz and Cullen, 1994:6). Because the existing Basic Law (Grundgesetz (GG)), with appropriate amendments, was adopted and the more radical alternative of entirely new legislation was eschewed, it is still formally correct to refer to the legal basis of United Germany as the 'Basic Law' rather than the 'Constitution', though the latter term is often used in less formal parlance. In fact Article 146 has been replaced by a new clause which envisages the possibility of a fully fledged Constitution at some future time: 'This Basic Law, which after the accomplishment of the unity and freedom of Germany is valid for the whole German people, loses its validity on the day on which a Constitution comes into force which is decided upon freely by the German people.'

The West German negotiator of the Unification Treaty was Minister of the Interior Dr Wolfgang Schäuble; the East German negotiator was Dr Günther Krause. In this Treaty, the whole corpus of West German law was systematically adopted to the requirements of unification in what Southern (1992), himself a lawyer, has admiringly called 'a juristic tour de force'. The Treaty had to be accepted or rejected *in toto* by the East and West German Parliaments. The Articles most relevant to the present study are numbers 37 (education) and 38 (higher education and research), while Article 31 deals with family and women. A so-called 'eternity clause' of the Basic Law, Article 79 (3), laid down prohibited amendments which were in contravention of Articles 1 and 20. Article 1 related to the protection of human dignity and Article 20 to fundamental principles underlying the Constitution: that Germany is a democratic and social federal state; that all state power derives from the people and is exercised through elections and referenda; that law-giving must be in keeping with the Constitution and executive power and that justice must be based on the law (making Germany a *Rechtsstaat*). No change in these Articles is ever to be permitted.

However, certain other changes to the Basic Law had to be made prior to unification; indeed, a number of subjects were extremely controversial due to the different traditions and values that prevailed in the two parts of Germany. The abortion issue was one such subject. Abortion had been used as a form of birth control in the GDR and had been allowed without restriction during the first three months of pregnancy. West Germany had always viewed itself as a Christian state and liberal abortion laws were abhorrent to many people there. Before a solution could be reached, soemthing had to give. The eventual compromise permitted abortions to be performed legally during the first twelve weeks of pregnancy in certain circumstances. In addition, there were new obligatory provisions for professional counselling, and the Court affirmed the 'protective duty' of the state towards the unborn child: serious efforts have to be made by health and social care authorities to encourage the mother to agree that the pregnancy should continue, and proper facilities are to be made available to her (Johnson, 1994:139). Johnson remarks that the Court's decision does not appear to pay much attention to the different attitudes towards abortion of doctors in the East and West and that this is bound to influence the practical application of the new provisions. Property was the other exceptionally controversial issue. Expropriations of property by the Soviet Union or the GDR between 1945 and 1949 were considered irreversible on the grounds that the Federal Republic could not be held responsible since its jurisdiction had been limited to the eleven western Länder (Goetz and Cullen, 1994:12). However, the Unification Treaty provided that property in East Germany which had been taken from former owners wrongfully or against inadequate compensation should be restored to those former owners (Southern, 1993). This decision was influenced by free market ideology, particularly as propounded by the FDP, which threatened resignation if restitution was not included in the unification settlement. Restitution proved a considerable problem in the economic reconstruction of East Germany, firstly because it impeded investment, and secondly because it resulted in all the financial benefit of restitution accruing to West Germans and people outside Germany, while all the disadvantages, such as loss or threatened loss of homes, fell on East Germans (ibid.:446).

Unification on the basis of Article 23 was an accession (*Beitritt*) of East to West; it was clearly a takeover of the GDR rather than a marriage of equals. The important consequence of unification on this basis was East Germany's assimilation into West Germany; henceforth, West German norms prevailed in educational as in other matters. The law of the Federal Republic was applied to the former GDR. Wolfgang Schäuble (1991) is quite clear about this: East Germans are welcome to join West Germans but it must be clearly understood that the Basic Law which has served the Federal Republic well is now being extended to the East. He adds: 'But there is no question here of a union of two equal states' (p. 131).

Unification increased the number of Länder from eleven to sixteen. It was possible to re-establish the 'New' Länder on a historical basis. The 1949 Constitution of East Germany set up a number of Länder – Brandenburg, Mecklenburg-Vorpommern, Saxony, Saxony-Anhalt and Thuringia – which were abolished in 1952 and replaced by fourteen administrative districts. When unification came about, the old Länder were revived. It was thus possible to introduce a structure which was not completely alien to the East German people and to claim that the Germany united in 1990 had a sort of continuity with pre-war Germany. However, the jurist Kelsen (1944) at the end of the Second World War had put forward the idea that as a result of its defeat and disarmament, Germany had ceased to exist as a state in 1945 and that the GDR and the FRG were new foundations (Southern, 1992). The question of whether the New Bundesländer (NBL) are really 'new' or are instead a genuine continuation of the past will assume great significance in a debate over values in the school curriculum to be described later in chapter 4 of the present volume.

The new Länder structure has certain implications for the position of Germany within the European Union which it regards as so important. In some ways the power of the Länder over federal policy and decision-making in the European Union has been strengthened by the use of Article 23 rather than Article 146. If exclusive competences of the Länder are at issue – which is the case for education – the Federal Republic will be represented in European Union matters by a representative of the Länder appointed by the Bundesrat rather than by a member of the federal government (Ress, 1994:51). The Länder thus have a potentially powerful role. Some scholars believe that they are not in a position to do justice to this role, whereas others believe that the Länder are now almost too powerful. Leonhardy (1994), of the former persuasion, states that many Länder lack the administrative and personnel capacities to cope with the volume and complexity of European business, and anticipates that inter-Länder disparities are likely to damage the Länder's influence in the Regional Committee of the European Union. Goetz and Cullen (1994:22), of the latter persuasion, take the view that the right of Länder government representatives to sit and speak for Germany in the Council of Ministers 'threatens to weaken the coherence of German European policy'; they anticipate the danger that particularist interests of the sixteen Länder might impede legislation which is in the interests of Germany as a whole. It is clear that many observers see in the increased number of Länder a potential for divisiveness which will make 'Germany' less effective at the European level.

Within the united Federal Republic of Germany, the tension between Bund and Länder, which existed even before unification, may well increase. The Bund of course does have its own modicum of power which derives from its willingness to take a large share of certain financial burdens. If less than one quarter of the costs of expenditure-relevant legislation falls on the Länder, then the consent of the Bundesrat – composed of Länder representatives – is not required and the Bund can legislate as it wishes. The resources commanded by the Länder vary considerably from one to the other. Leonhardy (1994:90–91) points out that unification – the addition of New Länder – has greatly increased inter-Länder disparities: the Länder borders are irrational, cutting as they do right across heavily industrialised and urbanised parts of the country.

The relative competences of the Bund and the Länder are important for any analysis of education which, after all, is one of the prime responsibilities of the Länder. The autonomy of the New Bundesländer means that in theory they should be able to act independently in the realm of education policy, but this autonomy is strongly mitigated by the need for policy coordination, mutual recognition of teachers and human mobility generally. Add to these factors the concept that the former GDR came into the united Germany not as a proud and equal partner but as one being 'assimilated' to Western structures, and it is clear that the pressure for conformity in terms of New Bundesländer education policy was and is very great. It can be difficult enough even for large Länder like North Rhine-Westphalia to exercise autonomy; this is due to the fear that its qualifications may not be recognised elsewhere in Germany. How much more difficult, then, for the New Bundesländer to insist on vigorous exercise of their autonomy in educational matters.

The East German Psyche

The fall of the Wall was greeted with almost universal joy and relief. When the euphoria died down, however, many Easterners experienced a feeling of loss, almost of bereavement, for the passing of their state and their socialist principles. The ideas and ideals which had guided their lives for so long were discredited. The result was a feeling of profound sadness and anomie. The *Wende* was a shock to the whole personality structure. The following personal letter written to a Western colleague by a highly qualified (*habilitiert*), middle-aged, female psychologist from East Berlin vividly reveals her disorientation and apprehension about the new regime.

Date: Christmas 1994

Dear Professor S.,

It is as though everything which in the East seemed like a castle walled-in for eternity has been swept away by a powerful storm. The five years since the fall of the Wall seem like a dream to me, although these five years have left many 'blue weals on my consciousness' (Max Frisch).

Since December 1992, I have been working … [here she gives the name of the department which employs her and a description of her job] … These tasks are very interesting and demanding. I have learned a great deal. I work as an education employee and have a so-called KW post ['KW' means *Kann-Weg-fallen*: 'can be dispensed with'] which means that I have no powers of decision. Because I have undergone a different education process, have a different curriculum vitae and have been taken in from a different system, I have no claim to an established post.

The social barriers are deeper than one thinks and many misunderstandings arise. Considering the misery in other former socialist countries, we former GDR citizens can be thankful, even if in an everyday sense there is as yet little to be seen of the so-called great freedom. Entry into this society means the end of employment for many of us, especially for the handicapped, for mothers with children (they have an especially tough time) and also for women in general. The legal experts now have the last word in everything. Almost all East Germans struggle to receive recognition for the education which they have acquired, for the right to equality of treatment, for the recognition of their years of work experience, for their pensions and so on. I have taken out two legal cases … for the recognition of my post-doctoral degree [*Habilitation*]. Now that most of the university posts are occupied by Westerners, it is only of hypothetical value anyhow because I cannot earn any money with it. The times are against me; I am too old for this society or born too early, however you choose to look at it.

So, my dear friend, you must try to understand that forty years of life experience have become invalid between one day and the next. Many people vote for the PDS [successor of the Socialist Unity Party] not out of nostalgia but because they need some kind of acknowledgement of the life they have lived up to now. Due to the fact that no one in our family is without work, we are all right, but the value of work had a different meaning in the GDR. Each person had a *duty* to work. People who did not work were regarded as antisocial, lazy, and had to be re-educated or punished by society…. The prevailing values of one society cannot be directly transferred to another. I well remember how at first we needed the help of acquaintances (West Berliners) in adapting to the new society: deciding on a health insurance company, filling out tax forms, even doing the daily shopping. It was as if we were in a foreign country, although we all spoke German. So we cling to old habits, for example to our holiday resort in Hiddensee, and to ties with family and friends. If one ... does not always adapt immediately to social circumstances, then 'good things take time' as the saying goes. (Copy of this letter given to the present author by its writer, 22 April 1995)

The society from which the GDR citizens emerged had been a profoundly authoritarian one in which people had no voice in determining the aims and functions of the state. The state was the instrument of the SED Party and promoted Party interests at every turn. People were subordinate to those interests and to the authority of Party and state. As Glaessner (1992:108) writes: 'Political culture was characterised by an almost uninterrupted transition between two dictatorships fundamentally different yet similar in their rejection of democracy. The democratic revolution of 1989 cannot hide the extent to which the people of the GDR had internalised authoritarian character traits.'

It must never be forgotten that the SED Party held the line by the use of physical violence or the threat of it, and by many unjust psychological stratagems, like 'systematic discreditation of public reputation', 'systematic organisation of professional failure for the purpose of undermining self-confidence', and 'production of mistrust and mutual suspicion within groups and organisations' (Schell and Kalinka, 1991:206). The Secret Police or Stasi were all pervasive – most public buildings had a special room for bugging devices so that the Stasi could exercise surveillance. It is estimated that in East Berlin alone, the Stasi had a staff of 1,500 officers and subordinates and 1,600 civilian employees; in the whole of the GDR they employed perhaps 17,000 people and had an incalculable number of informants (Fulbrook, 1991:262). The Stasi's omnipresent influence is conveyed by works of art as well as by statistics. In a small Berlin museum near the site known as Checkpoint Charlie, there is an exhibition of paintings about the Wall which portray the feelings of those who suffered from its divisive power. One of these depicts the Wall in flat, grey, almost monochrome colour. It is pierced by a substantial hole and through this hole oozes a flow of congealed blood – thick, heavy, tangible, almost three-dimensional. The painting thus brings together images of gloomy uniformity (grey) and of violence (red) – a reality experienced by many East Germans. In such an atmosphere, it is not easy to preserve civic courage.

One of the most controversial – and famous – books about the East German psyche was published after the fall of the Wall by the psychotherapist Hans-Joachim Maaz (1990). It must be pointed out that in retrospect Maaz came to see his book as rather one-sided, and in a subsequent book written with West German psychoanalyst Michael Lukas Moeller, his criticism of the East was counterbalanced by criticism of the West (Moeller and Maaz, 1991). Maaz's central argument is that external repression by the Party and state apparatus led to inner repression and alienation from true feelings on the part of the East German people. The breaching of the Wall was a catharsis for pent-up feelings. In his own profession, even medicine was used for repressive purposes and psychosomatic factors were discounted in favour of monocausal physical explanations of illness. He himself could not obtain a post as a chief doctor in the GDR because he would not join the SED Party. Psychotherapy was not considered respectable and anyone in a leading position who became ill expected a doctor to help him or her regain the 'right [political] attitudes' – not subversive or anarchic ones as psychotherapy might imply. Doctors would have needed enormous civil courage if they were to admit the true reasons for their patients' illnesses, some of which were clearly sociopolitical in nature.

'Our emotions were walled in just as the Berlin Wall had closed off our country', Maaz writes (p. 96). He indicts schools as being very much part of the repressive apparatus. Schools were an instrument of compulsion in which the values of discipline, order, control, punctuality, cleanliness and subordination were paramount, and parents backed the school rather than their children when conflict between the two arose. Women's jobs and the external well-being of the family took precedence over the true spiritual and social well-being of the children. Often success hid alienation because the more public forms of success in areas such as sport and culture were intended to glorify the GDR and promote its recognition internationally. As such, the success of the individual was subordinated to that of the state. Individualism was repressed even to the point of sending children home if they wore red clothes (though this was the colour of the Party). Red was too cheeky, too lively, too American and could not be tolerated, just as loud manners were a threat to the grey sadness and narrowness of life in the GDR (ibid.: 29, 101). Strength of character was officially valued as it served to dam up indignation and block the overt expression of opposition. The spontaneous expression of feeling could be allowed only when it took place under ritualised conditions such as at concerts or ballets. This explains the frenetic applause which was sometimes manifested at such functions. In Maaz's opinion, it was a displacement activity for more personal emotions which could not otherwise be expressed.

Maaz is scathing about the shortages that were endemic in East German everyday life. Long queues and hours of waiting made people feel subordinate and small. Searching for commodities wore people down. Restaurants and shops had continually to disappoint their customers and this led to gruff manners on the part of staff and waiters, probably as a defence mechanism against customers' frustration. All of this was exacerbated by television with its tantalising glimpses of Western prosperity and by the proximity of the Federal Republic. Of course, East German citizens were not supposed to watch West German television and teachers had trick questions to find out which pupils were doing so. Yet Maaz is not uncritical of Western capitalism. It is wrong, he believes, to assume that social security, happiness and the protection of the environment can only take place under circumstances of the highest productivity. In one of the book's most touching and memorable paragraphs, he points out the painful absurdity of waiting half a lifetime for a Trabant car (Trabie) only to see this aspiration rendered ridiculous by the introduction of a Mercedes economy (ibid.: 181). Where are the Westerners, he asks, who will tell us about the shortcomings of their own system?

Maaz's book found many critics who disliked its sweeping generalisations, its emotionalism and its stigmatisation of a whole people as 'repressed'. But other authors too produced work indicating that young Easterners – school pupils – were suffering from turbulent, conflicting, rebellious feelings, and that their counterparts in West Germany were often unsympathetic or even hostile to them. From October to December 1991, Böhm et al. (1993) chose a sample of one thousand pupils in East and West aged fifteen to nineteen and gave them forty-five minutes to write an essay on 'German Unity – What I Think of It'. Opinions were diverse and revelatory. The following is a reasonable, balanced statement from a West German grammar school pupil (male, ninth form):

> The inhabitants of the New Bundesländer invested too high hopes in reunification. There are large problems which simply cannot be solved in a short time. That is why I find it rather unjust that the Chancellor is criticised so much. He has not been able to keep all the promises but really expectations were just too high. I do not want to defend the regime, for many things happened against the wishes of the citizens of the Old Bundesländer, for example drastic tax rises or the huge rise in the standard of living in the New Bundesländer. But unification has positive sides too, for example the reduction in the period of military service because of disarmament. However, many citizens of the Old Bundesländer were very annoyed about the consequences of unity because many Easterners came to the Old Länder and there was then a lack of jobs there. All in all I value unification very much and if people could be a bit more patient, I think positive developments would take place more quickly. (p. 52)

Against this must be set the following hate-filled statement made by a male West German from a lower secondary school (ninth form):

> I think it is very bad that the Wall has fallen and that they can come from over there and take our jobs away. And we are supposed to pay for all that; it is nice for some people [Easterners] to be able to see their friends or acquaintances or other family members again but on the other hand everything which is our very own has to be shared with them.... It would be better to send them back and

build another wall 10 or 20 meters high with barbed wire all round and soldiers armed with machine guns and when someone wants to escape they should fire on him immediately as Hitler did with the Jews. The same should happen to them or much worse. That is my opinion. I hate them and when I see one of them coming I could hit them one.... What I like doing is when they give up their Trabie and buy a Mercedes with our money, then it's fun to put a scratch down the whole car with a key and bash in the windows and break the star. (p. 33)

The East German pupils were on the whole less visceral and more aware of the advantages and disadvantages of unification. Thus, a secondary school pupil (female, tenth form) wrote:

It is good that we can travel and see a lot of new things. The disadvantage is that so many businesses have gone bankrupt; that many people are on the street without work. It is still hard to get on with the others; some cut you off because you come from the other part of Germany. We need to learn how to get along. What's bad is that there are now a lot of drugs. I think criminality is on the increase. In that respect the Wall wasn't bad. I hope that drugs will not become so plentiful as in the Old Bundesländer. (p. 19)

Other pupils, like the following East German girl (ninth form), were worried about a whole variety of issues though they were overwhelmingly positive about the Wende:

Much has changed in my life through unification. I feel better than before and can give my opinion about what pleases me and what does not. Really it is much better than before. However, there are a lot of problems like the wave of foreigners, skinheads, AIDS, lack of accommodation and unemployment.... All this is terrible especially the foreigners who come and take our jobs away; rape and drugs are very widespread with us. I think AIDS is very bad. It could affect anybody, and many people have died of it or committed suicide out of fear of a painful death. I find the good sides of reunification totally great.... It is really super now. If the division were to be reintroduced, I would have no pleasure in life. (p. 50–51)

Pupils' opinions in the Böhm study cover quite a wide spectrum but it is clear that the children are vividly conscious of social issues and that they have strong views on them. They are very concerned with material matters and to them the problems of unity centre on money: broadly speaking, for the Westerners, subsidies to the East, and for the Easterners, exploitation by the West. The fact is that at first only a minority of young East German people were in favour of unification. A survey carried out by the Central Institute for Youth Research (ZIJ) (Bütow, 1995) found that in November 1989, only 46.2 per cent were for unification though this had changed to 86.8 per cent by 3 October 1990. Older people who had known a reality different from socialism were keener on it than young people. For youthful Easterners, the turning away from socialism in the 1980s was from the reality of socialism, not from the theoretical concept: GDR youth still wanted social security together with material well-being and personal freedom. It is sobering to note that in a survey conducted by the German Youth Institute (DJI) (1992), almost 40 per cent of young Westerners were against unification.

The GDR had an enormous network of child care institutions (KITAs) which accepted even tiny babies so that their mothers could go to work. In 1988, the degree of coverage was 94 per cent, and 83.2 per cent of women were gainfully employed outside the home (BLK, 1993b). Since the state assumed much of the burden of child care, Krüger (1996:107) remarks that whereas East German childhood was 'state-dominated and standardised', West German childhood was 'market- and media-dominated'. Indeed, it would be tempting to assume that a great sociopsychological difference existed between young Easterners and Westerners, but this is not necessarily so. On both sides of the Wall during the 1980s, family forms had been pluralised and individualised. In the former GDR, cohabitation was widespread: in 1987, 28.7 per cent of women and 26.5 per cent of men aged eighteen to forty were cohabiting, and as many as 50 per cent had children. By the mid 1980s, the divorce rate was one of the highest in the world: 30 per 10,000 inhabitants as opposed to 20 per 10,000 in the FRG. The proportion of children born out of wedlock had by 1970 risen to 13.3 per cent and by 1989 was almost one-third of all live births – three times higher than in the FRG (Winkler, 1990; Schneider, 1994). In the circumstances, it is not surprising that the parent-child relationship had moved from a command to a negotiation paradigm. Uhlendorff, Krappmann and Oswald (1997) speculate that differing macrosocial structures might have affected the social relationships among children on each side of the (former) Wall, and they set out to investigate friendship patterns among East and West Berlin primary school children. They did indeed find that East German parents control their children more tightly than those in West Germany, but this trend does not impede the children's integration into the outside world. In fact, children's relationship networks are remarkably similar in the East and West. Oswald and Krappmann (1995) state that having a good family life was a dominant objective in the GDR, and that in the New Bundesländer it is still very important: adolescents there rate their parents higher than do those in the Old Bundesländer.

This brings us to a phenomenon of great importance in the former GDR. Its totalitarianism was mitigated by the fact that it was a 'niche society',[3] that is a society in which enclaves existed where people could escape

3. Schmitz (1995) disparages the concept of the niche society on the grounds that it plays down a totalitarian regime and was not the result of a free decision ensuring tolerance and acceptance of those who thought differently from the crowd.

from ideological and social control, and find scope for independent action and alternative experience. Although the classroom and informal relationships between pupils could form a sort of niche, it was the family *par excellence* which offered protection to the hard-pressed individual from the sociopolitical pressures of the larger society (BFSFJ, 1994:p. v). This was especially important for the young because the SED was extremely mistrustful of youth (ibid.:p. x). The family formed a counterbalance to the state-permeated society, and offered an opportunity for diversity, individualism and self-realisation. The niches which it provided allowed a covert pluralism to develop that became overt after the fall of the Wall and asserted itself in a plethora of differing points of view and aspirations, especially between 1989 and 1990 as we shall see in the following chapter.

Chapter 2

REFORMING THE
SCHOOL STRUCTURES

The GDR's Unified School System

E ducation in the GDR was regarded as of supreme importance in the construction of a socialist society. The SED as the party of the working class claimed a monopoly of political power and authority over educational matters. Its inner structure was totalitarian and was dominated by the Politburo which made all the important decisions about education. The wife of the Party First Secretary, Margot Honecker (née Feist, b. 1927), became Minister of Education in 1963 and remained in that office until her resignation was announced on 2 November 1989 (Ninth Youth Report, 1994: 110). In the circumstances, it is scarcely surprising that education was supposed to be sacrosanct and immune from criticism. The general principles and parameters of educational development were determined by the political agenda. Conflict was suppressed and as a result the major institutions of society were broadly in harmony with each other, at least on the surface. This homogeneity dated from the origins of the East German state during the post–Second World War period. After 1945, the GDR was ruled by only one occupying power, not three like the future Federal Republic. This meant that there was less room for conflicts to develop, and that educational development was smoother than in the FRG (Ramm, 1990:35). Until 1963, even the birth rate in East Germany was steadier than in West Germany (MPI, 1994:207). Given macropolitical consensus about goals and values, what remained to be done was simply to fine-tune the educational system at the microlevel; this Margot Honecker did very effectively.

Latent conflict – regional, cultural and social – did, however, exist. There were cleavages between North and South, between different classes and different age groups, and the capital city tended to be privileged compared with the more remote regions (Glaessner, 1992:86). The dominating principles of democratic centralism, collectivism and statism were supposed to reduce class and regional inequality. The guiding concepts were equality of opportunity and the abolition of a class-ridden society. All educational sectors of general, vocational and higher education were governed by powerful ministries: for general school education, the Ministry of Education; for vocational education and apprenticeships, the State Secretariat for Vocational Education; and for third-level education, the Ministry for Higher Education and Specialist Colleges. Education and the economy were viewed as symbiotic, and a monistic Marxist-Leninist ideology prevailed (Anweiler et al., 1990:13/27). With the collapse of the SED as the ruling party in 1989, the three Ministries were melded by Modrow's transitional government into one unified ministry, the Ministry of Education and Higher Education.

The system was anything but pluralist. According to the East German Constitution, the state was supposed to consist primarily of workers (*Arbeiter*) and peasants (*Bauer*), but in practice these were supplemented by intelligentsia (*Intelligenz*) such as doctors and teachers, and independent artisans (*Handwerker*) involved in private manufacture and trade. The latter two categories were not highly valued because they did not fit in with the desired proletarian class basis of the GDR population. The artisans, even those who merely ran small family businesses, were not totally acceptable in a political sense because they possessed the means of production and employed others; this brought them too close to capitalism to be respectable in a socialist ethos. Society made few concessions towards them: their life was made hard by punitive taxes and the difficulty of obtaining materials. They and the intelligentsia experienced especial difficulty in obtaining admission to the upper forms of secondary school and thence to higher education. The intelligentsia were usually paid less than skilled workers; it was quite usual to find that in schools the caretaker (*Pförtner*) had higher wages than the teaching staff. It is important, however, to note that the 'working class' in the GDR was politically, not sociologically, defined lest the SED be seen to be betraying its own principles. Leading Party functionaries and officers were called 'workers' just like those involved in production (MPI, 1994:289). Erich Honecker's own daughters were categorised as working class.

The legal basis of the GDR school system was the definitive Law on the Unified Socialist Education System of 25 February 1965 (GBl. I, 1965). This 1965 Law superseded all others and remained valid until 1989–90. It contained all the basic decisions from which specific regulations could be derived and was broad enough to provide a framework for ongoing new developments. In the preamble, the Law refers to the historic socialist tasks set by the SED's Sixth Party Conference: the mastery of technical revolution, the development of socialist society and of the national economy, the steering of work productivity, as well as the stimulation (*Aufschwung*) of the arts and sciences. The 1965 Law sees education (*Bildung*) and character-formation (a free translation of *Erziehung*) as a unity and uses both terms in tandem, even for those students who have reached the age of maturity. The aims of education and character formation are to produce the *all-round developed socialist personality* whose attributes are in harmonious balance: ready for revolutionary struggle, gifted with a high socialist consciousness, highly qualified, healthy, intellectually and physically capable, cultured (Döbert, 1995:8). Moral traits are friendliness, politeness and cooperation, respect for parents and all older persons, and honesty and decency in the relations between the sexes. Social traits are ability to do worthwhile work, willingness to engage in continuing education, and readiness to assume responsibility; free time must be used positively in pursuits such as cultivation of the arts. The socialist personality is patriotic, truly devoted to the GDR as the fatherland and always prepared to strengthen and defend it (Ramm, 1990:42). This doctrine of the all-round socialist personality had been promulgated back in 1952, and was one of the all-pervasive concepts in GDR rhetoric.

The first principle of the 1965 Law was the unity of the system. The concept of unity encompassed objectives, the educational provider (the state) and the educational structures. The principle of equality was also of cardinal importance and was interpreted as the creation of equal opportunity for all the country's children (subject to socialist principles, of course). In pursuit of this equality it was important that school and higher education be free. For progression to the next-highest stage of education there were three main principles: achievement, social criteria and regard for the social structure of the population. This meant that the children of various social groups such as workers should be promoted (for example to upper secondary school or higher education) in proportion to their representation in the population as a whole. What was not wanted was *over*-representation of children from the bourgeoisie and intelligentsia.

The 1965 law describes the following as the components of the socialist education system:

- pre-school education establishments
- unified ten-year polytechnic upper schools
- institutions of vocational education
- educational institutions preparing students for entry to higher education
- engineering colleges and Specialist Colleges (*Fachschulen*)
- establishments for further and in-service education and training
- special schools for children with physical or psychological handicaps

The core of the education system was the General Polytechnic Upper School (*Allgemeine Polytechnische Oberschule* (POS)). The term 'Upper' was a politically motivated attempt to communicate to the population a notion of a 'higher', that is an academically high-grade, education for everyone, but it was an incongruous term because the POS included the stage of primary education which, far from being 'Upper', was known as the 'Lower Level' (*Unterstufe*). The term 'polytechnic' implied practical, vocational education - understandable in a system that regarded education and the economy as interdependent. This linking of education with socialist production went back to 1958–59 when the concept of Polytechnic Instruction (*Polytechnischer Unterricht*) was first legally introduced. It encompassed Introduction to Socialist Production, Productive Work and Technical Drawing.

The POS was divided into three main sections: the Lower Level (*Unterstufe*): forms 1 to 3; the Middle Level (*Mittelstufe*): forms 4 to 6; the Upper Level (*Oberstufe*): forms 7 to 10. In practice, the important division came after form 4 when secondary, subject-specific education began. At that point, too, compulsory Russian lessons were introduced together with some Science and Geography. The second foreign language, which was necessary for the 'leaving certificate' (*Abitur*), was introduced in form 7 on a voluntary basis. The relative proportions of time devoted to different subject areas at that stage were as follows: 25 per cent, Languages; 34 per cent, Mathematics and Sciences; 12 per cent, Polytechnic Instruction (Polytechnischer Unterricht); 15 per cent, Social Sciences like Geography, History and Civics; 6 per cent, Sport and Arts subjects such as Music and Painting. The importance attached to Maths and Sciences increased as children continued their school career; by form 9, the ratio of Languages to Maths/Sciences was 19:42. (Note: All the above figures are from Hörner, 1990a:13.)

Post-compulsory secondary education took place in the Extended Upper School (*Erweiterte Oberschule* (EOS)) which was attended by only a small proportion of the age cohort: in 1984, 9.5 per cent. The sociopolitical function of the EOS was to educate an ideologically sound, leading cadre which could be deployed politically and professionally as needed. Intrinsically, this had overtones of elitism, and indeed the EOS went against the hallowed principle of unity because it was selective. There was, therefore, a principled resistance in the GDR to curricular differentiation, and for a long time the EOS was merely supposed to extend, deepen and complete the POS. In 1959, compulsory education was lengthened from eight to ten years, and the question arose as to whether the EOS was to be four years or two years long. In 1965, the decision was taken to make the EOS a two-year structure consisting of forms 11 and 12. This decision, however, was not actually implemented until 1982–83, thereby reflecting a pronounced reluctance to make the EOS a distinct stage with its own curricular specialisation.

Until the two-year EOS was implemented, forms 9 and 10 of the POS offered some preparation for the transition to the EOS, and indeed a 1966 guideline assumed that selection for the EOS began after the eighth form (Baske, 1990:210/215; Hörner, 1990a:18). The subject range of the EOS was almost the same as that of the upper section of the POS, except that a second foreign language was taught for three hours a week and Polytechnic Instruction was offered as an option. The Creative Arts were represented in an even more attenuated form than in the POS: Art Education or Music was given only one hour a week, though in defence of East Germany, many lessons in these subjects were cancelled in the West as well (MPI, 1994: 270). There was a strong bias towards mathematical and scientific subjects because originally the intention had been to connect general and vocational education so that pupils emerged with Abitur and an apprenticeship. This was abandoned about 1966, though the principle of associating learning with productive work was retained. The commitment to equality, interpreted broadly as the *same* curriculum for everyone in general schools, was in tension with excellence and with special talents (though admittedly these were developed in a number of specialist institutions).

Despite the existence of several alternative routes into university, the EOS remained the most important and the shortest. Subject-specific admissions committees decided on access to higher education. The number of university places and who got them were regulated by central planners. In order to preserve the coherence of the planning, it was assumed that all those who obtained Abitur would proceed to higher education. There was, therefore, a particular onus on teachers to ensure that everyone passed (Hörner, 1990a:11). The Constitution stated that social factors and the social structure of the population as a whole could be taken into consideration in admitting candidates to the next-highest level of education. The criteria for admission to the EOS were therefore broadened from the purely academic to the (class-based) non-academic. Children of clergymen had special difficulty in gaining access since the SED did not welcome those with a world-view ideologically opposed to theirs. Children of the intelligentsia in general had problems in this respect, and since admission to the EOS was a necessary preselection (not merely a preparation) for higher education, those unable to gain access to the EOS found it very difficult to gain access to higher education. Failure to gain admission to the EOS could thus have a disastrous effect on one's life chances (though for the resourceful, there were ways of circumventing this obstacle).

An important difference between the education system of the GDR and that of the FRG was that the former took twelve years to obtain Abitur and the latter thirteen. The thirteenth year had been abolished by the Nazis and was never reintroduced by the East Germans (MPI, 1994:184). Another difference was the existence of the GDR youth organisation, the Free German Youth (Freie Deutsche Jugend (FDJ)), which was meant to help build the all-round socialist personality. Based on the principle of democratic centralism, it was founded on 7 March 1946. The Young Pioneer Organisation 'Ernst Thälmann' was subordinate to the FDJ. Although supposed to be voluntary, the various youth organisations encompassed almost all pupils, apprentices, students and young skilled workers (Döbert, 1995:37, 55). The activities of the Pioneers took place in the Pioneer palace of Berlin, Pioneer houses, stations and clubs for Young Technicians, Young Natural Science Researchers, Young Tourists, etc., resulting in a massive and elaborate youth infrastructure. In 1964, a law on the education and upbringing of young people was introduced which required that a secular ceremony, the Consecration of Young People (*Jugendweihe*), become mandatory as a permanent feature of preparation for life and work in a socialist society (Ramm, 1990). The Jugendweihe was a continuation of earlier workers' movements, and was very deliberately designed as a secular equivalent to church confirmation in order to alienate GDR youth from church and religious observance.

Moderate change was already on the agenda even before the fall of the Wall and had been blandly discussed at the three-day Ninth Education Congress of the GDR (13–15 June 1989) at which Margot Honecker stated in her keynote speech that, if necessary, young people should defend socialism by force (Fuchs and Reuter, 1997:11). A new emphasis had already been laid on Information Technology (IT) and computers in Business and Mathematics, and from 1987–88 apprentices and students in higher education were required to do a basic course in 'Informatics'. However, IT has always been rather problematic for Marxist theoreticians because it challenges the primacy of the factory worker in the manufacturing industry by shifting the centre of gravity away from engines and machine tools (Fishman and Martin, 1987:30). However, the ideological and political basis of education was reasserted at the Congress. Education was still 'oriented towards Marx, Engels, Lenin and the great tradition of German history and school history' (Honecker, 1989:9); the last item in the conference book had the subheading: 'In loyalty to the GDR and in responsibility for our Youth, the revolutionary work goes on' (p. 89). Christine Lost (1993) in a retrospective glance at what she terms the 'totalitarian claims of GDR education' shows that this 1989 internal review of East German education was merely geared towards removing one-sidedness and rigidity in the existing system without questioning its fundamental structure. In the end, she believes, the GDR education system was too monolithic, too firmly bound in state politics and ideology, to be capable of reform. Ineffectual East German attempts at self-renewal were swept aside by the imposition of West German structures and content (p. 147).

Utopia in Sight? GDR Reform Aspirations after the Fall of the Wall

For a short period – from October 1989 to early March 1990 under Modrow and from April to September 1990 under de Maiziere – all kinds of education reform seemed possible. Suddenly, the secrecy of the niche society was cracked open, and ideas nurtured in the niches were fed into public political discourse. Those who had lived in niches took centre stage and showed that they were capable of civil courage and independence of mind. It was one of the most creative periods of the century in terms of its ferment of thought and intensity of communication. The old prohibitions and fears had been removed; reform and relief from frustration were certain, and with them the realisation of hitherto impossible dreams. After the fall of the Wall, there was huge interest in education matters and much public discussion about education issues. A fundamental reassessment took place of the aims, methods, structures and curricula of education as it had existed in the GDR. Loose forms of communication and cooperation sprang up like, for example, the People's Initiative in Education (Volksinitiative Bildung) which was based on the impetus given by K.F. Wessel. Those involved in this Initiative held their first big meeting in the Berlin Congress Hall on 9 November 1989 just hours before the fall of the Wall. Afterwards, grassroots groups were formed in Berlin, Leipzig, Jena, Rostock and Dresden, incorporating those which had existed long before the Wende (for example, church peace groups). New Forum played its part as did independent groups such as the Citizens' Education Reform Initiative Karl-Marx-City (Bürgerinitiative Bildungsreform Karl-Marx-Stadt).

By 31 December, about eight thousand communications from groups and individuals had reached the Ministry of Education. The groups, expressing a great need to communicate, had a tendency to be critical of the status quo. Although they had lived in a society isolated from Western ideas and were not used to democratic processes of debate and consultation, they underwent a personal process of development in which they quickly acquired social competence, self-assurance and energy. They passed from being compliant subordinates to independent-minded citizens. This movement is analysed and chronicled by Hofmann et al. (1991) in 'The Future of Education and Educational Politics 2000', an *Enquête-Kommission* prepared for the eleventh session of the German Bundestag and compiled between January and August 1990. In the present chapter the focus will be on what it says about school structure.

For the analysis of the material on which the Enquête-Kommission is based, 132 documents consisting of about two thousand pages were chosen. These documents were made accessible through the People's Initiative in

Education and the Independent Contact Bureau of Educational Initiative Groups in the 'House of the Teacher', Berlin. The analysis was conducted by forming categories based on theoretical constructs. After several stages of preliminary work, an instrument was developed which could be divided into twenty-four superordinate concepts with 150 different subheadings. There were three main types of concept: (1) subject areas such as holidays, pre-school education, free time; (2) sub-divisions of an area such as the rights of pupils or the rights of parents; (3) attitudes towards issues such as school leadership structures. The documents were interpreted in three stages. First of all, each was independently assessed by three researchers; then they were discussed with a view to reconciling individual interpretations or discovering new interpretations; finally, elements of the separate documents were coded and slotted into the conceptual framework as seemed most appropriate, thus permitting certain hypotheses to be checked. A data matrix was established for the whole set of documents and in order to establish the importance of each concept, a frequency analysis was conducted of its occurrence throughout the whole data set. (This, however, excluded plural references to each concept within each document.)

The most pervasive theme of the whole grassroots movement was social justice 'a topic made controversial by the fact that more and more [politically defined] 'workers' had got into positions of power and left the real working class behind (Hofmann et al., 1991:42). 'Worker' had become all too often a phoney label that high Party officials attached to themselves and their families in order to achieve sociopolitical respectability. Poorer people, less privileged and genuinely working class, were being left out as were church members and those who had the temerity to protest about the environment. The grassroots groups and individuals strongly felt that access to education should be independent of social origins, religion or world-view. People were preoccupied with basic questions of principle like reconciling the demands of society and the individual (Hofmann et al., 1991:84). About 40 per cent of the respondents wanted a less uniform school system and called for the introduction of options and specialisation. They wanted increased access to Abitur, and many, but not all, believed that the way to do this was to introduce grammar schools which would select and cultivate talent. No attention, however, was paid to the fact that promotion of the more gifted involved relegation of the less gifted to less prestigious school types such as the Main School (*Hauptschule*) (Hofmann et al., 1991:152). It was feared (though not empirically proven), that the POS had promoted the average and below-average students to the detriment of the gifted. To the East German people, this neglect of the more able was one of the most important deficits in the outgoing system that had to be remedied.

However, once the East Germans became more familiar with West German school types, they were less inclined to reject all aspects of their own system and more inclined towards a synthesis. A survey (Rolff et al., 1992) carried out by the Institute for Research in School Development (Institut für Schulentwicklungsforschung (IFS)) of the University of Dortmund in October to November 1991 included for the first time the population of the five New Bundesländer. The IFS survey covered 2,850 citizens, East and West, of whom 1,597 were the parents of children in general or vocational education. It revealed that although only 5 per cent of the East Germans called for a continuation of the old GDR system, they were sceptical about the wholesale import of West German educational structures to their Länder. The Easterners wanted a state system with a strong emphasis on achievement, discipline, politeness and good communication skills (whereas the Westerners wanted good general education). They also wanted high-level leaving certificates: 51 per cent wanted Abitur, whereas only 13 per cent wanted the Main School (Hauptschule) Certificate and 36 per cent wanted the Modern School (*Realschule*) Certificate. Only 18 per cent in the East as opposed to 26 per cent in the West envisaged a university qualification as the ultimate form of certification for their children. It therefore looked as though the Easterners' expectations were conditioned by the historically low age participation rates at upper secondary/pre-university level in the GDR. There was strong support for Polytechnic Instruction, with only 13 per cent of the East German parents stating that it had *not* proved its worth. Rolff, the editor of the 1992 volume presenting the research, calls it 'the most spectacular feature of the GDR system'. The interviewees were invited to give a rating to different school types on a six-point scale. The highest mark in all categories – either East or West – was given by East Germans to the EOS (Erweiterte Oberschule), 75 per cent approving of it strongly or very strongly. The problem was that under the old regime, there had been insufficient access to it. When asked whether it would be better to continue educating children together after primary school, 60 per cent of East German respondents agreed to common education whereas only about 40 per cent of West Germans did so. So a strong majority of East Germans voted against a highly differentiated lower secondary school.

Of course, the most natural successor to the non-differentiated POS would have been the comprehensive school. Although this was the option which would have caused the least possible disruption, it was not the option which was eventually adopted. Emotions were as important as reason in accounting for the change which eventually took place. East German parents were weary of uniformity – one school type for everyone – and wanted choice. There was a widespread, (though not empirically proven), feeling that the unified school had not done justice to intelligent, high-flying pupils, and had invested too much effort in promoting those of slow to average intelligence. Democratisation was taken to mean getting rid of the old centralistic, dogmatic, unified school system (Kluge, 1995:348). Intellectually gifted parents who themselves had felt undervalued as pupils did not want the same to happen to their children; they could see that their own society which had traditionally protected the weak was about to be transformed into a competitive society based on the West German model of market values. Their reaction was quoted in the words of Marianne Birthler, first Minister of Education in Brandenburg: 'We live in a society based on achievement. My child must be fit for such a society.' (speech at the Franz-Fühmann Comprehensive School, 27 April 1995; author's field notes). Such parents wanted the most prestigious school type in West Germany, namely the grammar school (*Gymnasium*). If this had been denied them, they might have been resentful and regarded any substitute as second best. At a deeper level than individual self-interest lay a desire to make a clean break with the past. The unified school had been the tool of a totalitarian regime and if a new society based on democratic values was to be achieved, perhaps change of a radical kind was necessary.

Legal Constraints on Change after Unification

The Unification Treaty (Jobst, 1991) in Article 37 refers to education and in Article 38 to higher education/science (*Wissenschaft*) and research (see Appendix I for text of relevant provisions). According to Article 37, paragraph 4, the Hamburg Agreement and certain relevant decisions of the Standing Committee of Federal Ministers of Education (*Kultusminister-konferenz* (KMK)) were to form the basis for the reform of the East German education system. The Hamburg Agreement of 1964 was an attempt to codify a framework for the school system in West Germany, which from the 1950s onwards seemed to be increasingly subject to centrifugal forces that were pulling it apart. The Länder had made vigorous use of their autonomy in educational matters as a result of which developments in the Federal Republic had diverged and caused difficulties regarding mutual recognition of qualifications and out-migration from Land to Land. There was a need for more central regulation, yet at the same time a desire to avoid excessive uniformity. As a result of these developments, the KMK prepared an agreement for the Länder prime ministers, the first version of which, when ratified, become known as the Düsseldorf Agreement (1955). The Hamburg Agreement (signed in Hamburg, hence its name) was a reworked version of the Düsseldorf Agreement which attempted to strike a balance between central regulation and respect for local freedom to innovate.

The Hamburg Agreement regulates a number of apparently simple factual matters such as the dates on which the school year is to begin (1 August) and end (31 July), the number of days for holiday (seventy-five), and the principle that holidays are to be regionally staggered. It sets out the terms by which different school types are to be known: the primary school is the Basic School (*'Grundschule'*) and the post-primary sector is composed of Hauptschulen, Realschulen and Gymnasien – a tripartite division each with its own leaving certificate. The function of the Hauptschule is not explicitly defined except for the fact that it finishes after the ninth form (when pupils are aged about fifteen) and must offer a foreign language, usually English, in the fifth year when its pupils enter the Hauptschule from their primary schools. Unlike the other secondary school types, it does not have the right to apply special admissions criteria. The Realschule is defined as 'going beyond the Hauptschule' and as giving general education (para. 6). The Gymnasium course is defined in terms of its right to equip school-leavers with the qualifications to enter higher education (*Hochschulreife*). In terms of prestige, the Hauptschule is obviously at the bottom of the list and has to take the pupils who cannot obtain entry in higher-ranked school types.

The maximum period of school education, including post-compulsory education, is stipulated as thirteen years (rather than the East German twelve years). Since pupils begin school at age six, this means that they normally leave school at nineteen if they do the full course leading to Abitur. Both the Realschule and the Gymnasium may exist in different forms: they may offer their courses to school-age pupils or to working people who attend in the evenings, or they may exist in a form designed to help pupils who have entered from other school types and wish to reach Abitur standard. Transfer must take place by the seventh year if pupils are moving from a Hauptschule to a Gymnasium and by the tenth year if they are transferring from a Realschule. University entrance qualifications and other types of leaving certificate are recognised by the Länder, as are teaching qualifications which correspond to the recommendations of the KMK. Categorisations of marks are laid down: for global assessments of teaching qualifications there are four designations ranging from Excellent to Pass; for specific subjects both in school and in teacher education, there are six designations ranging from Very Good to Inadequate.

The Unification Treaty and the Hamburg Agreement formed the legal basis for the restructuring of the unified school system in East Germany. As such, they had an important enabling function, yet they also had a restricting function. They set limits to the possibilities discussed during the 1989– 90 period and introduced West German patterns for reform. The speed with which unification was introduced precluded a more gradualist approach in which the Easterners could have tried out various possibilities and devised more distinctive solutions to their problems. The number of options open to them was limited by the legal framework given to them, which was the same as that in West Germany. With its introduction, the period of romance ('Let a thousand flowers bloom') came to an end and that of realism began.

New Schools for Old

When the Wall fell, the West Germans were relatively ignorant about East German education, for which there was now an urgent necessity for reliable information. A small number of West German centres for comparative education existed, notably at the Universities of Bochum and at Oldenburg, which helped to disseminate knowledge about the GDR. The Bonn Ministry of Education (BMBW) commissioned a short descriptive booklet by Wolfgang Hörner (1990a) from Bochum (who later took up a Chair of Education at Leipzig) to help explain to West Germans the existing ethos and structures of education in the East. Copies of the booklet were sent for distribution to Berlin where they were first seized upon and eagerly read – *not*, strangely enough, by Westerners but by Easterners who knew all about their own system! This may seem difficult to understand until one realises that East German terminology had been permeated with the rhetoric of class struggle and Marxism. Because of the changed situation, Easterners needed new terms and conceptual schemata which the booklet helped them to acquire. Stevenson (1995) uses text analysis to demonstrate how in the GDR communication, even in 'real', everyday, social relationships, was filtered through forms of language – 'thinking templates' – used in state-controlled newspapers or official documents. He argues that the supposed 'common bond' of language created an invisible wall between the East and the West German communities, and that East Germans had to enter what was for them a wholly new 'discourse world' (their own discourse being so thoroughly permeated by ideology). They perceive West Germans as having a slower, more emphatic speech style and a wider vocabulary, as being more skilled at speaking and more self-confident. Their own speech is seen as more refined, more elegant, more sophisticated, but also more long-winded and more pretentious with a predilection for display (ibid.:109). He concludes that clashes in German-German interaction can be accounted for, at least to some extent, in terms of intercultural communication and a resistance to what many still perceive as cultural colonialism.

When it came to the first free elections held on 18 March 1990, most East Germans aligned themselves with the ruling West German Party, the CDU/CSU. The exception was Brandenburg, which gave the SPD a majority.

Brandenburg's Land constitution was liberal and left of centre in some respects. It protected the right to strike and the freedom of collective bargaining. It went beyond the minimum obligation to protect the environment by stipulating that animals are to be respected as fellow creatures; it stated that abuse of economic power is forbidden, and that each person is to render assistance to others in case of emergency (Starck, 1994). As we shall see, the education policies of Brandenburg are distinctive and in many ways progressive. Each Land had one or more West German partner/Länder which cooperated closely with them, gave advice, and helped them to adapt to structures and regulations in the old Federal States. The New/Old Bundesländer selection was partly determined by geography and convenience; thus the northern New Länder tended to choose North German partners and the southern New Länder, South German partners, though this was not an infallible rule. The partnerships were as follows:

Partnerships between New and Old Bundesländer

East Berlin	West Berlin
Brandenburg	Berlin, North Rhine-Westphalia and Hesse
Mecklenburg-Vorpommern	Schleswig-Holstein, Hamburg, Bremen
Saxony	Bavaria, Baden-Württemberg, Hesse
Saxony-Anhalt	Lower Saxony and Hesse
Thuringia	Hesse, Rhineland-Palatinate and Bavaria

Each New Bundesland had the right to introduce its own structure within the limitations placed on it by the Unification Treaty and the Hamburg Agreement. To some extent, the school structures corresponded to party-political positions with the CDU supporting a tripartite division at post-primary level, and the SPD tending to support comprehensive schools. The party-political divisions were not, however, absolute. A case in which party affiliation did not correspond to educational policy was that of Wolfgang Nowak, the first State Secretary of Saxony, who, although he was SPD and came from the progressive North Rhine-Westphalia, believed the comprehensive school created more problems than it solved and championed the grammar school. However, the typical CDU preference in the West was for a structure which consisted of the Gymnasium for the most academically oriented pupils, the Realschule for those wanting more vocational courses and the Hauptschule for those of a more practical bent. The very name 'Hauptschule' (Main School) implied that it was to take the majority of all secondary-age pupils, but this was not so and its critics pointed to serious flaws. Parental choice had operated in the West in such a way that the grammar schools were in great demand, the Realschulen were reasonably successful and the Hauptschulen had been reduced to schools for a minority – often the children of foreign workers – who could not obtain entry into a higher-ranked school type. These shortcomings were well known, and in some of the new Länder there was a desire to avoid their effects by introducing distinctive new structures (notwithstanding the Hamburg Agreement).

A scholar who influenced the debate was Klaus Hurrelmann (1991; 1992). He cautioned against wholesale Utopian reform which would be a leap in the dark and would have no guarantee of success. He weighed up the relative merits of comprehensive and grammar schools and rejected the notion of comprehensive schools for everyone. Firstly, this would be undemocratic in that there was no possibility of parental choice, and secondly, the Gymnasium was the strongest and most successful school type in most of the Old Bundesländer: attempts to replace it would likely be doomed to failure. What he proposed was a so-called 'Two-Way Model' consisting of a grammar school and a non-grammar school sector. In view of the fact that many parents are primarily interested in getting their children into grammar school, some positive discrimination was needed to make non-grammar schools attractive in their own right. A distinctive identity would be conferred on them by making at least some of them all-day schools and prestige would accrue from giving them their own post-compulsory upper secondary forms. It was emphasised that the Gymnasium, too, needed to change in order to keep pace with the times. Although demand for the Gymnasium was strong, it was now taking in a wider ability range than had traditionally been the case; there was therefore a need to take account of such differentials. The Gymnasium should of course continue to prepare its students for entry to higher education but should also give preparation for non-academic, practical and vocational careers as well as for the theoretical pursuits. This 'Two-Way Model' was adopted in three of the New Länder: Saxony, Saxony-Anhalt and Thuringia. They were therefore, nominally at least, bipartite at post-primary level. Each Land had a different term for this new-style secondary school: Saxony called it the *Mittelschule*, Saxony-Anhalt the *Sekundarschule* and Thuringia the *Regelschule*. The decision about which leaving certificate to take was implemented in form 7 after a two-year, secondary school-based cycle of guidance and orientation in forms 5 and 6 during which pupils were normally taught in undifferentiated classes. These guidance cycles (*Orientierungsstufen*) were not free-standing in East Germany, as they sometimes were in West Germany.

All the New Länder except Brandenburg chose a four-year primary education course. East Berlin was joined with West Berlin after unification and therefore naturally adopted its structures. Brandenburg followed East/West

Berlin by going for a six-year primary school; at the time this seemed sensible in view of a planned referendum to merge the two Länder, though the citizens eventually voted against the merger. West Berlin, like all of West Germany, already had a thirteen-year course to take pupils up to Abitur and found that a six-year primary school balanced the seven-year secondary course better than a four-year primary course. Some Länder adopted comprehensive schools (*Gesamtschulen*) which came closest in ethos to the old unified school in the GDR, but in two respects now occupied a different position in the education ecology. First of all, they were no longer the sole, all-embracing school type; they existed alongside other types of secondary school with the result that the comprehensives were always 'creamed' of the most able pupils who entered grammar schools directly. Secondly, there was no internal streaming by ability in the GDR unified school, whereas there *was* in the Western Gesamtschule. Streaming resulted in a homogeneous, single age-group class where it was difficult to use a technique that GDR teachers had deployed to good effect: the more able pupils had tutored the less able to the advantage of both parties. In terms of numbers, the comprehensive school did not feature significantly in the new school landscape. In Thuringia, for example, its establishment was permitted only if the normal school types were already set up, so in essence it was an alternative. This of course ran contrary to the very spirit of comprehensive education as schooling for *all* pupils, not just for those left after the best had been sent elsewhere. Secondary school structures in the New Länder were set up as follows:

Secondary Education Structures in the New Bundesländer
(Excluding Post-Compulsory and Vocational Education)

	No. of Years to Abitur	Names of School Types
East Berlin	13	Hauptschule Realschule Gesamtschule Gymnasium
Brandenburg	13	Gesamtschule Realschule Gymnasium
Mecklenburg-Vorpommern	12	Hauptschule Realschule Gesamtschule Gymnasium

Saxony	12	Mittelschule
		Gymnasium
Saxony-Anhalt	12	Sekundarschule
		Gymnasium
Thuringia	12	Regelschule
		Gymnasium

Following unification, all the new Bundesländer except Berlin and Brandenburg had a pattern leading to Abitur at the end of twelve years as had been the case in the GDR. The political parties differed in their attitudes towards the time taken to complete Abitur: the CDU/CSU tended to favour twelve years (which was supposed to be 'harder'); the SPD rejected this as elitist, and favoured thirteen years on the grounds that it afforded the less gifted the maximum time to perform successfully. Added to this, the SPD had a trade-union argument: thirteen years' school study was likely to maximise the number of teachers' jobs available, especially in view of falling student numbers. The education authorities insisted that pupils' courses should last for the same aggregate number of hours, regardless of whether twelve or thirteen years were taken to obtain Abitur. At the time of writing, Saxony and Thuringia intend to retain their twelve-year pattern, whereas Mecklenburg-Vorpommern will move to thirteen years.

The actual formation and establishment of new schools was swift, highly pressurised and almost dramatic. Ex-GDR teachers had to apply for school types in which they were not formally qualified to work, and perhaps not all teachers were initially aware of the far-reaching personal consequences of their choice of school type. The Lower Level Schools (Unterstufen) usually became primary schools, and the EOS became grammar schools usually running from the fifth year, while the middle level POS commuted into various secondary school types. However, far more grammar schools were needed than there had been upper secondary sections in the GDR, and it was therefore necessary to form some of them *ab initio*. Sometimes there was a mismatch between the existing buildings and the new school types which had to be organised in them. All school principals and their deputies were removed from post but could reapply for their jobs; in fact between 40 per cent and 50 per cent of them were reappointed (Ninth Youth Report, 1994:112). The procedures which typically had to be followed in the formation of new schools are illustrated by the following account from a Headmaster of a Saxony-Anhalt grammar school in the Land capital, Magdeburg.

Case Study: Establishment of a New Grammar School

In May 1991, Jörg Lösel heard officially from the Ministry of Education that he was to become head of a Gymnasium from August 1991. The Ministry immediately gave him a task: he was asked to calculate how many teachers he would need to staff his new school and what subject combinations they would teach. He worked this out on the basis of the projected timetable and planned numbers of classes in the school. He had only a weekend to do this and his work was promptly checked by the Ministry.

At this point, all the teachers in Magdeburg had to decide what sort of schools they wished to work in and submit an application to the Ministry. In GDR times teachers were installed by the appropriate authorities, so drawing up and submitting a job application was an unfamiliar procedure and a real challenge to most people in this situation. The school principals got a single consolidated list of all the teachers in Magdeburg who were eligible for employment and from this long list, they had to choose which teachers they wished to employ. Since there were about two thousand names on this list, Jörg Lösel knew only a very few of the teachers: those who had been teaching at his school or those whom he knew socially. He had to choose staff without interview and had only written documentation on which to base his judgement. Of course he was aware which teachers were the best at his own school but even so he was not always in a position to obtain the staff he wanted. There was a particular teacher whom he knew to be very good but at one point during her studies she had been given a mark of 4 [poor] in a main subject. This colleague was regarded as 'not suitable' for a grammar school; anyone with such a mark had almost no chance of being accepted as a Gymnasium teacher and went down to the bottom of the list. She was an excellent teacher in practice but the school principal was not permitted to accept her even though the low mark occurred twenty years ago. He was, however, able to decline to accept certain teachers from his own school who were mediocre but he was then exposed to the uncertainty of accepting other teachers whom he did not know personally at all. Of all the former colleagues at the school only seven or eight out of the post-Wende total of forty-five had been at the same school in GDR days. There was a certain amount of tension between the Magdeburg school principals because the appointments had to be made very quickly and there was competition for the best teachers.

The speed at which the whole exercise had to be conducted was in fact breath-taking. It was on a Friday that Jörg Lösel heard he was to be headmaster and on the following Monday, Tuesday and Wednesday, he had to choose the new teachers for his school. Within the space of a single week in mid-May everything had been decided. After that, there were still possibilities of minor staffing adjustments, for example in staff shortage subjects like

Music and English, but the main decisions were made within that crucial week. Groups of Ministry officials and school principals sat in the Ministry working on the staffing plans until 10 or 11 o'clock at night. The criteria which Lösel used for his appointments were as follows: he tried to employ men as well as women (because men had been in the minority in the GDR), and to mix the age structure so as to have both young and experienced teachers complementing each other. The younger teachers are closer to the pupils because the generation gap is not so great, and the older teachers can share their many years of experience with the younger staff. In covering the full range of academic subjects, Lösel always chose teachers with an eye to ensuring the greatest possible variety of subject combinations. English teachers, for example, were chosen with History or Geography as a second subject, not necessarily another language.

At first, he was only permitted to make provisional appointments of his deputy and of the coordinators. Later these posts were advertised and the danger arose that his choices might not be ratified. However, his chosen deputy did in the end keep her position even after open competition for the post. In the selection process, she had to do an examination similar to teacher training finals which involved assessment of practical teaching (in her case, one period of German and one of Russian). She also had to show competence in some of the tasks associated with the leadership of a school: e.g. knowledge of law, of school planning and organisation. Although she had already gained experience of all these activities, she had to *demonstrate anew* that she could do them. Legal knowledge was important: the old GDR laws had to be forgotten and new ones learned. There had not been the same pressure in the GDR to relate concrete incidents and decisions to the Constitution. In the new regime, all staff – and even the pupils when necessary – were familiarised with the content of the new laws.

At their first staff meeting, there were many pleased faces because teachers were delighted that they had found employment; their future seemed relatively secure and they had obtained a post at their chosen school type – the grammar school. The fact that so much was new – school building, textbooks, pupils and staff – caused considerable pressure. During that summer, the headmaster took only one week of holidays and that was in the nearby mountains so that he would be readily available to come home should problems arise. At the inaugural staff meeting, he told the teachers straight out that the work burden would be very heavy and that they would be subject to a lot of stress, so they must prepare for a rough ride.

Source: Interview conducted by the author in Magdeburg, 2 May 1995. 'Jörg Lösel' is a pseudonym.

❦ ❦ ❦

The challenges of this transitional period usually had to be faced by newly recruited staff who did not know each other. Händle (1996a:53) believes that this fact made it more difficult for staff to cope since cohesion took time to develop and at first they could not rely on each other; psychologically this rings true. There is, however, both anecdotal and research evidence that schools composed of predominantly new staff were more innovative and in the long run more successful than schools which were not subjected to the turmoil of wholesale staffing change.

Plath and Weishaupt (1995) carried out a study which addressed the fundamental question of how to establish a new school with teachers coming in from outside. They took three schools, A, B and C, of which B was the only one where the majority of pupils liked school. The staff of school B was completely new and its members had been working together for only three years when the research was carried out. School A was composed of merged parts of other schools, and the staff of school C had not changed at all since the fall of the Wall and the attendant upheaval. The researchers sought to analyse the factors which contributed to the inter-school differences. They distributed questionnaires, conducted interviews and carried out visits to extracurricular school activities in an attempt to explain school B's success compared with A and C. The teachers in all three schools took their responsibilities seriously and tried to do their best for the slower pupils. In school B, however, the pressure towards conformity and discipline was less intense than in the other two, and pupils more often stated that they got on well together, that the strong helped the weak and that no one was excluded from the social community. The staff were young and cooperated efficiently with each other in matters such as joint preparation of lessons, exchange of materials and observation of each other's classes. In common with most GDR teachers, they did not really approve of early academic differentiation and were not used to handling pupils who were quite homogeneous in terms of their ability. In GDR times, there had always been a number of high achievers who were now of course attending their local grammar school. Of the three schools, B was the only one which was coming to terms with the changed situation and was trying to devise a programme for the more 'demanding', less gifted pupils. The researchers conclude that the wholesale staffing changes, although initially upsetting to those involved, in the end were conducive to innovation and creativity. The role of the school principal of course was also important.

The Demographic Decline

Reduction in the School Population

In most places, the net effect of the new structures was a substantial increase in the absolute number of schools. Where there had been unified schools before at secondary level, there were now bipartite, tripartite or even quadripartite structures (for example in Mecklenburg-Vorpommern). These structures were sustained for a short period until a development occurred which was as unwelcome as it had been unforeseen. A dramatic reduction took place in the East German birth rate, as shown in Table 2.1.

Table 2.1 Population Decline in the New Bundesländer

	Live Births in Thousands	Excess of Births over Deaths	Number of Births per Thousand Inhabitants
1987	226.0	—	—
1988	215.7	—	—
1989	198.9	-0.4	12.0
1990	178.5	-1.8	11.1
1991	107.8	-5.9	6.8
1992	88.3	-6.5	5.6
1993	80.5	-6.7	5.1
1994	78.7	-6.6	5.1

Source: Grund- und Strukturdaten, 1995–96.

By 1994, the number of births per thousand inhabitants in the New Bundesländer was less than half of what it had been in 1989. At 5.1 per 1,000, it was less than half of the corresponding figure of 10.5 per 1,000 for the Old Bundesländer. Between 1993 and 1995, about 60 per cent fewer children were born in the NBL (not counting Berlin); this is a demographic decline of a magnitude unique in history which will by the year 2003 reduce the primary school population by 60 per cent. The drop in the East German birth rate was clearly a product of the unification process, its stress and its influence on employment. The strains of the Wende were immense and people's greatest fear was unemployment. In 1993, there were about 8.8 million employable men and women in East Germany of whom about 27 per cent had no work. The real figure is much higher if one counts those forced into premature retirement or not registered as unemployed (Weishaupt and Zedler, 1994). Women were especially affected: in January 1994, almost twice as many females as males were registered as unemployed. Women in the GDR had been used to combining work and family, and the plummeting birth rate was interpreted as a protest against dwindling opportunities for this combination. Even for those who were employed, nervous tension increased and the sense of personal security decreased.

The effect of the population decline has been to reduce recruitment to schools, starting at pre-school and primary levels, and gradually rising up the age scale. Sparsely populated rural Mecklenburg-Vorpommern has been particularly thrown into disarray. It has an elaborately differentiated secondary school system, an increased number of schools to maintain and a falling number of children to fill those schools. Weishaupt and Zedler (1994:411) show that even before the demographic decline hits secondary level, the Haupt- and Realschulen in Mecklenburg-Vorpommern already have pupil numbers under the prescribed minimum. This situation will become *more* critical when the decline in feeder primary school numbers begins to affect the secondary level. Baumbach, Holldack and Klemm (1994:53) anticipate that about 20 per cent of primary schools in Mecklenburg-Vorpommern (M-V) will have to be closed, if the principle of one class for each year cohort is retained. For the Realschulen, 40 per cent would have to be closed after the turn of the century, while between 50 per cent and 100 per cent of the Gymnasien could survive only in a reduced form. However, like most of the other New Bundesländer, M-V is resorting to strategies of mixing school types and ages, especially in rural areas. In Thuringia, for example, over 90 per cent of all communities have fewer than two thousand inhabitants, and its education law permits the organisational combination of Grundschulen and Regelschulen so as to be able to retain schools (Ninth Youth Report, 1994:122).

Brandenburg and the Jena Plan

The demographic decline poses a challenge of massive proportions to education planners whose work is bedevilled by many imponderable factors such as the changing birth rate, regional out-migration, school structures, behaviour relating to school choice and education participation, and the speed at which people go through the system. The magnitude of the demographic decline is extraordinary and unprecedented. Special measures are required to deal with it, and the educational planners sought inspiration from scholars and reformers who had lived and worked in East Germany but had been outside the Marxist-Leninist tradition. One such was Peter Petersen, the father of the so-called Jena Plan. (For a detailed description of Petersen's life and works see Dietrich (1995) from whom the following account is drawn.) Jena is in Thuringia but the influence of the Jena Plan is widespread, resulting in its being adopted farther afield.

Petersen (1884–1952) was a North German from Flensburg who grew up in a rural farming environment, went to a village school and thence to

Flensburg Gymnasium as a poor boy. His life experiences shaped his opinion that basic education should be free. In 1904, he entered Leipzig University where he studied a wide variety of subjects, but principally theology, philology, English, history, philosophy and psychology. He did his doctoral thesis on the work of the psychologist Wilhelm Wundt and since Leipzig did not accept theses based on contemporary authors, Petersen therefore completed his work at the University of Jena where fifteen years later he was to be taken onto the staff. He became a grammar school teacher in Hamburg where he was exposed to the ideas of the reform movement, especially the notion of child-centred education. In 1920, he became head of a Realschule in Hamburg-Winterhude which subsequently became known as the Lichtwarkschule. In 1921, he completed his post-doctoral thesis on the 'History of Aristotelian Philosophy in Protestant Germany'. This work is still an authoritative one on the subject and gained for Petersen in 1923 the Chair of Education in Jena where he lived and worked until his death in 1952.

Associated with the Chair was responsibility for a 'model' school which from 1926 was known as the Jena University School. It continued to exist until 11 August 1950 at which time it was closed by East German authorities against the wishes of parents. Petersen was deprived of the right from 1949 onwards to conduct state examinations at the University. The Chairholder reformed the school according to his own educational principles and schemata. The term 'Jena Plan' was conferred on his model by English nationals at the Fourth World Conference for the Renewal of Education in Locarno. He was consciously opposed to the approach which Herbart and his followers adopted towards education and drew his inspiration instead from Froebel, Pestalozzi and Rousseau. Whereas Herbart had attached much importance to the teacher, Petersen insisted that education consisted in helping people to develop from the inside and believed with Froebel that educational processes operate in all domains of human life throughout the entire life cycle. Whereas Herbart had emphasised a cognitive approach, Petersen placed human development in the position of prime importance and subscribed to Pestalozzi's doctrine that learning must be with 'head, hand and heart'.

The Jena Plan is many-sided (for a description see Dietrich, 1995). Its forms of grouping pupils are of particular interest to those in post-unification East Germany who are charged with the responsibility of managing shrinking schools. Petersen rejected as 'fossilised' classes based on year-groups and introduced instead three broad bands: years one to three, four to six and seven to nine. (He introduced the ten-year school from 1925–29.) Within these bands were 'affinity groups' (*Stammgruppen*) intended to provide a spiritual and emotional 'home' for the pupils. The children's roles within the affinity groups resembled those of apprentice, journeyman and master and were especially useful in supporting and socialising new entrants to a school (see Dietrich, 1995:71). The groups featured carefully organised forms of inner and outer differentiation for academic activities (ibid.:176). The mixed-age groups were formed by design, rather than by 'necessity'. Petersen encouraged pupils to join learning groups of different levels according to their ability and attainment and based his notions on a combination of theory, practice and research.

Petersen's ideas have been much used in the Netherlands (Kluge, 1995: 359), and have been adapted in the New Länder to help cope with demographic decline. The situation differs somewhat from one Land to another and in the present work the strategy has been adopted of illustrating the problem by detailed reference to one Land: Brandenburg. All the following data are from BB MBJS, 13.6.95. Brandenburg bases its forecasts up to the year 2015/16 on the Eighth All-German Population Prognosis which it has analysed for its own purposes. The lowest point of the demographic decline was reached in 1993 with 12,238 births; in 1994, there was an increase to 12,443 showing the beginning of an upturn. From 1998, a gradual recovery in the birth rate is predicted which will continue to the end of the time frame covered by the calculations. The fertility rate of East Germany will gradually reach the same level as that of West Germany but will never attain the high figures of the years up to 1989. The situation is, however, rather different from one educational sector to the other.

In primary schools there will be a numerical decline, at first gradual and from 1997/98 more perceptible. This will continue until 2004/05 in which year the number of primary pupils will reach its lowest point. In the years with the lowest school numbers (2002–07), the school population will be only about 40 per cent of what it was in 1994. From 2005/06 until 2015, pupil numbers will continually increase until in 2015, they will constitute about 58 per cent of what they were in 1994. The development of pupil numbers will be such that when the sixth year has reached the lowest point, the first year will already have begun to rise to about 45 per cent of the 1994/95 figure. The decline in new school entrants relative to a baseline of 1994 is shown in Table 2.2.

Table 2.2 Decline in New Primary School Recruits Relative to 1994

Year	Per Cent
1997	70
1998	50
2000	40

Source: BB MBJS, 1995:3.

The developments in lower secondary education follow the same pattern as in primary education. At first numbers rise slightly, then a slow decline sets in which stabilises around the turn of the century. The most serious decline begins during the school year 2003/04 and continues until the year 2009/10 when it reaches its deepest point corresponding to about 40 per cent of what numbers were in 1994/95. Then the numbers will rise slightly and by the year 2015 the secondary school population will constitute 52 per cent of that in 1994 (BB MBJS, 13.6.95:4).

In the upper forms of Brandenburg secondary schools, the addition of a thirteenth year has led to an overall increase in numbers. Interestingly, a result of the introduction of the thirteenth year was that in 1994, there were almost no *Abiturienten* because they were all doing an extra year at school. Since 1992/93 the transfer rate from the tenth year has run at about 42 per cent. This high demand for upper secondary education and the introduction of the thirteenth year support an upward trend in student numbers which will be sustained until 2005 and will then fall slowly until 2015 when it will settle at about 60 per cent of 1994/95 figures (BB MBJS, 13.6.95:4).

In the vocational sector, student numbers are less at the mercy of the demographic trends because they are increased by mature students and those changing and repeating courses. Since 1992, there has been a continuous growth in this sector which will reach its maximum in 2001/02 when the total population of vocational students in Brandenburg will be 32 per cent *more* than during the baseline year 1994/95. It will then decline until 2015 when it will be 57 per cent of the 1994 figure (BB MBJS, 13.5.95:5).

The demographic trends pose a great challenge to planners. The situation regarding staffing is a painful one: the overall level of staffing remains high while the need for teachers declines. The picture is, however, different in different school sectors. In primary education there will be a superfluity of teachers, whereas in lower and upper secondary schools there will be shortages of staff, especially in certain subjects. The Land of Brandenburg is adopting two main strategies to cope with this difficult situation. The first is to encourage teachers whose jobs are in danger to take continuing education courses which would enable them to earn new subject qualifications, thereby opening up the possibility of teaching at a different level. A major continuing education programme was initiated in 1994 with seven hundred participants and is expected to build up to three or four thousand. A second coping strategy is to develop models of part-time work. To this end, discussions are continuing with the unions and professional associations. Further education centres are being merged to ensure that vocational education continues to be offered, and cooperation is being encouraged between small upper secondary forms of grammar schools which may involve sharing space.

The decline in pupil numbers will be variable according to sector and indeed locality. There is no escaping the fact that some schools will have to be closed. Yet because an upturn is predicted in the medium-term, it is important not to destroy educational capacity by closing too many schools, only to have to reopen them later if or when they are needed again. From the social, cultural and economic point of view, small rural schools have a valuable role to play, and in these terms it may be more cost effective to maintain existing small schools than to concentrate provision in one location. All reasonable attempts will, therefore, be made to prevent a thinning out of primary schools in rural areas. A special 'Model of Small Primary Schools' project has been developed for sparsely populated areas with less than ninety pupils. The ideas of Peter Petersen are being actively implemented, for example in schools such as the all-day Jena Plan Primary School in Lübbenau (see Sommer, 1995). The distinguishing characteristic of such schools is mixed-age classes encompassing forms 1 to 3 and 4 to 6, especially for subjects like Sport, Music and Art Education. Syllabuses are thematic and the pupils are made to take responsibility for their own learning and for helping each other. The teacher's role changes from being an 'up-front' authority to being a facilitator and resource person. Every attempt is made to enlist the support of parents. There is strong demand for enrolment at this school (about ten applications for each available place), and it is often visited by teachers whose own schools are being threatened with closure and who need to study examples of new coping strategies.

It is one of the ironies of the education system in East Germany that the mixed-age classes place a premium on mutual help which is reminiscent of the socialist Collective. It is also ironic that whereas the socialists were proud of having got rid of mixed-age classes, the authorities in the New Bundesländer will have to reintroduce them in order to preserve schools! Sceptical East German parents will place an onus on school managers to ensure that small primary schools are well conducted and do not become redolent of nineteenth-century teaching methodology (Fickermann, Weishaupt and Zedler, 1998:29–30). Certainly, the decline of the school population calls into question the whole restructuring of the secondary school sector in the New Bundesländer, and intensifies fears of job loss and involuntary transfers among staff. For pupils, the restructuring has often meant longer journeys to school, and for the public authorities, high costs in school transport. Hoffmann and Chalupsky (1991) remark that the more teachers feel threatened in their job security, the less they feel able to cope with all the changes, and Kluge (1995:34) states: 'The experience of real socialism is almost abruptly and mercilessly replaced by the experience of real capitalism. Bitterness and disappointment link up with a new, hitherto unknown broadening of the horizons which is well-nigh painful because it is so sudden.'

Striving for Institutional Survival

Competition between Schools

At the onset of school restructuring the demand for Gymnasien was strong, particularly in large cities, and at first they were overwhelmed by popular demand. This was especially so in Länder like Brandenburg, Mecklenburg-Vorpommern and Saxony-Anhalt where, according to school law, the parents are supposed to have free choice of school and transfer depends on school recommendations and face-to-face consultations with their children's primary school teachers rather than on examinations. Weiler et al. (1996:40) make the point that there has been a most profound change in the balance of power between teachers and parents. Whereas formerly the teachers had the upper hand, now the parents have it. In Saxony and in Thuringia, the conditions for transfer are stiffer in that they include academic criteria: if parents wish to send their child to a grammar school against the school's recommendation, then the child must take an entrance examination and will be on probation during the first year at grammar school. The initially very high percentage seeking grammar school education has gradually fallen back to more reasonable levels as the new school types become better established and as some parents realise that the grammar school is academically too difficult for their children. From having been 50 per cent in some localities, the percentage of children attending the Gymnasium is now settling at between 35 per cent and 40 per cent (Ninth Youth Report, 1994:117). Even with the decrease in enrolment, the grammar school is still developing into a mass school, and the existence of such a sector continues to make it difficult for other less prestigious school types to prosper.

The popularity of the Gymnasium is scarcely surprising in view of the educational attainments of East German parents and their aspirations for their children. Weishaupt and Zedler (1994:399–400) point out that in the 1980s about 80 per cent of the GDR school-leavers had a qualification which was comparable with that of the present-day Realschule; they quote figures showing that whereas 19.5 per cent of West Germans in a 1992 survey had no formal qualification, this was the case for only 7.3 per cent of East Germans. In a population that values education and in which the majority have solid educational qualifications, it is clear that school types other than the Gymnasium will have to struggle hard for acceptance. This has indeed been the case: within the non-grammar sector which offers the choice of Hauptschule or Realschule leaving certificates, the Hauptschule option has, predictably, been a casualty. As is well known, the Hauptschule was already unpopular in West Germany and before long it was under pressure in East Germany too. In 1990/91, 34.2 per cent of pupils in forms 7 to 9 in the Old Bundesländer were at a Hauptschule (HS) or HS track, whereas in Mecklenburg-Vorpommern the figure was only 13.2 per cent. Weishaupt and Zedler (1994) pose the rhetorical question as to whether the social basis for acceptance of the Hauptschule is present in the East German population at all, since the adults are well qualified and ambitious for their children.

Some school principals in the non-grammar sector feel themselves in competition with the grammar schools and try to hold onto their pupils rather than encouraging them to change to a 'higher' school type if they turn out to be talented late-developers. Because the unified school has been abolished and a differentiated school system introduced, it is particularly important in the interests of social justice to ensure that as far as possible the correct decisions are made about allocating pupils to school types. Any faulty decision needs to be put right, and transferability is important as a means of rectifying wrong courses of action. Inertia and the fact that different school types have different curricula can mean a low rate of transfer between school types, both 'upwards' and 'downwards'. In Thuringia, transfer can take place between secondary and grammar school after the fifth or sixth years. In 1992 about 5 per cent of the Regelschule fifth year pupils moved into the sixth year of the Gymnasium, and after the sixth year another 6.7 per cent moved into the seventh year of the Gymnasium (Weishaupt and Zedler, 1994:401). These numbers are quite small, but the numbers leaving grammar schools for ordinary secondary schools (Regelschulen) are even smaller. In 1992/93 only half a percent of the pupils in forms 5 to 9 of the Gymnasium changed over to the Regelschule (ibid.:404). It is possible under Thuringian school law for pupils to transfer 'down' from the ninth year of a grammar school to the tenth year of a Regelschule if success in Abitur seems uncertain and they wish to make sure of a Realschule leaving certificate; in 1992/93, however, only 2.5 per cent of grammar school pupils made use of this possibility (ibid.:405). Any upward move has to be 'paid for' by making the pupils spend extra time at school. In Mecklenburg-Vorpommern, Saxony, Saxony-Anhalt and Thuringia, pupils with a good Realschule leaving certificate can transfer to a grammar school and take their Abitur, but since the structure of their curriculum is somewhat different and they usually do not have a second foreign language, they are made to repeat the tenth year, which results in taking an extra year to reach Abitur standard: that is, thirteen rather than twelve years.

There is a real unease about the appropriateness of academic standards which are applied to the pupils in different school sectors. Stenke et al.

(1995) state that the level of work for Hauptschule pupils is felt to be too demanding and at the Realschule level insufficiently rigorous. Since parental will is a crucial factor in admission to the Gymnasium, access is rather liberal. This results in a school population which is officially assumed to be homogeneous – so streaming is not 'respectable' – yet is in practice heterogeneous, hence hard to manage without streaming. The fact that teachers' jobs are related to pupil numbers makes some teachers reluctant to fail pupils and send them 'down' to other school types (Weiler et al., 1996:79). The education authorities are all too aware that they need to make special efforts to give the new school types better status and they set about this in a number of ways. In Thuringia, for example, grammar school pupils are denied the opportunity to take the leaving certificate for the Regelschule; it is Abitur or nothing. This ruling is intended to give the Regelschule a distinctive value in its own right; moreover, efforts are also made to ensure that class sizes are actually smaller in the Regelschule than in the Gymnasium. Yet even these attempts at positive discrimination have proved ineffectual. The Gymnasien have tended to have the best buildings, the best teachers, the best working conditions and the best social prestige. Their creation was almost universally welcomed: in a survey of parents, teachers and pupils in Thuringia conducted by the Institute for Research in School Development (IFS), the Gymnasium was rated – at 73 per cent – more highly than any other school type, old or new. By contrast, the new Regelschule was less popular than the school type it had replaced: the secondary phase of the old POS was rated 'good' or 'very good' by over 70 per cent of parents compared with only 36 per cent for the Regelschule (quoted by Weishaupt and Zedler, 1994:420). This division between grammar schools and other post-primary school types was intensified by the fact that the providers were at different administrative levels. In Sachsen-Anhalt, for example, the *Landkreise* were the school providers for the grammar schools and the *Kommune* were the providers for other school types.

There are regional inequalities in the provision of grammar schools across the country, and in some rural areas access is incompatible with a manageable length of school journey, so the pupils are denied the chance of a grammar school education. Weishaupt and Zedler (1994:409) show that grammar schools in Mecklenburg-Vorpommern and in Thuringia tend to be concentrated in urban rather than in rural centres. In both these Länder, transfer to Gymnasien is 10 per cent higher than in other communities. In general, the more accessible the school, the easier it is for pupils to participate in it. The differentials between areas are sometimes startling. Thus in Thuringia, the transfer rate to Gymnasien varies between less than 10 per cent and 60 per cent. Even within one city, transfer rates vary: in Erfurt in 1991/92, the transfer quota from primary to grammar school ranged between 16.7 per cent and 67.6 per cent (Kuthe and Schwerd, 1993:39). Regional disparities are sharpened by the development of a free housing market which is conducive to social segregation; the decline in the birth rate, however, makes it more difficult to reconcile the cause of social justice and access with that of school viability.

Profiling

Because of the drop in birth rates not all schools can survive; some have to be closed and it is up to the state authorities to decide which ones. This puts pressure on the schools to prove that they have something special to offer. Both in order to survive and in order to enhance their educational offering, they are encouraged to profile themselves and in some Länder can obtain state-funded extra teaching hours if they do so successfully. Profiling is interpreted in different ways by different Länder, and in a country like Germany where, in both West and East, many schools – particularly vocational ones – have been known merely by identification numbers, it may seem somewhat alien. Yet successful profiling can make the difference between being closed and staying open. Profiling can be accomplished in a number of different ways, some general and some more specialist. A whole school can attempt to build a distinctive identity for itself by finding associations which will stick in the public mind. If this identity is based on a worthwhile concept, then it can be deepened in a pedagogical way which enriches classroom life and is much more than a mere label.

INFORMAL PROFILING. An example of generalist profile-building is provided by the F. Fühmann Comprehensive School in Potsdam. Franz Fühmann (1922–1994) was an East German novelist and poet who was deeply interested in children and did a great deal for them. Armin Schubert, director of a children's art gallery called the 'Sonnensegel', in 1992 suggested naming the Potsdam school after Fühmann. The relationship with the gallery turned out to be fruitful: the children made ceramics, wrote poems and a book, and designed and painted murals on the outside walls of their school, under the guidance of an American artist, William Walsh. A competition was held to find a suitable logo for the school, and a pupil came up with a simple but effective image. A poem of Fühmann's, 'In Praise of Disobedience', stimulated both visual and verbal creative production, the latter assisted by two novelists: Walter Flegel and Gerd Eggers. The moral of the 'Disobedience' story is that sometimes it is necessary to ignore prohibitions in the interests of self-preservation; following one's own path can be positive if it is in the service of humanity and independent thought. Fühmann's 'Marysas', a mythological story, has been used as a metaphor for the relationship between East and West, and was illustrated by the children in an anthology issued for the school's naming day which took place on 27 April 1994 in the presence of Fühmann's daughter and of the writer Christa Wolf, who had been personally acquainted with the poet. Marianne Birthler, then Brandenburg Minister of Education, wrote to the school on the occasion of the Nameday, and a year later attended its first anniversary. By such efforts, the school tries to profile itself in a distinctive way and enhance the quality of its children's educational experience.

FORMAL PROFILING. An altogether more formalised profiling takes place in Saxony on a Land-wide basis. The Mittelschulen (but not the Gymnasien) have six subject-based profiles which are as follows:

- Technical education
- Social/domestic science
- Economics
- Language
- Art/music (creative and expressive subjects)
- Sport

Not all schools offer the full range of profiles; on average they have proper facilities and equipment for about two profiles each per school. A science profile is being developed on a trial basis. A number of profile centres exist independently of particular schools and are used by several schools in a region; pupils and their teachers travel to these centres and the journeys are somewhat controversial due to their length – sometimes judged excessive. Long journeys result in block-timetabling and this too is the subject of criticism because lessons are crammed into four-hour periods rather than broken into shorter periods which would make it easier for the learners to assimilate knowledge. Pupils opt for particular profiles at the beginning of form 7 (age thirteen). This is an important choice which may prompt students to change from one Mittelschule to another to achieve a more preferable arrangement, and may even cause difficulties in continuity of educational pattern if parents move house to a neighbourhood whose Mittelschule carries different profiles from those where the child started out.

On the surface the profiles seem a creative idea, but in practice they cause many problems, the greatest of which is that they introduce new forms of division apart from that based on achievement. Differentiation takes place according to gender because girls tend to take the social/ domestic option, whereas boys take the technical option. Thought needs to be given to means of making the technical option more appealing to girls. Since more girls are accepted by grammar schools anyhow, the Saxony Mittelschulen have a majority of boys who are sometimes unmotivated and difficult to deal with. Melzer and Stenke (1996:324) state that the percentage of boys in the Mittelschule is 55 per cent, in special education classes 65 per cent, and in the Gymnasien 40 per cent. The regional differences in terms of access to the grammar schools are very sharply raked, and Melzer and Stenke (ibid.) quote a range varying regionally from 5 per cent to 50 per cent. The Hauptschule classes often have quite a number of pupils who are repeating the year and manifest problems such as bad behaviour and lack of motivation (ibid.:322). In short, some of the Hauptschulen resemble what in British educational parlance are sometimes called 'sink schools'.

Profiles are linked to the type of leaving certificate which pupils eventually take and to their job aspirations; this too has become a basis for differentiation. The less prestigious technical and social/domestic science profiles are associated with those intending a Hauptschule certificate whereas the economics and language profiles tend to be taken by those doing the Realschule certificate (though there is, of course, no bar to 'cross-overs'). There is a tendency to teach the Haupt- and Realschule pupils in separate classes and this, combined with the divisive effect of profiling, forces apart the two main constituencies of the Mittelschule in a way which could eventually threaten its unity. If it were not for the falling birth rate and school enrolment, Hauptschulen and Realschulen might have a better chance to become established. Indeed, the inability to offer all profiles limits pupils' choice, and some schools are therefore pondering ways of increasing the number of profiles on offer, of changing their profiles or of combining them (Stenke et al., 1995).

Tensions within the School System

The expansion of intake into the university-preparatory school sector was undoubtedly a considerable step in the direction of social justice, because access to the EOS had been so limited in GDR times. However, increased opportunity for the more able has to be balanced against the interests of the less able who lost the intensive tutoring, small classes and close teacher-parent liaison which in GDR times had helped them to realise their potential. The popularity and success of the grammar school cause serious problems for other school types: it is difficult for the less academic school types to define their own identity and impossible for them to achieve parity of prestige with the Gymnasien. International experience (not least in Northern Ireland) shows that this is normally the case when grammar schools 'skim off' the most talented pupils, and the other school types have to carve out their existence alongside selective schools for the most able. Years after the fall of the Wall, the structure of secondary education continues to be controversial and a matter for debate.

The Ninth Youth Report (1994:114) states that the school restructuring as a result of the Wende constituted the most enormous upheaval in pupils' lives.

Existing classes and school communities were dissolved, friendship groupings and the composition and membership of school staffs changed, academic selectivity was introduced, and many children had to undertake longer journeys to school. Evidence exists (BIJU, 1994) that the rapid transformation of the school system was destabilising for pupils in the New Bundesländer (NBL), at least in the short term. The BIJU research project was based on data collected in 1991/92, and covered the subjects of German, Mathematics, Physics and Biology in both New and Old Bundesländer (OBL). Pupils in the NBL were emotionally burdened by the reorganisation of the whole school structure. At the beginning of the school year, it was found that a greater proportion of pupils in the NBL than in the OBL clearly manifested fear of not succeeding. This was especially true for NBL girls and for the less able who lacked confidence in their own ability. By the end of the year, however, differences between the NBL and the OBL had diminished substantially. The grammar school pupils in the NBL showed a high level of belief in their own self-efficacy, to an even greater extent than their counterparts in the OBL. In a sense, they were the 'winners' in the reform of the school structure. Pupils were asked to respond to the statements: 'The very thought of school puts me out of sorts in the mornings' and 'There is not much that I can really enjoy in school.' The non-grammar school pupils in the NBL were the most negative in their attitudes towards school, and school type differences were significantly greater in the New than in the Old Bundesländer (ibid.:33). Yet in comparison with their peers in the OBL, the non-grammar school pupils in the NBL manifested a higher level of academic achievement. Despite this fact, they still had a more negative self-evaluation (ibid.:13), and the school type was the greatest influence on their self-concept.

The Institute for Research in School Development (IFS) mentioned above conducted surveys in 1991, 1993 and 1995 into attitudes towards schools, taking soundings of opinion in both East and West Germany (Rolff et al., 1992; 1994; 1996). The same questions were asked from one survey to the next so that trends in the formation of opinions could be observed. By 1995, it had become obvious that in retrospect the Easterners had come to value certain elements of their former school system very strongly. They were asked (Rolff et al., 1996:51) whether they would have preferred to see: (a) the GDR system retained unchanged; (b) change in both the external school structure and the internal curriculum; or (c) the external school structure of the GDR to be retained but divested of its Party-political ideological pedagogy. Option (b) was what had *actually* happened but by 1995, only one-fifth of respondents chose this option. By far the favourite was (c), and 21 per cent of the parents even went so far as to choose (a). The proportion wishing 'no change' has even risen since 1993. The higher the school qualification of those surveyed, the stronger the tendency to go for option (b). Over 70 per cent of the research subjects endorsed the concept of common education for all children up to age sixteen (form 10), and working-class people were keener on a unified post-primary sector than more middle-class people. The Easterners emphasise the values of achievement, discipline and social justice to a greater extent than the Westerners. They seem dissatisfied with the way in which their new school structure is developing, and their attitudes and values diverge in some important respects from those in the Old Bundesländer (Rolff et al., 1996:54).

It may well be that the objectives of maximising all pupils' potential and mediating a positive self-concept to as many children as possible are no longer attainable using the organisational concepts of the early 1970s. The Hamburg Agreement was taken as an unconditional legal 'given' from the onset of the restructuring. It laid down the different school types, each with its corresponding leaving certificate. Schools in East Germany with their mixed school types of Mittelschule, Regelschule and Sekundarschule actually deviated from the Agreement and to the extent that this is true, the NBL produced more liberal regulations. The new hybrid school types are distinctive for the New Bundesländer, but the crucial fact remains that they are obliged to cater for two different types of leaving certificate: those of the Hauptschule and the Realschule. This vitiates the reality of a 'Two-Way Model' such as Hurrelmann had suggested. The existence of these different leaving certificates has a divisive effect which tends to re-create tripartitism (Abitur track plus two others) within a nominally bipartite system; moreover, shrinking school numbers can make the formation of viable classes impossible if pupils have to be taught in separate classes for two different leaving certificates.

Most pupils have a more subtly differentiated achievement profile than is allowed for in the division between two different school certificates. They may be poor at French but good at Informatics, or good at Geography but mediocre at Science. Such pupils would be well served by a type of examination which reflects their varying levels of performance in different subjects. This possibility is offered by examinations such as the Republic of Ireland's Leaving Certificate with its Pass and Honours levels or by the British General Certificate in Secondary Education with its Basic and Higher level. The Hamburg Agreement stands in the way of such integrative examinations which are good for pupils and would make the diminution in pupil numbers much easier to cope with in the new Bundesländer. This Agreement served a useful purpose in West Germany in the 1970s and 1980s but is less appropriate for the East Germany of the year 2000 and the new millennium. In some West German Länder, too, the division between school types is becoming blurred. Surely the time has come to replace the Hamburg Agreement with another more modern manifesto which takes account of the circumstances in the united Germany.

≈ *Chapter 3* ≈

SCHOOL LIFE AND LEARNING

Educational Practice in the GDR

Education was the primary means of inducting the young into Marx-ist-Leninist values and reproducing East German society on socialist principles. According to Lenin, school was to become an instrument for the dictatorship of the proletariat. The transition to 'existing real socialism' made it very difficult to think in any terms other than socialist, and since socialism had to be accepted as an undisputed 'given', the only way for-ward was to fine-tune or perfect the system within its existing ideological parameters. This led to a concentration on classroom practice at the ex-pense of more general debate about theory and principle which could not be questioned.

The GDR possessed a detailed series of syllabuses which had their gene-sis in the 1960s and remained essentially unchanged for twenty years. Each syllabus was meticulously built up according to its objectives, content and methods; in addition there were teaching guidelines (*Unterrichtshilfen*) which gave such detailed help that they were almost fail-safe. By the end of the 1980s, there were more than 150 guidelines which gave such firm, clear directions on schemes of work and teaching methodology that nothing was left to chance (MPI, 1994:263). Such works were published by the state press, *Volk und Wissen* (People and Knowledge), in shabby and uninspiring-looking volumes carrying pictures of farm machinery or Lenin addressing the masses or Erich Honecker talking to school pupils – sometimes with all three types of picture on the same cover.

Teaching was efficient and discipline was normally good: all but a few pupils mastered the basics – and indeed far beyond – and East German pupils were particularly good at Maths and Science (BIJU, 1994). Yet, despite the system's merits and achievements, problems existed. Sometimes teachers found that the children of top Party officials flouted their authority and demanded special attention. There was a quality of regimentation about classroom life which was ill-adapted to producing independent-minded citizens. Even little children were disciplined by being shamed in public, and the Collective was used to build group norms sympathetic to the sociopolitical aims of the Party. After the fall of the Wall, when Western educational theories became current, the term 'symbolic violence' was extracted from the work of Bourdieu (1977) and used by some Easterners, for example intellectuals at the University of Leipzig, to characterise the spirit of the educational process in the GDR. This, however, must not be allowed to obscure the fact that GDR teachers had an enormous and unremitting concern for their pupils (MPI, 1994:339).

The giving of marks in East German schools was more than a mere recording of pupils' performance. It was also a means of deciding on their life chances and motivating them to achievement. The latter was accomplished more easily by good than by bad marks and, since teachers were judged by their pupils' level of achievement, there was a tendency to inflate marks. The mark scale was 1 to 5, and if a young person needed an 'Excellent' mark (1) to get into university, then it was a matter of solidarity to give it to him or her. In 1982, 42 per cent of those embarking on higher education programmes had obtained the mark 'Very Good' in their Abitur (Ninth Youth Report, 1994:109). Teachers felt under immense pressure to get through a crowded curriculum, to attain the official learning objectives, and to ensure that as few pupils as possible failed and therefore had to repeat classes. They were supposed to toil at the chalkface just as labourers toiled in the streets or on the coalface, and they shared with the proletariat the same constraint of meeting 'production targets' – though teachers produced not commodities but (eventually) skilled workers. The socialist ethos of the whole society imbued the teachers with a special concern for the weak and disadvantaged whom they devoted many hours to helping *gratis* out of school hours. They also undertook personal visits to the children's homes to ensure home-school liaison. On the one hand, this assistance to the less able was humanitarian, but on the other hand, it was necessary for professional self-preservation in the face of an overtly critical, not to say hostile, school management system which could and did hold the teachers responsible for their pupils' failure. Pupils knew how to exploit these norms, and it was not infrequent for a teacher to be told by a lazy, under-achieving pupil looking for better marks than she deserved: 'You won't be *allowed* to let me fail!'

The youth organisations such as the Pioneers, and for older pupils the Free German Youth, were drawn into the process of helping those who had difficulty in meeting the academic demands of the school or those whose behaviour was in any way problematic. Matched partnerships of pupils, one high ability and one lower ability, were used for peer teaching and the consolidation of material. This was especially necessary since all classes were mixed ability and streaming was not permitted. The Youth Initiation Ceremony (Jugendweihe) was a *rite de passage* analogous to confirmation of Christian pupils and all were expected to undergo it. Only members of religious organisations were exempted and to them it was clearly communicated that this withdrawal was not socially or politically acceptable. FDJ activism was regarded as a positive factor in the selection process for the EOS – to which, of course, admission took place on social and political as well as on academic grounds.

The values which the GDR education system endorsed are vividly illustrated by the following school report on a girl who had just finished her period of ten-year compulsory education at the POS:

> The Collective values Cornelia for her open and honest manner and her constant willingness to get involved when FDJ tasks have to be accomplished or class problems solved. She thinks and acts with a consciousness of class issues. In her three-year function as the FDJ secretary, her endeavours to drive forward the Collective and to imbue it with new ideas for FDJ work deserve special recognition. Cornelia also showed the highest sense of responsibility in her school work. She studied very diligently and ambitiously to reach the highest goals. Despite her successes, she is constantly polite and modest. She accepts advice and criticism willingly, reaching the right conclusions about what will enable her and the Collective to develop. Cornelia has developed the characteristics of the socialist personality to a significant extent. She is capable of leading and guiding a Collective.

One of the most hated GDR subjects was *Staatsbürgerkunde* (SBK) (Civics; a free translation, Civics for Socialists, gives a flavour of SBK's political overtones) which had been the carrier of much of the Marxist-Leninist and SED Party ideology. It taught, for example, that

> We live in the era of transition from capitalism to socialism, at a time in which all forms of human existence will be renewed in a long-drawn-out historical process. The revolutionary transformation of the world through the abolition of capitalist exploitation is associated with the eradication of the roots of national oppression and annihilating wars. (Grundmann et al., 1989:41)

> In our country, there are many Collectives which deliver exemplary achievements in resource management and in the most economical deployment of national income. One can observe how they raise productivity above average, how they build homes cheaper and faster than elsewhere, how they achieve an equal or superior level of efficiency with smaller input, how they avoid complacency once a certain level has been reached and instead constantly aspire to new heights so as not to be left behind in international competition. (ibid.:101)

The power of the working class, its leading role in society, are realised not only through the state but also in other organisations. In first place stands the SED as the party of the working class. The parties and mass organisations in the National Front of the GDR are ranked alongside it. They all function closely together under the leadership of the SED and form the political organisation of socialist society. (ibid.:147)

History was a hegemonic discipline which was consciously used by the Party to help legitimate the political system and create social identity. Marxist historiography was based on the concept of dialectical, revolutionary change, and had its distinctive periodisation. Whereas western European historians divided time into prehistory, antiquity, the Middle Ages and modern history, Marxists analysed it into primeval, feudal, bourgeois, socialist and communist periods, and rarely presented political history in terms of concrete governmental issues and foreign policies (Ahonen, 1997). Sirkka Ahonen (ibid.:48) demonstrates the manner in which ideologically slanted terminology helped keep historical discussion safely within the Marxist-Leninist frame of reference: the Berlin Wall was 'the assurance of peace in Europe'; the American War of Independence was 'the first bourgeois revolution in America'; the annexation of Belorussia, Moldavia, Latvia, Lithuania and Estonia into the USSR was called 'the growth of the friendly family of the Soviet people'; while German unification in 1871 was 'the final bourgeois revolution in Germany'. This rhetoric had to be used in public, but in private people had their own interpretations which eventually led to the rejection of the 'double-faced' and narrow, manipulative teaching.

The environment had always been a sensitive issue in the GDR, though officially the Constitution protected it. Local Studies (*Heimatkunde*) informed pupils about the struggle for a socialist fatherland; the life of Karl Marx and Friedrich Engels; the heroic struggle of German workers under the leadership of the communists against oppression, war and fascism; the good results of socialist development in industry and agriculture; the importance of water for plants, animals and humans. Children were adjured to use as little water as possible, to turn off taps immediately after drawing water, not to let water run unnecessarily, not to rinse dishes under running water, to shower rather than bath and to be especially economical in the use of water on warm days (Motschmann et al., 1985). The country tried to become self-sufficient in energy and used the lignite which existed in its territory as fuel for industry. Lignite, since it contains so much moisture, did not give good heat and caused a lot of air pollution but the Party didn't want to draw attention to this fact. In 1982, a law was passed entitled 'Decision of the Ministerial Council on the Secrecy of Environmental Data' (No. 47,1.2./82, 16.11.1982), according to which all topics in this field were state secrets. All discussions about the visible change for the worse in the GDR's environment were seen as attacks against the received wisdom of the Party. Those who reproached the regime over its lack of consideration for nature were sometimes subject to dire punishment from the Secret Police, even extended on occasion to the *families* of the protester. This proxy punishment – which could involve deliberate, serious injury to a son or daughter – was intended to absorb the time, emotion and energy of the dissidents so that they would be less effective in opposing the environment policies of the Party (Personal interview, 27.2.93; Schell and Kalinka, 1991). Subjects like School Gardening and Astronomy had been offered with ulterior motives in the GDR: the former was intended to train children in means of food production for the socialist nation (useful if it became necessary to 'Dig for victory' in case of war), and the latter to sensitise them to issues connected with the space race against the United States, thereby building up sympathy with the SED against the country's 'imperialist enemies'.

The West Germans set out to introduce a new spirit of freedom into the schools; to remove fear from both teachers and pupils; to liberalise the curriculum; to modernise materials and methodology in subject teaching; to introduce pupils to the concept of a market economy and to democratise education – surely a massively ambitious agenda. It was handled by the New Bundesländer Ministries of Education in collaboration with the federal government, the teachers themselves and the Institutes for Continuing and In-Service Education, of which there was one in each of the New Länder. In the remainder of the present chapter, an attempt will be made to probe the extent to which the reform of external school structure described in the previous chapter facilitated the reform of inner content: that is materials, curriculum, syllabus and methodology, understood as classroom practice.

New Books

One of the most successful schemes in the renewal of East German education was also one of the simplest in concept: the West gave the East large numbers of free textbooks. This project, known as the Action for School Textbook Supply (*Schulbuchaktion*), was a personal initiative of Dr Eberhard Jobst, a senior official at the Federal Ministry of Education and Science in Bonn. Jobst liaised with the Association of School Textbook Publishers in Frankfurt am Main to select and transport 2.46 million books to the new Bundesländer. It was a huge logistical exercise but was implemented technically almost to the point of perfection. The Ministry provided 32.8 million Deutschmarks for the purchase of the books, while the Association of School Textbook Publishers gave a rebate of 50 per cent off the shop price, which meant that 6,992 East German schools received books to the value of 66 million Deutschmarks (BMBW, 21.1.1991). The books covered an enormous range of disciplines. These included the most obvious like History, German, Geography and Economics, as well as vocational subjects like metalwork and its subdisciplines such as plumbing and soldering, floristry, electronics and pastry-making for the catering trade.

It was difficult for the East Germans to know which books to select and how to use them, so Jobst collaborated with the Association of Seminar Leaders (Bundesakademie für Studienleiter (BAK)) in setting up a series of introductory sessions in thirteen central locations to induct the Easterners into textbook selection and use. A condition of the scheme was that the East Germans should have the right to decide freely on the choice of books when they came to the point of ordering for their schools; another condition was that only books approved for use in West German classrooms were included in the scheme. Even with this help, mistakes were sometimes made and schools ended up with incomplete coverage of a subject or a form of presentation which proved unsuited to their pupils. More seriously, the new materials were available chronologically *before* the new syllabuses, and the two often did not match. As a result teachers had to copy whole sections of other books which seemed to correspond better to their pupils' courses (Döbert, 1995:152).

The Association of School Textbook Publishers received many written expressions of thanks from grateful teachers, and the project attracted attention in the world's media, being featured in newspapers, for example, in New York and Singapore.[1] Classroom interest in the glossy new Western books was intense and the enthusiasm which they aroused eclipsed the dowdy Volk und Wissen publications. This was, however, temporary. Volk und Wissen did not die: once freed from the constraints to which it had been subject under the old regime, the press reinvented itself and after a period of development began to produce smart, modern books which met teachers' needs and were popular in schools. In Thuringia, for example, it became a market leader, among the top three educational publishers. A sense of residual loyalty and the need for books attuned to the local environment (and perhaps a consciousness of the troubled East German economy) made some teachers choose an East German publisher over a Western one – given equal merit in content and presentation.

---

1. It is only fair to point out that sometimes the West German publishers sought to offload books which they did not want onto the East German schools! They also hoped that some of the schools to which they gave books would eventually become clients and place orders with them in future.

New Curricula and Syllabuses

Newly produced syllabuses were eagerly snapped up by teachers for use in the classroom. In the former GDR they would have placed almost total reliance on such documents and were thus preconditioned to do the same after unification. They found, however, that the new-style syllabuses and guidelines were much less directive than they were accustomed to. They were not used to planning their own material nor to working in an inter-disciplinary way. Some of them had fretted under the constraint of the old syllabuses and teaching guidelines, but along with that constraint had come a degree of support and security which was no longer available to the same extent in the new regime. Now teachers have to learn to work much more independently and creatively on the basis of certain general principles, objectives and outline syllabuses. The Land Brandenburg (BB MBJS, 30.4.1994) adumbrates the following guiding concepts for the plan-ning, execution and analysis of teaching: pupil orientation, action orienta-tion, problem orientation, a holistic approach (*Ganzheitlichkeit*), selectivity in teaching and learning (*Exemplarität*), academic orientation, open learn-ing, differentiation, project-oriented work, and thematic work. Although these educational core principles are most impressively articulated, teachers do not always find them easy to put into practice.

In GDR times, syllabus guidelines had been delivered to schools as from on high, but after the Wende the process of producing them became more consultative. In Saxony-Anhalt, for example, the Ministry of Education coordinates the work of 150 syllabus guideline committees a year, each con-sisting of five to seven members drawn mainly from the teaching profession and higher education. Over one thousand persons are involved in the process, including parents and other members of the public. The Land Par-liament has to approve the guidelines, typically taking about eight months to do so. Naturally the consultation and the parliamentary scrutiny slow up the process of syllabus production, but at least the Land population cannot complain that it has not been consulted. The guidelines are now firmly based on broad consensus. Once finalised, they are intended to be used for four to five years. The role of the universities has become an advisory rather than a formative one as it was in the GDR where the universities actually wrote the syllabuses. It could be argued that the contribution of higher edu-cation has now been marginalised compared with what it was before the fall of the Wall, but the positive element in the reformed situation is the active contribution made by classroom teachers. Curriculum development in the New Bundesländer stimulated nationwide interest in the process with regard to quality and comparability, but because of the need to produce new syllabuses rapidly, there was little opportunity to try out new subjects or interdisciplinary combinations. It was easier to play safe by simply adopting conventional, existing West German models (Döbert, 1995:149).

The number of lessons offered per week varied from Land to Land. In forms 1 to 4, the NBL offered fewer lessons than had been given in the POS; only Thuringia came close to the POS, and Brandenburg had substantially fewer periods a week (Döbert, 1995:164). The same trend held true for forms 7 to 10 of post-primary school: in absolute terms a smaller number of periods was offered in the NBL than in the former GDR (ibid.:207). A North/South divide existed in the NBL, with the South offering more weekly lessons than the North (Döbert, 1995:163–4). No doubt this was intended to lighten the heavy load which had prevailed in GDR times, but it has been pointed out by Lynn (1988) that Japanese children work significantly longer than their contemporaries in Europe and the United States, and that their high educational standards are at least in part due to the greater length of their school year. Therefore, reducing NBL pupils' contact with subjects may make it more difficult for them to achieve as high results as before. Class sizes have risen in the NBL. Before the Wende, the POS had an average of twenty-one pupils per class, and the EOS, seventeen (Döbert, 1995:153). Although the regulations vary from one New Bundesland to another, the general guidelines lay down larger units, for example about twenty at the post-compulsory level in forms 11 and 12.

The balance of subject matter within the curriculum was adjusted to give more emphasis to expressive subjects which call upon pupils to use their imagination. Compared with the POS, the NBL offered fewer hours' instruction in German, Maths, Science, History and Political Education, whereas the number of hours in foreign languages and artistic subjects was increased (ibid.:208–9). In Saxony-Anhalt, the proportion of time devoted to the latter was at 9.37 per cent – double what it had been in the GDR (ibid.:210). Some of the controversial subjects in the GDR curriculum were retained in the new curriculum, but in a changed form. Astronomy was taught purely as science and dealt with matters such as the developmental stages of the cosmos. School Gardening was divested of its ideological content, and was either integrated into another subject or left in its free-standing form. It was regarded as especially appropriate in Thuringia which is famous for its fertile soil and has a long horticultural tradition. Its capital, Erfurt, boasts a permanent Garden Exhibition dating from 1961 which is visited by over a million and a half people a year. One of its citizens, Johann-Christian Reichart (1685–1775), was responsible for the introduction of scientific seed production and the establishment of gardening as a commercial concern. In such an environment, School Gardening can put pupils in touch with their past as well as orienting them towards the future.

A SCHOOL GARDENING LESSON. A lesson randomly sampled by the author in Thuringia, which took as its theme 'Weeds', was taught to a class of eight-year-olds sufficiently few in number (sixteen) to perform practical tasks like planting and hoeing; (the class was divided in half for this particular subject). The lesson happened to be taught on a rainy day when the pupils could not get outside into the real garden. It began with an attention-focusing poem on dandelions, followed by a definition of 'weeds' elicited from the pupils in Socratic style, then confirmed and restated by the teacher. Next the children were given samples of various weeds – living green plants – which they identified at their desks; thereafter pictures of the weeds were labelled and stuck into the exercise books, and the children wrote a little about each plant. Then came the most original element of the lesson: the pupils were invited to taste a warm sweetened infusion of nettle tea which they all enjoyed and which helped to drive home the message that weeds are useful and can be humankind's friend rather than enemy. The lesson thus made use of several different sense modalities such as taste, touch, sight, smell and sound. It was very effective in arousing the pupils' interest and developing the target concepts.

CIVICS. From 31 October 1989 – so still under a GDR government – the syllabus for Civics for Socialists was suspended and exposed to censure, and the subject was summarily abolished (Ninth Youth Report, 1994:111). Its purpose had been to socialise people into a socialist society. With the Wende, the objective of political socialisation changed: the process was no longer directed towards socialism but rather towards a free democratic society. Just as the new society was pluralistic, so the agents of socialisation were plural and diffused in a sort of permeation model. Political socialisation was mediated through teacher training and government law-making. At school it was carried in textbooks, in subject content, and also in school conventions and procedures. An apparatus of committee structures for pupil and parent representation had long been current in West German schools, and was introduced in the New Bundesländer in an effort to give pupils a taste of participatory democracy and a limited degree of self-government (see for example Brandenburg's *Die Demokratische Schule: Zur Mitwirkung im Schulwesen*). Article 2 (1) of the Basic Law – 'Everyone has the right to the free unfolding of his or her personality, insofar as s/he does not infringe the rights of others' – was supposed to guarantee the right to one's own opinion or world-view, in short to plurality. No one single school subject existed which was supposed to teach clearly articulated democratic values, and the various concepts of 'freedom' which a growing child could discern in the new society seemed to, and indeed did, contradict each other. New school laws held out the possibility of joint decision-making power, and a Bund-Länder-Kommission project sought to involve children in environmental planning in Leipzig and in Frankfurt. Yet in Leipzig, property restitution problems prevented the use of a wasteland area for an extension of a school playground. Authors Mauthe and Pfeiffer (1996), reviewing general attempts at school democratisation in both East and West Germany, conclude that the real possibilities for pupils to exert influence on school structures and content are very limited. They believe that for children the motivational effect of having any say at all in school affairs is so great that attempts at school democratisation are well worthwhile, especially since pupils are usually satisfied with relatively little. What children – and adults too – initially hoped for was freedom in relation to the pursuit of desired ends and lack of compulsion in relation to personal beliefs. Pluralism implied absence of pressure to conform. Berndt (1990) points out that the East German population had been very much conditioned to live in harmony with societal norms and this preconditioning created the danger of new conformity, based on the different values currently in vogue in the NBL. Freedom, prosperity and justice were hoped for, and when this Holy Trinity proved elusive, many East German people felt steam-rollered (ibid.:227).

HISTORY. In many cultures history carries heavy ideological baggage, and the GDR was no exception. Rust (1993; 1995) has made a special study of the subject in East Germany before and after the Wende and begins by pointing out its strengths in GDR times: it was highly integrated, was articulated between all grade levels, and had a clear theoretical and conceptual framework running through the entire series of textbooks. On the down side, it was normative and authoritarian, and did not allow for alternative perspectives in any way. In fact, texts were essentially political tracts using History for ideological purposes (ibid.:208). *En passant*, Rust also notes how puzzling it is in retrospect that the GDR textbook writers failed to highlight some of their state's achievements: the attempt to change the status of women, the institution of a comprehensive social welfare system, child care centres, medical care and so on. Despite ideological bias, it is interesting to note that high standards had been achieved in GDR History classes: in 1990 Borries and Lehmann (1992) conducted an empirical study of historical awareness among pupils of the same age in East and West Germany, and found that the Easterners showed superior achievement in terms of 'cognition' and 'basic value orientation'.

The fall of the Wall meant that Easterners were at liberty to revise their syllabuses as they saw fit, and in November 1989, the old History syllabus was suspended. By February 1990, the programme had been largely revised for forms 5 to 10 with the orientation away from 'service to the state' towards strengthening the individuality of each pupil. It was no longer dedicated to a single ideological orientation. Up to the summer of 1990, therefore, it was the East Germans themselves who took the initiative in syllabus reform. From the school year 1990/91 onwards, however, a Western approach was asserted. Although Volk und Wissen revised its history books, Rust (ibid.:212) states that West German authorities pressurised the East German Länder to forbid their use. In a review of fourteen History textbooks, Rust concludes that up to 75 per cent of the content is about West Germany, and that the young Easterners are learning little about their own environment and development. Accounts of how West German agricultural, industrial and service production exceeded East German trends were scarcely calculated to imbue Easterners with civic pride. He calls for a History which reflects the reality experienced by all its people, and which is written from a new, more all-encompassing, multicultural (East and West) perspective. Brandenburg, he believes, provides a particularly good lead in this respect, in that its new syllabuses allow the exploration of both East and West German interpretations of critical events after the Second World War without imposing a clear-cut, predetermined interpretation.

GEOGRAPHY AND ENVIRONMENTAL STUDIES. The type of Geography which the East German teachers had known was 'scientific' physical and regional Geography, which evaded political issues and was perceived as a politically neutral subject (Mai and Burpee, 1996:31). To many East German teachers, this was the 'real' Geography, and they had little understanding of human and social Geography. Cartographic conventions in socialist countries were different to those in non-socialist countries, and in the old days, the authorities had treated large-scale maps as confidential documents not available for non-military uses like local geographical studies in schools (ibid.:35). In West Germany, reforms of the 1970s aimed at incorporating more democracy into educational institutions had resulted in fundamental changes in the conceptualisation of Geography as a subject. Regional Geography was replaced by topical Geography, transferable skills were emphasised, and knowledge of location of specific places was discredited as 'postal Geography' (Niemz, 1996:45). By the 1990s, a survey on Geography teaching in West Germany (Niemz, 1989) revealed widespread teacher dissatisfaction with syllabuses and textbooks in their Länder. An international project (Inter Geo II) by the Commission on Geographical Education of the International Geographical Union (IGU) provided data on the Geography achievement of pupils in East and West Germany. On each subtest, except Human Geography, East German pupils scored higher; they even scored higher on geography skills, although these had been a major objective in West Germany since the 1970 reform, and scored considerably higher on regional Geography (Niemz and Stoltmann, 1992).

After the fall of the Wall it at last became possible to discuss environmental problems openly, and young NBL people found them of great interest since they brought up moral as well as scientific issues for consideration

(Protze, 1994:33). Indeed, environmental studies made an important contribution to values education, doing so in a practical non-doctrinaire manner which was stimulating to both teacher and pupil. Heimatkunde was no longer taught in the same form as before; some of its functions were subsumed in Geography which after the fall of the Wall became much more popular as a subject. Though travelling was now so much easier, the Wende brought problems as well as pleasures for Geography teachers. With little consultation, they were given new syllabuses containing concepts which were the product of many years of discussion in West Germany, and were expected to understand and to be able to use them without further ado. Predictably they found this quite difficult and longed for a more prescriptive approach, with the result that some teachers dusted off their old textbooks and brought them back into use. The new textbooks were West German oriented, and in a survey conducted by Mai and Burpee (1996) few examples from pupils' local environments were found. Thus, the issue of brown coal was dealt with in one textbook by elaborating on mining near Cologne, whilst neglecting the importance of this industry in Saxony (ibid.:30). Moreover, the textbooks were sometimes out of sync with the syllabus. Because the new Geography was problem oriented, the teachers felt that it carried a political message of some sort, and this tended to discredit the subject to a certain extent (ibid.:33). Mai and Burpee (1996:35) point to NBL teachers' 'striking lack of understanding' towards Geography as a pedagogical tool to strengthen pupils' autonomy in school and society alike, and they state that the subject was introduced too quickly for teachers to become convinced about the values and benefits of new approaches.

ECONOMIC AWARENESS. Efforts are being made to teach East German pupils economic awareness and to acquaint them with the principles of the market economy which differs so much from the planned economy in which their parents grew up. This is tackled routinely in the mainstream classroom where teachers explain the laws of supply and demand, the flow of money and goods, the stock market and private enterprise. A special experimental project is led by Dr Antje Lüben (of the German Trust for Children and Youth at the Comenius Institute, Radebeul), in association with the Ministry of Education in Dresden, Saxony, as part of a wider scheme promoted by the Bund-Länder-Kommission. Here the pupils form companies to carry out certain economic tasks. For example, there is a travel agency called 'Power Tours' in Hoyerswerda which arranges school trips, excursions and journeys for classes, children, youth groups (and teachers too). It has been able to obtain sponsorship to buy equipment, and the agency now boasts a computer, fax, telephone, printer and videocamera. It produces posters, curriculum vitae, job applications and commercial materials to order. Penalties are prespecified in its terms of business if the work is not completed efficiently and punctually; if it is, then all employees of the firm participate in the profits. Such school minibusinesses are not unusual in the West but in East Germany they are exciting and stimulating because of their novelty; by their nature they are well fitted to become self-sustaining once the initial support of Dr Lüben and the Ministry has been withdrawn. These projects certainly play a useful role in socialising pupils into a new economic order.

New Approaches to the Methodology of Teaching

Methodology is by no means ideologically neutral. Klingberg (1996) points out that East and West Germans have a common tradition in education emanating from such classical thinkers as Comenius, Herbart and Diester-weg. In its philosophical background and theoretical orientation, the East German theory of didactics was in the 'Western' mould, but the GDR tended to neglect general educational questions in favour of classroom teaching influenced by the Soviet dialectical-materialist model. Here one can discern a form of Abgrenzung against the West with its allegedly '*bürgerlich*' theories said to be rooted in National Socialism (ibid.:502). The East German approach to methodology had been firmly teacher-centred and whole-class teaching was the norm. In the 1980s, however, there had been a move towards a more pupil-centred orientation (Hörner, 1990a:13) and this trend was continued in the united Germany. Immediately after the Wende, East German teachers' attention was almost totally absorbed in matters pertaining to their very livelihood, such as whether they were going to be made redundant and in what school type they would teach. However, they were eager to observe classroom reality in the West and, as soon as it was practicable, they poured into West Germany – usually heading for a Bundesland with which their New Land was partnered. There they were warmly welcomed and given every help and support; they spent time observing classes and opened up a dialogue with their Western counterparts. Indeed there was so much travel to the West by teachers, pupils and their parents that Saturday morning lessons in the East had to be cancelled or rescheduled.

At first, East German teachers were disposed to admire all they saw and were impressed by lavish classroom equipment, but soon a counter-reaction set in. The Easterners became critical of undisciplined Western pupils and contrasted this unfavourably with their own traditionally well-behaved pupils back home (though the latter were becoming somewhat rowdy too as a result of their perception of 'freedom'). Methodologically, teaching in the West seemed to lack the rigour and authority of teaching in the East; more emphasis seemed to be placed on participation than on the acquisition of a body of knowledge. The Easterners had not known what the standard of comparison was and, when they experienced it at firsthand, many of them lost incipient feelings of inferiority and gained a new self-assurance: they argued that what they had been doing all along was sound enough.

Their positive self-assessment was supported by some research. Shortly after the Wende, a major longitudinal study (BIJU, 1994, 1996; Schnabel et al., 1996) of educational success and psychosocial development was launched, comparing pupil achievement in selected East and West Bundesländer. The researchers used their own measures of achievement rather than taking them from the class teachers. The project, which ran over a period of five years, began collecting data in 1991/92. That school year was still sufficiently close to the Wende to measure the effect of the POS rather than the reformed system. The interim report (BIJU, 1994) stated that in German, Maths and Biology, East German seventh year pupils performed better than their West German counterparts. NBL girls outperformed OBL girls in Maths and Physics. The spread of marks in the West was greater than in the East where pupils' marks tended to cluster around the mean and avoid the very low achievement categories. It is sometimes argued that the GDR system disadvantaged the more intelligent pupils in favour of the average, and the researchers therefore investigated this issue. They were not able to find any empirical evidence that the top-level pupils were under-achieving (BIJU, 1994:27). In the second and summative report, the authors demonstrate that achievement orientation and a positive motivational syndrome ('good feelings') can coexist perfectly well. Teacher-centred procedures can be conducive to achievement and if these are combined with a warm emotional climate in which the socioemotional commitment of the teacher is obvious, and due weight is given to the social relationships between teachers and pupils, then there should be no question of cognitive goals being attained at the expense of the pupils' emotional well-being. The BIJU authors state (BIJU, 1996:42): 'If teachers succeed in balancing a combination of pupil- and teacher-centred approaches so as to create a positive emotional climate, without abandoning demands for subject achievement, then the essential conditions for the promotion of achievement without loss of motivation are fulfilled.'

This insistence on the balance between intellect and emotions is very important. In GDR times teachers worked hard and successfully at subject teaching; they maintained close relations with parents and demonstrated an immense concern for the well-being of their pupils which went far to mitigate the leaning towards cognitive subject mastery. They had achieved their own equilibrium between the human and the academic. Now the question is whether they will be able to maintain all of this after the fall of the Wall.

Already their contacts with parents have changed. Either they have become more tenuous (no more home visits by teachers), or else the parents have assumed greater power than heretofore through parental choice and through the committee structures for codetermination. This can, though it does not necessarily have to, lead to tension rather than cooperation. It is well known that East German teachers prefer tightly organised teaching that adheres to a plan based on subject content (Rase-Schefler, 1996). In West German teacher training, by contrast, there is a very strong emphasis on pupil participation which sometimes threatens to outweigh cognitive development. Pritchard (1992) shows how teachers and their trainers attempt to promote school democracy through 'open' lesson planning and non-directive teaching, but expresses concern lest the pursuit of a democratic ethos be allowed to cover up vague lesson planning and failure on the part of student teachers to develop proper pedagogical skills. She questions whether social interaction should be allowed to become more important than the knowledge gained by those who are being taught. There is pressure on NBL teachers to adopt new styles of teaching compatible with Western norms, and the danger is that these may jeopardise the traditional balance between psychosocial well-being and intellectual progress. The new way of specifying syllabus guidelines certainly constitutes a great contrast to the GDR way. The GDR specifications were usually in terms of subject coverage, but the new specifications emphasise '*exemplarisches Lernen*' which involves a selective choice of content geared to the interests, knowledge and experience of the pupils (BB MBJS, 30.4.1994). 'Exemplarisches Lernen' is not always easy to handle.

The new Western methodology comes with its own ideological loading: it is supposed to contribute to the democratisation of school and society, so it has to be taken seriously in the New Bundesländer (as well as in the Old). Two of the 'buzz words' are 'Open Instruction' and 'Project Work', both required in the Brandenburg Core Principles (ibid.). Project work was not popular in the GDR. It was regarded as 'bürgerlich', revisionist thinking which undermined the principle of systematicity and the desired high level of academic general education. Moreover, it gave both teachers and their pupils an increased scope for decision-making and action; this eroded the pivotal position of the teacher and was intrinsically resistant to central direction and steering (Bastian and Fuhrmann, 1992:176). Yet ever since the 1970s, East German educationalists had been thinking of ways to make learning more flexible and closer to life. To this end, the Institute for Didactics of the Academy of Educational Science mounted, over a period of several years, an experiment which was to all intents and purposes project-oriented but was camouflaged by terms such as 'Raising the Level of Pupil Activity'. Thus, despite all appearances to the contrary, the ex-GDR did not begin from zero in the domain of project work. Active attempts were made by New Länder governments to promote such work, and Tosch (1996) reports on a post-Wende 'Innovative Learning Project' set up in 1993 by the Brandenburg Ministry for Education, Youth and Sport. This scheme sponsored no less than 506 school projects intended to change the existing school culture and humanise the school – though Tosch notes (p. 522) that in some schools the effect of the projects was to challenge the existing self-concept of the school administration to its very limits! He takes the fact that 385 of the 506 projects were carried out in the six-year Grundschule and in the Comprehensive School as an indication that the more innovative outer structures (i.e. those particular school types) facilitated inner innovation in terms of content.

It would, however, be a cardinal error to equate 'open' teaching with 'good' teaching, and Haedayet (1995) stresses in this connection how important it is not to indulge in a general negation of whole-class teaching. The BIJU research too (1996:42) emphasises that a positive motivational climate is much more important than 'open' forms of teaching, especially if the latter appear unstructured, chaotic and undisciplined to the pupils. Clearly, training is important in making a success of the new methodology, and Döbert (1994:37) indicates that younger teachers are better at it than the older ones; also that university-trained teachers seem to meet the new challenges better than those trained at the former Institutes for Teacher Training (IfLs). It is vital that the East German teachers retain their existing competencies alongside the new ones which they are acquiring. Certainly, they should be encouraged to broaden their pedagogic repertoire but without jettisoning the subject-teaching skills which have served them so well in the past.

Pupil Classroom Norms in East Germany

The interface between teachers and pupils in East Germany is a delicate one: both have assumptions, expectations and a habitual way of acting which sets them apart from West Germany. As one might expect, pupils in the former GDR have been socialised differently than those in West Germany, both at home and in the classroom. There is some evidence (Ahonen, 1997:50; Friedrich, 1990) that in GDR times highly educated young people identified more strongly with socialist society perhaps because they at least had a modicum of job satisfaction, whereas young industrial workers suffered more from the economic failure of their society and so had neither much job satisfaction nor money. Researchers have hypothesised that young people in the East might be more authoritarian than in the West, but

Rippl and Boehnke (1995) find no persuasive evidence that state socialism in the GDR produced distinctly more socialist personalities than Western democracies such as the US and the FRG. Klein-Allermann et al. (1995) in an empirical study found that, in contrast to their expectations, adolescents in both parts of Germany did not differ substantially in their proneness to violence and anti-foreigner attitudes, although East German adolescents were more strained by environmental factors. These authors point out that at present there are relatively few foreigners in the NBL and this fact, combined with the internationalism promoted by the philosophy of socialism, results in a low NBL level of anti-foreigner discrimination among young people. The Ninth Youth Report too (1994:192–3) shows that only a tiny percentage of youth, either in East or West, has actually taken part in violent deeds (4 per cent and under), though most youth (NBL 75 per cent; OBL 58 per cent) do want stricter controls on immigration (ibid.:198). Though these findings are broadly reassuring, it should be noted that the percentage of youth justifying violence or willing in principle to engage in violent acts is larger in East than in West Germany (ibid.:192–3).

A complex, multiphase research project in the Max Planck Institute (Oettingen et al., 1994; Oettingen, 1995) has been devoted to studying how factors associated with school performance affect school children in East and West Berlin. (Empirical work was carried out in the former GDR in July 1990 and in the latter in 1991.) The study has been extended to include Russian and American as well as German children (Little et al., 1995). The researchers adopted a conceptual schema devised by Skinner et al. (1988 a, b and c) postulating three basic belief systems linking actors and means:

1. *Causality beliefs (or means-ends beliefs)* refer to children's beliefs about what factors influence success or failure in school. The factors involved in the study were effort, ability, luck, teachers and 'Unknown'. (This last category yields high values when children say that they do not know what causes good and bad school grades.)
2. *Agency (efficacy) beliefs* refer to children's beliefs about whether they personally can gain access to means of assistance which can be expected to influence school performance. The four a priori defined performance-related means were: effort, ability, luck and teachers' help.
3. *Control beliefs* resemble the notion of 'expectations for success' in achievement motivation literature; they refer to children's convictions about whether they are generally able to achieve success in school and avoid failure. This third belief system is a syndrome of a general nature in which causality and agents are not specified.

Some of the findings (Oettingen, 1995) indicate that pupils in East Berlin are more dependent on their teachers' judgement for concepts of self-efficacy than pupils in West Berlin. Easterners at the lower but *not* at the higher level of intelligence believe that they are capable of achieving only as much as their teachers' opinions suggest. Authority bears down very heavily upon their estimates of their own competence and likelihood of success. In comparison with their West German counterparts, they believe themselves to be less smart, to have lesser capacity to exert effort in school, to attract less luck, and to attain less help from their teachers. Interestingly, there was a gender difference in perception of teachers as agents: girls believed that they had more access to teachers than boys. The lower perceived self-efficacy begins in third grade and is pervasive for the rest of the school years.

Oettingen et al. (1994) account for the East-West Berlin differences in a number of different ways, though they prefer to focus on the school context rather than on the general societal-political context as an explanatory framework. First of all, they recall that in East Germany, it was the custom to announce praise and negative sanctions publicly in front of the class. In case of low performance, children had to accept from their peers unsolicited help imposed by their teachers, despite the fact that such measures can lower children's evaluations of their own competence (Graham and Barker, 1990). Thus, academic self-perception and self-concept were directly linked to public respect granted by the teacher and the class Collective. The influence of school was intensified by the high degree of overlap between school and social life – most children of one classroom met each other again after school. Teaching style too was important in accounting for East/West differences. In East Germany, the tendency was towards full-class teaching which Oettingen et al. (1994) term 'unidimensional' as opposed to more varied patterns of teacher-class, small-group, pair and individual interaction which are termed 'multidimensional'. They claim (ibid.:590) that differences between unidimensionally taught pupils in the same class tend to be more transparent and more highly differentiated than in multidimensionally taught classes. Moreover, they quote Rosenholtz and Rosenholtz's statement (1981) that pupils in the latter category of classroom demonstrate higher evaluations of their own potential which are less strongly linked to teacher and peer evaluations than in unidimensional classrooms.

Oettingen at al. (1994) speculate that the East Berlin children's dependence on teachers may not ultimately operate in their favour, particularly as they enter the world of a unified Germany. If pupils do not have a strongly held belief in their own self-efficacy, they may give up more easily in the face of set-backs and failure. Western perspectives suggest that children should keep a positive view of their potential as long as possible. However, the psychosocial comparison between Germany and the US indicates that

East Berlin pupils' perceptions may not be altogether dysfunctional. They are at least *realistic* in their self-perceptions, and this is likely to be a strength to them. Little et al. (1995) demonstrate that pupils in Los Angeles displayed a very low correspondence between their self-related appraisals and their actual school performance. Although this is in keeping with general macrolevel influences in American society toward optimism and individualism, pupils in the United States are ill-served by having self-beliefs which are illusory. If they have been nurtured in an academic fool's paradise, they are likely to receive a rude shock when they go out into society to exercise their all too modest competencies. It is important not to forget that in terms of school achievement level, the Easterners show up well in East-West comparison (BIJU, 1994). The ideal objective in the united Germany must be to maintain Eastern students' good performance whilst trying to promote a self-image which is less deterministic and more life-enhancing without becoming totally unrealistic.

Youth Policy in East Germany

The Ninth Youth Report (BFSFJ, 1994) devotes itself particularly to the issue of young people in the New Bundesländer after the Wende. This Report was researched and written by independent experts, but in a commentary at the beginning the federal Ministry for Family, Old People, Women and Youth (BFSFJ) takes up a stance in relation to the Report's findings and recommendations. Whereas such reports are often fully accepted by the government, in this instance the Ministry takes sharp exception to some of the assertions made, for example in the experts' criticism of policy relating to welfare and poverty in East Germany. It is freely admitted that families with numerous children have problems, as do incomplete families and those in which the parents are unemployed. In such circumstances, there is no alternative to welfare. The Ministry points out, however, that being in receipt of social welfare is usually transitional, has a preventative function and enables people to participate in social and cultural life.

The government believes that there is little point in comparing economic prosperity in East and West Germany because the East started from such a low base. It chooses to highlight the fact that buying power and incomes have greatly increased in the NBL: between 1991 and 1993, the percentage of parents claiming to earn over DM 3,000 a month increased from 25 per cent to 68 per cent (BFSFJ, 1994:vii). In 1991, the federal government provided DM 20 million for the programme 'Summer Encounter' to bring young Easterners and Westerners together; 20,000 jobs in youth work were provided by 'ABM' job creation schemes, and a further

18,000 under the programme 'Work Promotion East'; properties and buildings for purposes of youth work can be purchased at up to 80 per cent of the market value; a Cultural Infrastructure Programme has been financed by the Ministry of the Interior; the Federal Youth Plan of 1991 mandated DM 47 million for voluntary providers of youth services; and the West German Bundesländer were given an extra DM 1 million for their work in developing youth structures in the NBL. Moreover, the investment programme *'Aufbau Ost'* will provide DM 6.6 billion annually for 10 years for youth, education and social work in the NBL (ibid.:iv–v). An action programme against aggression and violence has been launched (ibid.:xii). In view of all this intense financial and social effort, the Ministry energetically rejects the proposal of the independent experts that 'special programmes' should be set up for youth work in the NBL. The creation of an entire new youth infrastructure is already under way, and the federal government believes that it has managed to cushion the process of economic transformation (ibid.: viii). It is only fair to quote these facts and figures in answer to accusations that the West is uncaring about the welfare of young people in the East, and has put nothing in the place of the previous structures which existed in the GDR.

The government does address itself to the problem of violence among East German youth. It is observed (BFSFJ, 1994:x) that the life cycle phase of 'youth' has been prolonged after the Wende because more young people are taking advantage of educational opportunities. They are not, however, keen on civic behaviour such as voting, and their integration into the adult world is hesitant, complicated and sometimes disrupted (ibid.:xi). Although aggression is sharpened by competition for scarce resources in East Germany, xenophobia is not explicitly neo-Nazi, though of course it could in future become so. In fact, deviant behaviour is almost as pronounced in the West as in the East, but the Ministry believes that '[The present young NBL generation] has only endured the pressures of the old regime briefly and will be able to enjoy the advantages of a democracy for a long time' (BFSFJ, 1994:vi).

Much has been done; there remains much to do, and of course many problems of a structural nature exist. The Ministry does not, however, see the well-being of young people purely in economic terms. It states with conviction that it would be wrong to limit the advantages of the Wende to material things, and that 'freedom and justice have been won back'. The tradition of ethical reflection among NBL young has been broken by constant regulation and overdirection in GDR times, and in the circumstances the Ministry is convinced that the best service it can render to young people is to make them self-confident and socially competent: 'If young people are enabled to master their lives independently, they will acquire the necessary inner assurance and serenity in their contact with the unknown and the unforeseen' (BFSFJ, 1994:xiv).

Yet the challenge to the government and its Ministry remains a substantial and urgent one: a majority of young people still think that the government is not doing enough for them (ibid.:192), and Bettina Westle (1995:240) predicts that if democracy cannot 'prove itself' in respect of individual freedoms, rights of political participation and the rewards of material well-being, then there is a danger of political abstinence and/or a turning towards violent, right-wing radical groups on the part of East German youth.

Chapter 4

RELIGIOUS EDUCATION, CHURCH SCHOOLS AND ETHICS

Religion in a Socialist State

The territory of the former German Democratic Republic was the heartland of Lutheranism and of the Reformation. Martin Luther was born in Eisleben (1483), took up his studies at the University of Erfurt and entered the Augustinian Cloister at Erfurt (1501), nailed up his ninety-five theses in Wittenberg (1516), worked on his translation of the New Testament at the Wartburg Castle in Eisenach (1521/22) and died in Eisleben (1546) (Bainton, 1955). In view of this historical background in the GDR, the reformed church in particular was the agency that confronted the SED Party over educational matters. Indeed, education, as the key to forming the outlook and value system of the young, was the most bitterly contested issue dividing Church and state. The SED Party claimed a total monopoly on education and used this monopoly to promote its own goals. Schools, colleges, universities, institutions, both formal and informal, and the laws of the land were made to serve the ideological monism of Marxism-Leninism. No private schools were permitted, and the Church was not accepted as a partner in policy-making or in shaping the curriculum. The state authorities defended this stance by pointing out that to give the Church a consultative role of this type would be to contravene the principle of the separation of Church and state.

The Protestant and the Roman Catholic (RC) Church differed in their ways of managing their relationships with the state. Though both of them had no alternative but to recognise the de facto existence of the GDR state, the RC Church was much less overtly confrontational than the Lutherans. It kept its distance from the SED Party, the block parties and the CDU, whilst preserving sufficient links with the state authorities to facilitate its charitable and pastoral work (Lange, 1993:4–5). It was in the nature of things that the Church had to have an official communication partner for contact with the Ministry for State Security; in the Berlin Bishop's Conference of the 1980s, this was Prelate Paul Dissemond, whose code name as an informal co-worker was 'Peter' (Deutscher Bundestag, 1995:932). However, the possibility of the Ministry influencing a large number of informal co-workers was greatly reduced by the organisational structure of the Church, which was so hierarchical that the Bishop of Berlin was almost the only person who counted for purposes of liaison with the Ministry (ibid.: 933). Under Cardinal Alfred Bengsch, the RC Church was almost completely politically 'abstinent'; for example, it made no public comment about the building of the Berlin Wall (ibid.:930). Bengsch's achievement was to preserve the unity of the Catholic Church in a situation in which he received little support either from the West German government or, more surprisingly perhaps, from the Vatican itself. The Holy See was disposed to recognise the GDR as a political reality and under Pope Paul VI there was a proposal to establish new East German bishoprics; this was subsequently somewhat downgraded from 'bishoprics' to 'Apostolic Administratures', but these Administratures were still merely the lesser of two evils to those who did not want to see an incipient split in the Church. In 1978, just as Cardinal Bengsch seemed to have lost the battle, Pope Paul VI died and was replaced by the Polish Pope, John Paul II. The former Cardinal Wojtyla had lived in a communist regime and had few illusions about concessions to an atheistic state. A visit of the GDR foreign minister to seal the agreement about the Apostolic Administratures, already planned under the previous Pope, was due to take place on 29 October 1978 but was aborted at the last minute: the new Pope had definitively broken with the concession policies of his predecessor (ibid.:929). Bengsch died the following year and was given a funeral celebrated by several cardinals from Germany and abroad. This was done at the express wish of His Holiness in order to emphasise the bond between the world Church and East German Catholics.

The 1980s were a time of relative stability for the East German Catholic Church. State Secretary Klaus Gysi had been the GDR's ambassador to Rome and, while not exactly supportive of the Church, was not especially anticlerical. The state itself enjoyed an increasing degree of international recognition which was conducive to feelings of self-assurance and reduced pressure to split the Church. The most notable event of the 1980s was the Dresden Meeting of Catholics on 10–12 July 1987, which was attended by about 10 per cent of RCs in the GDR. The price which had to be paid for the state's allowing this function to take place was that political themes were scarcely touched upon (ibid.:935). This passivity continued right up to the fall of the Wall which actually coincided with a change of leadership – the appointment of a new cardinal, Bishop Georg Sterzinsky, on 24 June 1989. As a result of its self-ordained political abstinence, the Catholic Church took little part in the Peaceful Revolution.

The GDR Roman Catholic Church's numerical fall in membership under socialism was much less dramatic than the GDR Protestant Church's decline. In 1964, nearly 1.4 million people were members of the Catholic Church, in 1979 there were almost 1.3 million, and in 1992, just over 1 million. The Protestant Church fared badly in terms of membership: in the late 1940s more than 90 per cent of the population claimed allegiance; in 1964, it had 11.5 million members (about 68 per cent of the total population, down from a high point of nearly 17 million in 1950); in 1979, 7.6 million members; and in 1992, 4.8 million members. Table 4.1 shows the percentage figures for Church membership in the East German population, including Berlin, shortly after unification (statistics taken on 31 December 1992).

Table 4.1 Percentage of the NBL Population Claiming Church Membership, 1992

Protestant	27.0
Roman Catholic	5.9
Other beliefs or no religion	67.0

Source: EKD, 15.10.94.

The enormous erosion of Protestants in East Germany, from over 90 per cent in 1949 to 27 per cent in 1994 took place despite the fact that the Protestant Church had a constitutional right to exist (as indeed did other churches). During the forty-odd years of the GDR's existence, the complex, embattled relationship between the GDR state and the Lutherans improved and worsened by turns. In the early post-war years 1945–49, the Church had a certain credibility rooted in its non-cooperation with fascism. The 1949 Constitution guaranteed freedom of religion and conscience, and Article 6 put religion in a special category. Thereafter, however, Church-state relations deteriorated into a sort of struggle, and in the 1968 Constitution, religion was mentioned merely as one category among other basic philosophies which were to be accorded certain rights and duties. The rights and freedoms granted in the 1949 Constitution disappeared. Only two areas of the Church's work were especially protected: its spiritual ministry and its charitable work. Article 39 (2) states that the Churches may order their own affairs, but must do so in agreement with the Constitutional and legal dictates of the GDR. Goeckel (1990:82) points out that in socialist states, constitutions have a different status to that in liberal democracies. They are revised in order to produce rather than follow change, and are intended to lay the ground for the next stage of development towards the goal of a communist society. In such a state, rights granted by a constitution can be all the more easily subverted in practice.

The GDR was an entity geopolitically wedged between East and West, and the Church was a sort of Trojan Horse within a socialist state, representing values alien to the SED: the Christian non-materialist and theist philosophy as opposed to the Marxist materialist and atheist philosophy. For the founding fathers of Marxism, religion was a false consciousness, the opiate of the people undermining their will to rebel, an unscientific ideology grounded in myths and legends, a fantastic reflection in people's minds of those external forces which control their lives. Ultimately, the Marxists' objective was to destroy religion and all of its manifestations. Nevertheless, despite militant atheism, both Marx and Lenin in their different ways advocated a limited cooperation with Christians. Lenin was in favour of letting Christians into the Party, and of cooperating with them pragmatically. Within the GDR, there was supposed to be complete separation of Church and state, yet Marxists and Christians were called upon to collaborate for the building of socialism (Goeckel, 1990:28). The attitude of the state authorities towards the Church was thus riven by contradictions. Sometimes, the state was utterly antagonistic towards the Church but at other times it looked for loyalty and assistance from it.

At the highest level, the relationship between Church and state was influenced by macropolitical developments, in particular the struggle of East Germany for international recognition, and by the diplomacy of German unity. In a dramatic series of developments, these tensions eventually split the German Protestant Church, and in 1969 the Eastern part became known as the Federation of Protestant Churches (the so-called *Kirchenbund* consisting of the Eastern *Landeskirchen* or church provinces). The build-up to this culmination of events began in the 1950s. During this time the Soviet Union continued to profess a desire for the reunification of Germany which was more tactical than real. By holding out an attractive possibility to the West Germans – that of a united Germany – it intended to loosen the FRG's commitment to the Western alliance. The FRG, however, continued to progress towards full sovereignty, which had the rebound effect of making the Soviet Union concede greater sovereignty towards the GDR. As each part of Germany sought the trappings and indeed the substance of nationhood, the two Germanys drew apart from each other. The FRG was integrated into the West's defensive strategy, while the GDR was incorporated into the Warsaw Pact. A milestone development was the Military Chaplaincy Agreement (1958) between the West German member churches of the Evangelische Kirche Deutschland (EKD) and the West

German army. This was controversial in both East and West, and the official SED interpretation was that it intensified the link between the EKD and NATO. Despite the fact that the Agreement did not include the East German Protestant Churches, the GDR, which regarded the EKD as treacherously fuelling the Cold War, used it as ammunition for splitting the Church. Tension between Church and state escalated. The Church was challenged to pledge its loyalty to the state, and in 1958 an agreement – a truce – was concluded between the two parties in which the Church promised to respect the development of socialism. This was a step towards the concept of 'the church in socialism', which involved some acceptance of the state's values on the part of the Church.

Pressure continued for the GDR to delimit itself from the FRG (Abgrenzung) and there was concomitant pressure on the East German Churches to separate themselves from West German Churches. The GDR state refused to deal with leaders of the EKD from West Germany, and after the erection of the Wall in 1961, such leaders were not even permitted access to the GDR. The splitting of the Church was a pragmatic result of the construction of the Wall. In 1967, the EKD made a declaration at Fürstenwalde in support of all-German unity in Church organisation, but it was itself internally divided about the policy. The dissident Bishop Mitzenheim of Thuringia, sometimes known as 'The Red Bishop', took the view that the boundaries of the East German Church should be isomorphic with the GDR state, thereby distancing himself from the Fürstenwalde Declaration. The new Constitution of 1968 was another weapon used to compel the Eastern Churches to separate from the Western by insisting that they should order their affairs according to the laws of the GDR. The state continued to play one Landeskirche off against another and threatened to make separate agreements with them. De facto separation eventually took place in 1969 when the Federation of Protestant Churches (Kirchenbund) was established.

Although intended to improve relations between Church and state, the Kirchenbund was not at first recognised by the state; in fact, recognition was delayed until February 1971. While there were a number of reasons for this reluctance, the most crucial one was that the state disliked the continuing ecumenical relationships and links with other churches in the West, all of which indicated that the process of ecclesiastical Abgrenzung was not yet complete. The formation of the Kirchenbund was a move which tended to unite the Protestant Church within East Germany, thus constituting a potential challenge to the state's strategy of *divide et impera*. There was always a possibility that Kirchenbund synergy would raise the profile and power of the Church in society, and the state would have to rethink its strategy for coping with it. A unified structure meant that the Kirchenbund had to be taken more seriously by the state.

However, the state was in no particular hurry to achieve a breakthrough in its relations with the Church; indeed the impasse increased the state's leverage on the Church. In the end, recognition of the Kirchenbund came about because the policy of playing the Landeskirchen off against each other ran into difficulties, and the state came to the conclusion that it could use the Kirchenbund for its own purposes, for example exerting influence and defusing criticism. Abgrenzung as a policy objective took precedence over 'divide and rule'. It is, however, important to realise that such recognition did not change the state's basically antagonistic stance towards the Church. As Goeckel (1990:157) put it: 'The initiative of February 1971 did not represent a change in the state's long-term goal of reducing the churches to mere ritual on a par with the churches in most Soviet bloc states.'

Despite recognition of the Kirchenbund, tension between Church and state still continued. Erich Honecker, no doubt in an attempt to define his profile clearly in relation to the West and to set himself off from his predecessor Ulbricht, began to emphasise ideological issues: the leading role of the working class, the GDR as 'the socialist nation' and the 'all-round developed socialist personality' (Goeckel, 1990:156). These ideological issues were divisive and exacerbated conflict in Church-state relationships. The GDR Protestant Church authorities handled these problems by avoiding public confrontations with the state. For example, at the World Council of Churches in Nairobi (1975) they opposed the proposal to hold a plenary debate on the issue of the religious situation in the USSR – obviously an embarrassment to socialist governments. At home and in private they did try to negotiate with the state about conflicts of interest, but these negotiations were out of the public eye and the impression arose among laity and some Church people that the Church was collaborating with the state to an unacceptable extent. On 18 August 1976 Pastor Oskar Brüsewitz of Zeitz committed suicide. His death was a protest against the pain caused by discriminatory state policies, and his burning was of great importance in discussions about the position of Protestant Churches in the GDR. The SED Party declared his action to be that of a mentally unsound person, but he was later regarded as a martyr by right-wing fundamentalist Christian groups.

The time had come for some action to reduce such a high level of discontent before it reached unmanageable proportions. On 6 March 1978, a summit conference was held between Erich Honecker and Bishop Schönherr, Head of the Kirchenbund, as a result of which important concessions were made to the Churches (Landeskirchen). They were granted access to television four times a year; they were allowed to visit ministers in certain prisons; they were to be compensated for Church lands now tilled by agricultural cooperatives; clergy and other established Church workers were to be integrated into the state pension scheme; Church congresses were to be facilitated; and the building programme begun in 1976 was to be continued. It was not just the actual concessions which were noteworthy; it was the fact that the state was tacitly accepting the Church's presence and according recognition to 'an allegedly anachronistic, ideologically taboo institution' (Goeckel, 1990:242). The recognition was, however, of a pragmatic nature and was not tantamount to giving the Church official status. This would have been contrary to state policy and would have undermined the leading role of the Party.

Education, Young People and the Church under Socialism

At the root of the Church-state conflict was the fact that the Protestant Church was unwilling to accept a curtailment of its role to the spiritual realm and to 'good deeds'. A number of its Bishops, notably Hans-Joachim Fränkel of Görlitz, Werner Krusche of Saxony-Magdeburg and Heino Falcke of Erfurt, took the view that the state should not attempt to make the Church politically irrelevant, and this naturally set Church and state on a collision course. The subjects of conflict between the Church and the regime were many and varied: Stalinist policies such as the collectivisation of agriculture and the socialist transformation of industry, abortion, human rights, the education of clergy and of their offspring, the ecological environment and socialist militarism.

A major purpose of the education system was to form the socialist personality. Socialist individuals had to have a firm class standpoint and a Marxist-Leninist view of the world, and this purpose was repeatedly reinforced by the Youth and Education Laws of the GDR and the SED Party Programme. Marxism-Leninism was atheistic and therefore incompatible with Christianity: a loyal supporter of the GDR must have a negative attitude towards the Church. Students in higher education were required to display personal commitment to the working class and the socialist state, and in 1950 Marxism-Leninism was made a compulsory subject at universities. Lecturers were forbidden to propagate religious doctrines. In July 1950, the SED decided at its Third Congress to base instruction at schools and colleges on the theories of dialectical materialism, and this policy was endorsed by a Central Committee resolution of 19 January 1951. A decree of 1 March 1954 declared that all teachers would have to be loyal supporters of the SED Programme (Maser, 1963:94–95). The Education Act of February 1965 reiterated that the objective of education was to produce convinced and committed Marxist-Leninists. The SED's Eighth Congress (June 1971) declared anew that the socialist personality was atheist and

Marxist-Leninist, and in 1975 courses on scientific atheism were introduced into universities and colleges. Atheistic propaganda work was reincorporated into the study programme of Party members in 1977/78 (Railton, 1986:79–81).

These legal prescriptions had direct consequences for GDR teachers. It was clear that they could not serve two masters, the state and the Church; the Minister for Education, Fritz Lange, stated at a teachers' conference that ideological coexistence between them was not possible. The consequence was a flight of teachers leaving school teaching. In the period following the uprising in 1953, and again between 1956–58, there was a great loss of Christian teachers and students from the system. In 1952–53, hundreds of Christian teachers lost their posts and 3,000 young Christians were expelled from secondary schools and universities. In 1954, 1,500 teachers were removed from their posts for political reasons, and it became clear that those who gave courses in Religious Education would lose chances for promotion and might be transferred to another locality (Railton, 1986:70–71).

The Church's potential as an alternative agent of socialisation was greatly reduced by the state's requirement for young people to join the FDJ and the Pioneer organisation. The Church's own efforts for youth were circumscribed by state restrictions: Christian youth groups were declared to be illegal organisations, and the sole newspaper for Christian youth, *Die Stafette* (1947–1953), was prohibited supposedly because of a paper shortage. An issue which became particularly divisive was that of the Youth Dedication Ceremony (Jugendweihe). The Jugendweihe had its roots in the 1848 Revolution and had begun in the mid-nineteenth century as a humanist movement instigated by freethinkers (mostly from the middle class) who had turned against the orthodoxy of official school religious education and wished to organise their own freethinking classes and associated school-leaving ceremonies. Eduard Balzer of Nordhausen popularised the term 'Jugendweihe' from about 1852 onwards, and by about 1890, it was quite widely used. The first Jugendweihe ceremony with a proletarian character took place in Berlin on 14 April 1889 in front of an audience of 1,500 in the Concert House in Leipzigstraße. Thirty-seven young people were 'dedicated' and promised to promote political and social progress (*Jugendweihe*, 1989:7).

In the early years of the twentieth century, the Jugendweihe became more closely linked to the Social Democratic Party. In 1921, the publication *Mein Genosse* (My Comrade) appeared; this was the first communist Jugendweihe book, and in the following years it reached print runs of 34,000 copies. The conceptual preparation of young people for the ceremony continued to develop, addressing themes like society, class, revolution, the origins and meaning of religion, and the revolutionary struggle. On 28 February 1933, all social-democratic and communist Jugendweihen were declared illegal, and subsequent ceremonies took place in deep secrecy. They resumed openly in the spring of 1946 and gathered momentum until in November 1954 the Central Committee for Youth Dedication of the GDR was constituted. The following year, the Committee promulgated ten themes for the preparation of young people and at that stage emphasised that participation in the Jugendweihe was open to all regardless of their religion or world-view (*Jugendweihe*, 1989:15). However, the book which was used as the supporting text for Jugendweihe preparation, *Universe-Earth-Human Being* (*Weltall-Erde-Mensch*, 1954) was based on atheistic materialism. By June 1955, 52,322 boys and girls took part in the Jugendweihe, and many local committees were formed to promote its development (*Jugendweihe*, 1989:18). This they did so successfully that between 1981 and 1985, 1,163,943 young people participated: that is, 97.4 per cent of all fourteen-year-olds (ibid.:22). It was, therefore, an almost universal experience. All teachers were required to encourage their pupils to participate in the ceremony.

The choice of age fourteen for the Jugendweihe was strategically important in terms of young people's schooling options. Until the GDR school reform of 1983, this was the stage at which decisions were taken about admission to the Oberschule. Later under the new law, the POS went up to form 10 for all except pupils in some selective special schools. Political as well as academic criteria were taken into account in deciding who should enter this vital university-preparatory stage of education. Failure to participate in the Jugendweihe seriously jeopardised one's chances of entering the EOS, and of course it was Christians, especially the children of clergy, who tended to abstain. Christianity and the associated decision not to take part in the Jugendweihe were rather like a *malus* which had to be compensated for. Of all the trials to which Christians were subjected at school, the most significant hardship was the difficulty of gaining entry to the EOS.[1]

At first the stance of the Church concerning the Jugendweihe was stern and unbending: the Jugendweihe was deemed completely incompatible with confirmation. Then an attempt was made to circumvent the problem by delaying confirmation until the ninth or tenth form, but some church provinces such as Saxony-Dresden refused to give even tacit support to the Jugendweihe. The Church's reaction was generally low profile; in tussles with the state it relied on an attempt to prove anticonstitutional discrimination in individual cases. Though the state's reaction was to deny that the problem

1. The children of clergymen had a small advantage over others: they could join the Kirchliches Oberseminar in Moritzburg, Naumburg or Potsdam-Hermannswerder and take a formal Abitur there, which opened the way to studying theology or church law at the Kirchliche Hochschule in Leipzig, Berlin or Naumburg.

was a real one, it shortly became obvious that the problem was anything but illusory. Between 1945 and 1949, many teachers had been dismissed as part of the de-Nazification drive, and were substituted by the badly trained *Neulehrer*. During the Cold War in the 1950s, there was a second wave of teacher dismissal that produced black-and-white opponents in all public areas, placing the Church on the side of the enemies. The Central Committee for Youth Dedication insisted that teachers publicise the Jugendweihe rite; otherwise they would be regarded as saboteurs of the workers' and peasants' state. In 1958, several thousand Protestant teachers were forced to resign for refusing to obey this order (Railton, 1986:71). Between 1965 and 1973, GDR-wide participation in Christian religious instruction dropped 34 per cent and confirmations 35 per cent. From 1971 to 1973, the number of children taking Christian religious instruction in Saxony-Magdeburg fell 26 per cent (Goeckel, 1990:236). The dramatic loss in support showed that the Church was clearly the loser in the battle over the Jugendweihe.

The state's rigorous insistence on Marxism-Leninism as the only acceptable world-view caused socialist schools and teachers to discriminate against Christian young people and their parents. It is interesting, but not surprising, that the new GDR teachers (Neulehrer) trained on short courses after the War were among the most assiduous in discriminating against Christians. As mentioned above, Christian pupils found it difficult to gain entry into the EOS, even if individuals had excellent academic records (though in order to disarm opposition some token pupils were admitted). They were rarely granted prizes or distinctions despite highly meritorious achievements. By 1966, parents were required by law to cooperate with the principles of socialist morality, and married couples were obliged to reject religion as the basis of their marriage (Railton, 1986:78, 159). The parents of Christian children were not acceptable as members of Parents' Committees because they were considered unreliable in supporting the Jugendweihe. Christian symbols and practices were outlawed. No religious songs like Christmas carols could be sung in school; religious emblems had to be removed from buildings, especially schools (ibid.:201); the badge of Protestant youth, the Cross and Globe, was intensely controversial, and those who wore it were pestered and beaten up by the FDJ (ibid.:202–3). In the early 1980s, the peace badge, Swords into Ploughshares, caused immense difficulties to those with the temerity to wear it. They were accused of strengthening pacifism and undermining the GDR's military preparedness. They were fined, removed from trains, refused apprenticeships, not permitted to take exams and sometimes forced to leave their education establishments (ibid.: 206–8). As a result of these strictures, the Church decided to discontinue production of the badge.

Christian pupils were not allowed to talk about their beliefs inside school buildings. In 1958, the Lange Order was passed by the Ministry of Education to limit Religious Education in the schools. The subject was allowed to be taught only to those up to fourteen years of age, and lessons could not be held until two hours had lapsed after regular school hours. Moreover, the church teachers of Religion had to apply every four months for permission from the school principal to continue their courses. This meant that pupils had the inconvenience of waiting around (though the state claimed that the pause was to avoid the pupils becoming exhausted!). It also meant that no Religious Education (RE) could be offered to senior forms. Predictably, attendance at RE fell. Religious Education on school premises became more and more difficult despite the Constitutional provision protecting it, and the Church was driven to develop strategies to counter these strictures. It did this by training a special corps of teachers called catechists (*Katecheten*) who differed from the traditional RE instructors in being more heterogeneous, less professional, trained on shorter courses and having a lower social status (Leschinsky, 1996:51). The nature of the subject changed, too. As delivered by the Church, it was called 'Christian Instruction' (*Christenlehre*), and was more devotional in content than RE. Whereas RE had dealt with Western culture and morality, Christian Instruction dealt with the gospel, the Biblical message, worship, belief and the integration of young people into the community. The Catholics, who had also been adversely affected by the Lange Order, had their own similar form of Christian Instruction called *Religionsunterricht*. This distinction between RE and the Church's own more 'religious' syllabus was to become conceptually important after the fall of the Wall when reforms took place.

In the autumn of 1968, the Lutherans re-evaluated their Christian Instruction courses. The *Goßner Plan* was critical of the catechists' work – especially the tendency to teach as if the Biblical message was timeless – and called for a syllabus which would relate Christian faith to the adolescents' world. The major concepts of the Goßner Plan were radical but they influenced the 1977 Lutheran Framework Plan for Church Work with Children and Young People (*Rahmenplan für die kirchliche Arbeit mit Kindern und Jugendlichen*). This was an impressive, carefully sequenced curriculum with content specified in detail for different ages and stages – very different from mere 'Sunday School'. It championed pluralism, freedom and individuality, and its aim was nothing less than a holistic blending of the emotional, the creative and the cognitive. As such, it posed a challenge to the rather fossilised official state pedagogy. Obviously, it made considerable demands on those who had to teach it, and many catechists were not up to the job so there was a gap between what the authors of the 1977 Framework Plan intended to happen and what actually did happen. However, Leschinsky

(1996:57) explains that despite their intellectual and educational limitations, many catechists were all too aware of the difficult circumstances which children faced at home and at school. They were anxious to create an atmosphere in which the children felt cherished and wanted; in this they were so successful that Christian Instruction became almost a form of social therapy and was attractive to those who had never been baptised.

So far in the present account, the emphasis has been on the decline of the Church in terms of baptisms, confirmations and marriages. This gloomy picture needs to be balanced by another: the Church was of use to non-members, especially young people. Railton (1986, Chapter 8) has conducted a special study of the attraction of the Church to the non-religious. He found that increasing numbers of the young took an active part in the Young Congregation, and quite substantial numbers of non-baptised children attended religion classes in the 1980s, to an extent which made some pastors feel that it was inappropriate to deny Holy Communion to the non-baptised. Peace seminars, environmental protection campaigns, Children's Church Days and Church book fairs were all popular with GDR youth who were disappointed with GDR society, bored with official ideology or had problems with their family and housing. Such young people longed for freedom to express their feelings, and wanted to be taken seriously. The Church had the merit of addressing ultimate existential questions, and the Party was aware of this strength. To help counter Church influence, the SED brought out its own literature about the meaning of life, *Wozu lebe ich?* (Kosing, 1983) and *Vom Sinn unseres Lebens* (Zentraler Ausschuß für Jugendweihe in der DDR, 1983).

The Church was therefore of use to dissidents, especially those concerned with peace and the ecology. Religion was the only sphere of private activity permitted by the SED, and newsletters could be legally printed and distributed if they were marked for church use. This was one reason why the Church played such a salient role in the peaceful protests leading up to the fall of the Wall. The rhetoric of the SED about ecological issues was that its government was founded on 'scientific laws' which would bring prosperity to all and solve environmental problems; yet data on air pollution were kept secret because they indicated that the air quality was damaging people's health (Maaz, 1992:61). The rhetoric-reality gap caused cognitive dissonance in the minds of socialists who observed pollution and environmental degradation with their own eyes. It was the Church which formed a front for protest about the environment, and when the government forbade the publication of environmental data in 1982, Church-affiliated groups took the responsibility of disseminating it themselves (Hager, 1992). This work on environmental issues was a blow for increased freedom and democracy in the GDR, and as such it constituted a form of anticipatory political socialisation which was useful after the Wende. This was stated by Pastor Steinbeck, leader of Leipzig Environmental Seminar, who later became *Regierungspräsident* in Leipzig (ibid.:108). The Church in the person of Bishop Falcke of Erfurt put forward a well-argued counterideology of respect for nature and reduction of material demands. According to him, 'the objectification of nature is the origin of the destruction of the living' (Goeckel, 1990:252).

Though the Church played an important role as a front for protest by both believers and non-believers, it was also on occasion deliberately used by the state for its own purposes in its quest for loyalty and for a specific GDR identity. For example, the 500th anniversary of Martin Luther was celebrated as if he were one of the patron saints of communism, reflecting the GDR's wish to emphasise its international legitimacy as a member of the community of nations and a part of the fabric of Western culture. Its desire to merge socialist and national tradition led to a debate on 'heritage and tradition' and to the emphasis of certain 'progressive' elements in figures like Luther and King Frederick II who had contributed to the prominence of eastern Germany in comparison to the West (Ahonen, 1997:49).

Mention of Luther brings us in a roundabout way to the Achilles heel of the Church under socialism: namely the accusation that it 'colluded' with the Marxist regime. Luther's concept of the Two Kingdoms – the spiritual of God and the temporal of the devil – implied that the state is ordained by God to help control wickedness; Christians should therefore submit to worldly authority. The political passivity associated with this doctrine was not a problem when the regime was a decent one but was invidious when the regime was brutal and totalitarian. The tension between Church and state had driven Oskar Brüsewitz to his death, yet the EKD played down that conflict, claiming that Brüsewitz's experience of the relationship between the two was not typical. A running sore was the fact that some senior members of the Church were allowed foreign travel. This highlighted the lack of privilege of those back home. When travelling abroad, Church hierarchy members were careful not to criticise the GDR in public and glossed over the fact that what was in Western European countries the rule – freedom to travel – was in Eastern European countries the exception. Maaz (1992:53) calls such privilege a 'small corruption'. More serious, however, was the role played by certain clergy like Bishop Mitzenheim of Thuringia who was decorated by the regime for his services to the state. He and another Church official, Gerhard Lodz – also decorated – connived at the building of the Berlin Wall and at the forced division of the all-German Protestant Church. Not for nothing was he known as 'The Red Bishop'.

Maaz (1992:49–53) pays tribute to the courage of the Protestant Church – for decades the only organised oppositional force – and admits that it provided space for an alternative way of thinking and feeling. The great ideals of love, peace, justice, the protection of Creation, and the taboos of society such as handicap, homosexuality, death, the military, the ecology, could be – and were – discussed and aired in a Church forum. Brave individuals from the Church took their stand against the arbitrariness of the state. Yet Maaz's admiration is not unconditional. He complains that the Church's search for a positive understanding with the state (such as the Schön-herr-Honecker meeting of 6 March 1978) effectively endorsed an unjust system, in return for certain concessions. True, the Church was frank and open in confronting social, political and global problems, but it used the religious imperative of faith and discipline to calm people and to keep a kind of order. This had the effect of subduing and managing discontent; indeed, the state depended on the Church to perform this role of defusing and containing protest. Maaz utters the suspicion that the Church's honourable protest compensated for lack of religious strength, thereby covering up weakness. He points to the contradictory Church attitudes towards the events of October 1989: on the one hand, the Church was in the forefront of protest; on the other, it had a tendency to try to keep revolution off the streets.

Religion in the United Germany

The role which the Church had played during the decades of the GDR's existence was a complex one. After the Wende, it was perceived by turns as 'cultural hero' and 'collaborator'; 'scourge of injustice' and 'societal safety valve'. During the 1970s and 1980s, political change continued slowly but surely and resulted in a more pluralistic society. A new generation of political functionaries came to power, many of them with an academic education, and this led to a more subtly differentiated, less oppressive handling of the Church. It was noted by Noack (1996) that students at universities were more preoccupied with retaining their places than with 'spectacular actions' and that there was a falling off in protest. After the Wende, the important new feature of the situation which the church faced was that the pluralism of society, long covertly under development, had suddenly almost overnight become overt. The Church was now only one option among many, whereas during the GDR's existence it had been the only available legal alternative to the state world-view. Of course, the Protestant Church had accumulated prestige by its steadfastness in suffering and its courage in adversity, but this had to be balanced against its occasional complaisance and collaboration with the regime. The 'cleansing process' revealed that not all its members were free from involvement with the Stasi, and its opponents naturally used such cases to undermine the Church's credibility. The fall of the Wall and German unification did not produce a great surge of sustained support for the East German Churches, despite their salient leadership role in the Monday Prayers and the peace demonstrations. Historically, the GDR population had been accustomed to using the Church as a vehicle for protest and did so to great effect in 1989. Once the downfall of the regime was achieved, loyalty to the Church faded.

Pluralism and the modernism of society had contributed to a declining Church membership in both the New and the Old Bundesländer before the Wende, and economic factors accelerated this trend after November 1989. Church taxes were collected by the state revenue offices in the Federal Republic, and this practice was extended to the East. The tax applied only to those who also paid income tax: 36 per cent of Protestant church members. It was a deductible expenditure in the yearly income tax return, amounting to 9 per cent of the sum calculated as income tax (at most 3 per cent of taxable income), and was gradated according to salary as shown in Table 4.2.

Table 4.2 Income-Linked Gradations of Church Tax Contributions

Gross Income per Month	Single	Married	Married, 1 child	Married, 3 children
DM 2.000	DM18.02	—	—	—
DM 3.000	DM 39.73	DM 23.45	DM 14.94	—
DM 5.000	DM 92.95	DM 59.22	DM 49.70	DM 31.24

Source: Protestant Church in Berlin-Brandenburg, EkiBB, July 1994:31.

The Church argued that these amounts were just and moderate; that the freedom of preaching and the Church's open and public support for the weak in society should not depend on the personal opinion of a few financially strong donors; and that the state had no influence whatsoever on the use of the Church tax. But many people, both East and West, were unemployed or under great financial pressure. Moreover, the so-called 'solidarity tax' to help finance the costs of German unification was very similar in amount to the Church tax, and those whose need for financial liquidity was stronger than their religious convictions decided to stop paying the latter. The solidarity tax was compulsory whereas the Church tax was voluntary, so the temptation to refuse the voluntary tax was overwhelming for many people. These economic pressures were a contributory factor to weakening Church membership.

Statistically, the proportion of non-believers in the German population has been greatly increased by unification as demonstrated in Tables 4.3 and 4.4. The proportion of non-believers has risen from 8 per cent to almost 30 per cent – a development to be attributed to the large percentage (67 per cent in 1992) in the New Bundesländer who have no religious belief at all. A notable trend is that the Protestants are losing ground to the Catholics. Protestants are older on average (perhaps a sign of low institutional vitality for a church) – in 1987, 41.6 years of age as opposed to 39.2 for Catholics – with the result that thirty to forty thousand more Protestants are lost through death every year. For Catholics, the balance of baptisms and burials is still just about positive. Numbers of those leaving the Protestant Church are much higher than those leaving the Catholic Church. The figures for Protestant Church-leavers were all the more pronounced in the years following German unification because the payment of Church tax forced people in the New Länder, possibly dormant church members, to make a clear decision about Church membership. Many decided against staying with the Church and of course there were far more Protestants than Catholics in the East German population, hence more withdrawals from that religion (EKD, 15.10.94).

Table 4.3 Population According to Religious Denomination on 25 May 1987: The Federal Republic before Unification (West Germany Only)

Religious Affiliation	Number	% of the Population
Total population	61,077,042	100.0
Protestant	25,412,572	41.6
Protestant Free Church	388,235	0.6
Roman Catholic	26,232,004	42.9
Other beliefs/no data	4,131,971	6.8
No religion	4,912,260	8.0

Table 4.4 Population According to Religious Denomination on 31 December 1992: The Federal Republic after Unification (East and West Germany Combined)

Religious Affiliation	Number	% of the Population
Total population	80,974,632	100.0
Protestant	28,875,180	35.7
Roman Catholic	28,127,672	34.7
Other beliefs/no religion	23,971,780	29.6

Source: 'Kirchenzugehörigkeit in Deutschland – Was hat sich verändert?' EKD, 15.10.1994:1–2.

Taking Protestants and Catholics together, about one-third of the population of the New Bundesländer professed a religious affiliation in 1992 (EKD, 14.10.94). By this stage, most of the population was ill informed about religious matters, because the level of religious knowledge had declined since 1949. This impeded understanding of cultural content in literature, music and art, and was a factor in dividing East from West Germany and cutting the Easterners off from their cultural heritage. The East German authorities had come to acknowledge this, and it is interesting to note that in January 1990, before unification was formally completed, they recommended the introduction of Religious Education as a school subject. There was widespread ignorance about religious matters, and children in particular had no notion of the most basic protocol in the unfamiliar environment of a Church. This is vividly illustrated by a noticeboard in St. Mauritius Cathedral, Magdeburg, bearing a typewritten set of instructions to young visitors on how NOT to behave: 'We can understand that you may find all this strange or even funny today because you are not aware of its significance, but try to remember that even kings used to come barefoot from the Kloster Berge to the cathedral out of sheer reverence. Of course, you may keep your shoes on but please accept that for us a place where altar, christening font and cross all stand is no ordinary place, and certainly not a skateboard rink.' Not infrequently, schoolchildren undertaking church visits were heard to ask: 'Who is "that man" hanging on the cross?', while towards the less doubting end of the 'atheism/belief' spectrum, one child's search for a toehold on the cliff of faith is exemplified by a short, slightly poignant note stuck to a pillar in St. Thomas's Church, Leipzig: 'Dear God, why do you make it so hard for me to believe in you?' (Author's field notes: Magdeburg, 2 May 1995; Leipzig, 17 June 1995).

It was in such an environment that Church schools and Religious Education were introduced to East Germany. There was not much support for the introduction of RE, yet there was a pressing need for some attempt to cope with the values vacuum left by the demise of Marxism-Leninism which gave rise to uncertainty about what to believe and how to live. Almost all ordinary people went through a process of change that challenged their values and actions. For children, however, the problems were of a different order. Most adults had been given a firm framework of values under the old regime, even if it was now rather discredited because of its ideological basis. Children, on the other hand, were at grave risk of growing up without any framework at all. They had less experience than their parents and it was not uncommon for young children listening to their parents discussing the current political situation to ask: 'Mother, what was the GDR?' It was necessary to give them some standards by which to judge right and wrong, and if Marxism-Leninism was no longer to be used as a basis for those standards then some other basis had to be found. The Basic Law of West Germany regarded the country as Christian, and two major political parties, the CDU and the CSU, both included the work 'Christian' in their titles. The

Constitution was extended to East Germany and with it the expectation that Religious Education would become a normal school subject.

The problem, however, was that two-thirds of the population was atheist and did not support the introduction of RE. There was a widespread abhorrence at the prospect of giving children ready-made opinions – yet again – and of substituting religious for political dogma. The fear encapsulated in a pithy sentence, 'Rot geht heraus, schwarz kommt' (Red out, Black in), was understandable, yet the need for some form of values education remained. Not the least of the difficulties was the lack of suitably qualified RE teachers, if indeed the subject was to be introduced. West Germany in its reform of education in the East had laid down the structural forms for freedom, but Western 'freedom' was often taken as licence, especially by the young, and there was a feeling that the legal forms needed to be combined with content if they were to be meaningful. Indeed, the West Germans found it hard enough in their pluralist society to agree upon the defining principles among themselves. However, the authorities of the New Bundesländer set out to initiate Religious Education and Ethics in East German schools, and to facilitate the establishment of Church schools if there was sufficient demand for them on the part of the local population.

Church Schools

Despite the doubters, there were still those who had preserved their religious convictions intact throughout the difficult days of socialism – often at the cost of much sacrifice. A number of people existed in East Germany who were passionately keen to see voluntary schools established after the fall of the Wall, and there was more demand for them than the Roman Catholic and Protestant Churches could satisfy financially. The Basic Law (Article 7) provided the legal basis for the establishment of Church schools and Religious Education.

Basic Law: Article 7

(1) The whole school system is under the control of the state.

(2) The parents or guardians have the right to decide on the participation of the child in Religious Education.

(3) Religious Education is a normal full school subject in public schools with the exception of non-denominational schools. Without prejudice to the supervisory right of the state, Religious Education is to be taught in keeping with the principles of the religious communities. No teacher may be forced to teach Religious Education against his or her will.

(4) The right to the establishment of private schools is guaranteed. Private schools as a substitute for public schools require the permission of

the state and are subject to the laws of the Länder. Permission may be granted if the private schools are not inferior to public schools in their learning aims and arrangements and in the academic education of their teaching staff; they should not promote a division of pupils according to the financial circumstances of the parents. Permission is to be denied if the economic and legal situation of the teaching staff is not sufficiently well assured.

The right to establish private schools had never existed in the GDR, so the Basic Law opened up new opportunities to found them. Such schools had to be of at least as high a standard as the state schools, hence they needed to be well funded, but they must not be 'elite schools' only accessible to the well-off. The Basic Law gave no support for ecumenism: Religious Education was viewed as denominational education, and Protestants and Catholics had little reason to make common cause in the foundation of Church schools. To give a flavour of how a Church school developed, a brief case study will now be presented.

Exemplar of a Church School

The Protestant School Centre in Leipzig, Saxony, nestles in the shadow of St. Peter's Church (the Petrikirche). It is three schools in one: a primary school, a grammar school and a Mittelschule. The founding headmaster, Burkhard Jung, came from West Germany where he was a master in the Evangelisches Gymnasium in Siegen. He, his wife and their children at first had reservations about uprooting themselves from their comfortable home in the West and setting out for an uncertain future in the East of Germany but they were won over by the enthusiasm of the Easterners who instigated the establishment of the school. The young future headmaster and his wife were also attracted by the rich heritage of German classical culture in the East, and by the idea of making a positive contribution to German unification. It was important to them, too, to bear witness to their faith. In a leaflet (1996) detailing the origins of the Evangelisches Schulzentrum, the complexities of the desire for a new sort of school are evident: there is a hope of achieving something better than in the past but also a fear of falling prey to new dangers.

> The demand for free schools unleashed unbelievable astonishment at first because these had been forbidden in the east of Germany for almost sixty years. From all parts of Germany, reformist advisors helped us to discover how to establish the Good School. Our own experience with the state's abuse of the school monopoly sensitised us to the dangers of

new indoctrination through the imported party-political struggle over structures, or alternatively through individual dogmatising 'saviours'.

However, three major demands crystallised for us: (1) freedom to be able to shape the entity as we wish; (2) a spiritual centre of gravity; (3) a community of teachers, pupils and parents which clusters round this spiritual centre voluntarily and with commitment.

What could be more natural for Christians than to want to see this spiritual centre of the gospel in all its liberating strength in the school as well as elsewhere? But the doubts and scruples of those same Christians promoting potentially a new constraint on world-view were very strong. It was a matter of proceeding with extreme caution....

The guiding concept and the composition of the teaching staff unite a very wide variety of school experience with the objective of developing something new, not yet present in the West. The Protestant Church authorities of East and West Leipzig will promote these objectives in their capacity as school providers. The venerable school building near St. Peter's Church will be able to take 900 pupils when it is fully developed. On the basis of very great demand the number of classes was expanded from 5 to 15 in the first school year. (Leaflet: Evangelisches Schulzentrum Leipzig, 'Entstehungsgeschichte', 1996)

Indeed the growth of the School Centre has been exponential, owing much to the two regional parishes in Leipzig which 'own' the schools and to the city of Leipzig which has a very open school policy conducive to the establishment of voluntary schools, such as a UNESCO school and a Bilingual Russian-German School. The Evangelisches Schulzentrum began with 121 pupils in 1991; by the 1992/93 year it had 411, and by 1996, 871 pupils. The intention at present is to hold enrolment to about 900 students. The denominational balance is a mixed one, as the following figures for 1996 show:

	Number of Pupils	Percent
Protestant	581	66.7
Catholic	104	11.9
Other religions	40	4.6
No religion	146	16.8
Totals	**871**	**100.0**

It must be emphasised that the school is open to all, regardless of ethnic and social origin or world-view, be it religious or otherwise. The buildings look a little drab on the outside, but inside the schoolrooms are bright, well decorated and structurally sound. The headmaster took a conscious decision to put the interior of the school in order before tackling the façade, on the grounds that this would enhance the quality of the pupils' lives much more. There is a need to purchase neighbouring land in order to build a gymnasium and a new primary school, and the price has been set at DM 410,000. The school managers have decided to raise money for the new project by the symbolic 'sale' of the ground at DM 500 for half a square meter. Constant fund-raising is stressful but it is the price of independence and distinctiveness. Academically, the school is sound: the first Abitur examinations were taken by the pupils of the School Centre in 1997 and they were in the upper third of the results table for Saxony as a whole.

✄ ✄ ✄

In the establishment of denominational schools, the Roman Catholic Church was quick off the mark. It is interesting to note that although its relations with its Protestant counterparts were good, it had rejected the possibility of establishing an ecumenical Christian school jointly with the founders of the School Centre described above. Table 4.5 shows the figures for the RC schools which had been established in the New Bundesländer by 1995/96.

Table 4.5 Catholic Schools in the New Bundesländer, School Year 1995/96

	BB*	MV*	S*	SA*	TH*	Total
Primary, Elementary, Main	2	1	0	0	0	3
Grammar	1	0	2	3	2	8
Special	3	0	2	0	1	6
Evening	0	0	0	1	0	1
Vocational	0	0	2	2	4	8
Health	0	0	1	2	2	5
Total	**6**	**1**	**7**	**8**	**9**	**31**

Source: Zentralstelle Bildung der Deutschen Bischofskonferenz. Figures supplied to the author at her request.

*See List of Abbreviations for key.

By 1996, the Protestant Church had established about twelve schools. Quite a large disparity existed, therefore, between the dynamic of Protestant and Catholic development. The Catholics were thinly dispersed through the population and if they were to have any impact, they needed to concentrate their strength. This they did by founding voluntary schools. They were organisationally in a better position than the federal Protestant Church to finance schools by virtue of the fact that they were a centralised, unitary Church with many rich dioceses, and thus were better able to back up their decisions about priorities with the necessary financial resources.

The Protestants, by contrast, were divided among themselves as to whether it was better to found denominational schools or rather to seek to influence the state's general educational policies and principles. For forty years they had had little influence on the state system of education, and there was now a real possibility of their constituting a pressure group to effect change at a high level. With some exceptions (human nature being what it is), the overwhelming majority of their adherents were politically 'clean' and thus suitable to take on leadership roles in the New Bundesländer. They did not necessarily want to go all out to establish their own schools; they wanted to improve state schools, making them freer and more liberal. They did not necessarily want to see Protestant families forming small 'ghettos' (school communities) and becoming detached from the world; they wanted to disseminate their influence throughout the body politic like the leaven in the bread, as it were. In short, they were of two minds about what was desirable and feasible. When confronted with vigorous demand by Church adherents for establishment of Church schools, they had to decide whether or not to meet that demand. Their response was rather more sluggish than that of their Catholic counterparts.

Although schools in the New Bundesländer were normally denominational, either Protestant or Catholic, a curious fact is that in practice they were usually mixed. Protestant schools included substantial minorities of Catholic pupils and vice versa; for example, Protestant clergy unable to obtain a place for their child in the first school of their choice would sometimes send him or her to the nearest Roman Catholic school on the grounds that they wanted a Christian education and were convinced that the Catholic school was the best possible solution under the circumstances. Usually there were also substantial minorities of pupils whose parents were not churchgoers at all but who believed that by sending their children to a Church school they were securing certain advantages for them. Many parents did not believe that existing state schools could change from within to become 'democratic' and preferred a modern, newly established school for their children. Such schools, by virtue of the fact that they had to raise part of their own funding, preserved an above-average degree of autonomy which could be conducive to creativity. They were able to develop distinctive profiles with specialisms like Classics or Music which diverged from the standardised state curriculum. Distinctiveness was welcomed in a society where in the past the overriding tendency was towards uniformity. Such schools had more than the usual modicum of West German-trained teachers, and this was attractive to East German parents who supposed that Western teachers could help socialise their children into the New Germany and ensure a smooth passage for them into the all-German labour market when the time came. Of course, the denominational schools had to be good academically to be considered seriously.

Ethics and Religious Education in State Schools

Churches were not the only bodies to address themselves to the issue of values education. The state did so too. As we have seen, Religious Education is a normal school subject guaranteed as such in the German Constitution. This state of affairs existed in West Germany before unification but it was in tension with the increasing agnosticism of the FRG population, especially following the Student Revolt of the 1960s in which antiauthoritarian ideas gained currency. In most Länder, school pupils had the right to withdraw from Religious Education on their own initiative when they reached the age of fourteen (in some Länder, like Bavaria, eighteen).[2] The problem which then ensued was that the children simply had an unfilled gap in their timetable: there was no other programme for them. A syllabus in Ethics was therefore developed and was given a legal basis in 1974/75. Consequently, it was no longer possible to avoid any ethics education; the choice was now not 'RE or nothing' but 'RE or Ethics'. Although the introduction of Ethics led to a decline in numbers of pupils taking Religious Education, the two great Churches had not been vehemently opposed to its introduction. They approved of the move to help young people explore moral values. The state too felt that Ethics could be useful in promoting homogeneous values conducive to the common good.

The legal situation in West Germany was that Ethics could be offered only as an alternative to Religious Education. Treml (1994) argues that this is now an unjustified anachronism deriving from the time when the Churches had the privileged role of *Volkskirche* (National Church) in Germany. It is high time, he says, that Ethics became a regular school subject and stopped being regarded as an appendage to Religious Education – a sort of penance for the refusniks who no longer wish to participate in Religious Education; time also that the training of Ethics teachers became professionalised and well developed. In order to avoid competition between Ethics and RE, Ethics may be offered only if RE is also offered (e.g. as in Hesse and Baden-Württemberg) and this can have paradoxical effects. Let us suppose that there are eight pupils wishing to do RE and twenty wishing to do Ethics: if an additional two pupils withdraw from

2. It was not possible for the author to find figures for numbers of pupils withdrawing from Religious Education.

RE in favour of Ethics, the Church can no longer teach RE because minimum viable numbers have not been attained. Since RE is not being offered, Ethics has to be cancelled too on the grounds that it is an 'alternative' to RE – an apparent injustice in view of possible strong demand for Ethics in such circumstances.

Treml (1994) lays out a number of different pedagogical concepts for Ethics and relates them to different German Länder.

PRACTICAL PHILOSOPHY. Ethics can be interpreted as practical philosophy. It is based on the Classics such as Plato and Aristotle, and does not necessarily take the pupils' interests as paramount. It is a training in how to philosophise – for example by using the Socratic method – and is especially suitable for senior classes. One great strength is that it derives from a well-established university discipline – philosophy – which is conducive to professionalism. A weakness is that pupils do not necessarily find it very motivational. Länder where this model is in use: Schleswig-Holstein, Bremen (in a rudimentary way) and the Saarland; also Mecklenberg-Vorpommern.

AN AID TO LIVING THE GOOD LIFE. Ethics can be regarded as a practical aid to living. This model is pupil-centred and derives from the source disciplines of psychology and education rather than from philosophy. Its concern is to help young people define their identity and their social behaviour. It is 'applied' rather than 'pure' ethics, and the teacher's role is less that of an academic and more that of a discussion partner and companion. There is a danger that the teacher may be thrust into the role of therapist without being trained for it. The subject lacks intrinsic cognitive and logical rigour and is difficult to assess: how can pupils' achievement in such an experiential subject be evaluated? Länder where this model is in use: in the vocational schools of Baden-Württemberg, in Brandenburg and in Thuringia.

MORAL EDUCATION. Ethics can be a form of moral education: its aim is to mediate binding values and norms which are taken as pre-existing and axiomatic. It is not and cannot be value-neutral; moral relativism is shunned and religion, especially the Catholic religion, is the object of special protection. Religion is viewed not anthropologically or socially from the outside but from within its own self-concept as a 'mystery'. Its premisses either have to be accepted or rejected. Ethics as a religiously grounded type of moral education is not well adapted for dealing with modern problems of doubt, and there is no logical connection between fundamental norms/values and classroom reality (though of course there may be a spiritual connection). The practical implementation of this model may be questionable: if the moral basis of education is implicit and latent and not amenable to explicit and logical treatment, how can it be 'produced' by conscious (pedagogical) means? Moreover, there is a problem about how to assess it as a school subject: if action and 'mentality' as well as knowledge are valued, then the question arises as to whether the actions and ideological alignment of the pupils should be assessed, in addition to their test papers. This might open the way to hypocrisy or to the punishment of ideological unsoundness. Land where this model is in use: Bavaria. This model, associated by Treml with religious underpinnings, is partially applicable to socialism too in that actions and the 'right' (i.e. socialist) mentality were valued in the socialist states of East Central Europe. Where the parallel becomes inapplicable is that Marxism-Leninism is grounded not in transcendent, spiritual religious authority but in history, philosophy and economics.

ETHICAL REFLECTION. Ethics can be interpreted as ethical reflection: an illuminating focus on ethical principles which aims to form ethical judgements (or 'competence') rather than inculcate values. Nothing is immune from critical reflection and nothing is sacrosanct. Ethical convictions cannot be transferred from teacher to pupil; they must be developed by individuals for themselves. This kind of Ethics can do no more than provide the classroom context for common reflection about good and evil and the exercise of practical reason. There is no single source discipline: the academic context is multidisciplinary and addresses itself to the social sciences and the humanities as well as to the natural sciences. This form of Ethics education which concerns itself with pupils' interests and preoccupations is not particularly pupil-centred; the teacher structures the syllabus by choosing certain ethical dilemmas thereby avoiding arbitrary content. It is difficult to train teachers for this type of Ethics education since it goes beyond practical philosophy and pedagogy. It is, however, at its best a way of striking a balance between absolutism and total relativism that takes account of intellectual scepticism. Länder where this model is in use: Hesse, Hamburg, Lower Saxony, the Saarland and Schleswig-Holstein.

Treml (1994) points out that these different approaches could all be used at different times in a child's development and at different levels of education: e.g. an aid to living in the primary school, ethical reflection in the middle form of secondary school and practical philosophy in the upper secondary school, though he himself personally believes that these dimensions are all components of Ethics as a whole. He demonstrates that the pedagogical orientation of Ethics is extremely heterogeneous in the West German Länder. There are clear differences in the legal and conceptual underpinnings of Ethics in Protestant and Catholic Länder, although in practice the classroom reality may be quite similar. He produces a grid showing which Länder offer Ethics as a substitute for Religious Education. All of the New Bundesländer offer Ethics (or an equivalent) as an option in its own right rather than as a substitute for RE. This is an example of the NBL departing from the OBL norm in a way which is highly appropriate development in the circumstances; it could serve as a stimulus for the OBL to change their own approach.

Obviously both Ethics and Religious Education depend on the training of sufficient teachers to enable the subjects to be offered, and progress towards provision of both subjects is incremental. Producing teachers of new subjects is a long-term process, and the picture is constantly changing. Table 4.6 gives an overview of the situation in the various New Bundesländer with regard to the take-up of Religious Education and Ethics.

Table 4.6 Participation in Ethics and Protestant Religious Education in Four New Bundesländer: School Year 1995/96

	No. of Pupils in State Schools	No. of Pupils Taking Protestant RE	No. of Pupils Taking Ethics	Provision of RE (%)
SA	383,859	11,359	28,329	3.00
TH	360,251	72,029	197,618	20.00
S	625,265	52,282	214,435	8.36
BB	403,417	8,226		2.04
			Subject offered is 'LER' (see discussion below)	

Source: Comenius Institut, Berlin, 1997. Figures supplied to the author at her request.

Note: Matching figures for Mecklenburg-Vorpommern for the year 1995/96 were unobtainable.

In some quarters, the take-up of Religious Education has been regarded as disappointing, but in view of the almost universal background of atheism in the East German population, it is important not to harbour unrealistic expectations about its potential. In Church circles, the figure of 20 per cent take-up rate for RE is often regarded as about the maximum that can be achieved. The East German Churches do not want to abandon their own Christian Instruction; in the Protestant Church of Berlin-Brandenburg, for example, there were 30,344 children in forms 1 to 6 taking such classes in 1995/96. The ultimate purpose of such classes is confirmation into the Church. Curiously, however, commitment to the Jugendweihe has not died out in the New Bundesländer. Since 1990, more than a quarter of a million NBL youths – that is about half of all fourteen-year-olds – have taken part in the ceremony (Mohrmann, 1996:197). Even before the Wende, the Jugendweihe had become less standardised and more diverse, as a reaction to boredom which threatened to make young people's participation merely formalistic. Nowadays there are quite a number of different commercial providers who compete for business and publicity; and the German Association of Free Thinkers (since 1991, a country-wide organisation) plays a salient role. The ceremony has been deritualised and depoliticised. It is no longer the atheistic counter-balance to Christian confirmation which it once was. There are probably two main reasons for the survival of Youth Dedication. Parents who them-selves took part in the GDR Jugendweihe believe that their children should have the opportunity to undergo the same experience. Many also believe that in continuing with the Jugendweihe, they are ensuring the survival of a tradition which is distinctive to the former GDR and thus helps consolidate a sense of identity at present under threat.

It is important to evaluate the success of Religious Education in the New Bundesländer schools, but so far no system-wide surveys have been carried out. Degen (3.4.95) notes that real difficulty is caused by a scarcity of RE teachers, and believes that if more RE were offered, it would help to stimulate demand. Often up to 50 per cent of those in RE classes have never been baptised and belong to no church. In Degen's view this beto-kens a growing openness. Decher (1995), a West German teacher from Worms who went to teach for a time at the Dr. Tolberg grammar school in Schöneberg, found her RE groups extremely heterogeneous and very stimulating. The pupils' expectations (Christians and non-Christians sit-ting side by side) were high, both because RE was a new subject and because they had burning existential questions. What concerned them most were two issues: the fracturing of families after the Wende, and unemployment which seems to rob people of their self-worth. Hanisch and Pollack (1995) have carried out an empirical study of pupils' reactions to Religious Education in Saxony. The sample consisted of almost 1,500 male and female pupils in forms 5/6 and 9/10, and was conducted be-tween February and September 1994. The numbers were just about equally divided between grammar school and Mittelschule. Almost 50 per cent of these children had no relationship whatever with the Church, but 81 per cent had a 'religious orientation' in that they believed in God at least 'sometimes'. Interestingly, 22 per cent of those who were not church mem-bers would seriously consider being baptised, so it hardly appeared as if school-based RE was robbing the Churches of support. The most com-mon reason for participating in RE was 'Because I was curious about the subject'. The subject was popular 'Because we discuss things a lot' (46 per cent), 'Because there is a lot of talk about God' (41 per cent) and 'Because a lot of stories are told'. RE teachers apparently make use of narrative and intense personal conversation, which not all subject teachers do, and 60 per cent of the pupils claimed that it could not be compared with other subjects. They regarded it as *sui generis* (though of course they did not use that term). When asked to rank their subject preferences, Sport came first, then Religious Education, then Mathematics. The high ranking of RE is encouraging for the subject's proponents. So far as can be ascertained, then, Religious Education is positively received in Saxony – and not just by those who come from church backgrounds.

Life Skills – Ethics – Religion: 'LER'

Of all the New Länder, it is Brandenburg which has adopted the most distinctive approach to values education. The impetus predated the Wende, stemming, as it did, from socialist times in the late 1980s and the transitional period prior to German unification. There had been a grassroots movement in favour of a compulsory subject which would offer pupils help in life skills and moral and religious education. The Volksinitiative Bildung and the Independent Interest Group for a Democratic Education and Upbringing contributed to the movement, as did the Initiative for Peace and Human Rights. Work undertaken by Protestant churchmen such as Eckart Schwerin and Götz Doyé in preparation for the Ninth Education Congress of the GDR nourished the concept; so too did the activities of the Association of Free Thinkers (1988). On 9 November 1989, representatives of these groups, together with parents, pupils and teachers, met in the Berlin Congress Hall to discuss the 'Education Emergency'. Various working groups were formed to advance certain ideas, and one of these was deputed to develop the concept of 'Life Skills' (*Lebensgestaltung*). This was understood to include such matters as conflict resolution, self-knowledge, suffering, health and sickness, life and death, love and marriage: in short, all the issues which adolescents address when defining their identity as future young grown-ups. The Modrow government was also working on the Life Skills concept and on 2 October 1990, one day before German unification, recommended the introduction of a subject 'Life Skills/ Ethics/ Religion'; this was the culmination of many different streams of development dating from the mid-1980s (BB MBJS, 1.2.96:7–8).

After the Wende, the New Bundesland of Brandenburg had a coalition government consisting of SPD, FDP and Bündnis 90 which agreed unanimously that it would be desirable to introduce a subject on the lines of Life Skills and Ethics but that denominational Religious Education should be left to the Churches. This of course was in contravention of Article 7 (3) of the Basic Law which obliged the Länder of the Federal Republic to introduce Religious Education as a normal full school subject. There was a legal justification for this departure. Brandenburg invoked the so-called Bremen Clause, Article 141 of the Basic Law, which states that 'Article 7, para. 3, sentence 1 does not apply in a Land in which a different Land law was in force on 1 January 1949'.

In 1949, the Basic Law of the Federal German Republic was introduced. Berlin (at that time Berlin-Brandenburg) and Bremen already had their Länder law in 1949, and it was agreed in the Bremen Clause that they should be exempt from the provisions of the Basic Law regarding Religious Education. On the criterion date of 1 January 1949, there was no denominational Religious Education in public schools in any of the Länder of the Soviet Zone of Occupation. This enabled Bremen and Berlin to follow their own paths in such matters, acting more independently and in ways which diverged from the other Länder. After German unification, the Land Brandenburg argued: (a) that it was in legal continuity with the Land Brandenburg before 1949 when East and West Germany were divided; (b) that it was like Bremen – not subject to Article 7 (3) of the Basic Law concerning denominational Religious Education; (c) that it was therefore legally empowered to seek its own distinctive path in the matter of Religious Education and Ethics in school.

After the Wende, the first Minister of Education was Marianne Birthler who had been a Protestant catechist and a member of the Initiative for Peace and Human Rights. She established a working group to refine and elaborate the 'Life Skills – Ethics – Religion' concept and the conclusion was reached that a hasty introduction of a new subject would be an error. Instead, it was decided to mount a pilot study over a period of three or four years in close collaboration with the Churches, both Protestant and Catholic. The new subject cluster was called Lebensgestaltung – Ethik – Religion: LER for short; it was to be non-denominational and for all pupils. The Churches did not agree with the decision to adopt Article 141 as the basis of policy. They believed that the Land should be bound by Article 7 (3) which would oblige Brandenburg to introduce Religious Education as a normal full school subject. However, the Protestant Church did agree to participate in the LER Pilot Study, initially for a period of one year, and formalised this in an Agreement of 9 July 1992 (BB EK 9.7.92). In the event, it participated until the Pilot Study was concluded. The Catholic Church dissociated itself from the project because the status of Religious Education was not defined to its satisfaction. Like the Protestants, the Catholics wanted it to be a normal full school subject according to Article 7 (3).

The LER pilot study was one of the most extensive in the entire Federal Republic of Germany in the early 1990s, and it attracted enormous public interest from the media in both parts of Germany. It was subjected to a concurrent academic analysis directed by Achim Leschinsky, until 1992 a professor at the Max-Planck-Institut and subsequently at the Humboldt University. Together with his colleagues, Professors Henkys and Bloth who were nominated by the Protestant Church, he presented a report published in book form to the Land government in spring 1995, which was entitled *Vorleben oder Nachdenken?* (Exemplary Living or Reflecting?, Leschinsky, 1996).

The experiment began in 1992 and ran until 31 July 1995. LER was offered on an experimental basis in 44 post-primary schools out of a total of 1,200 in Brandenburg. In terms of school type, 17 were grammar schools, 6 Realschulen and 21 comprehensive schools. School principals who entered the project did so in order to help their pupils reflect upon and come to terms with their lives. There were two lessons a week in lower secondary school (the project did not extend to primary schools), and the lessons sometimes took place outside the normal timetable, sometimes within it. No marks were awarded for the subject. LER was a conglomerate with a common, integrated core. A differentiated phase in which Religious Education was undertaken was a compromise developed in order to keep the Protestant Churches on board; the balance between the integrated and the differentiated phases varied between one school and another. No defined syllabus existed, but by the end of the third year there were Guidelines (*Hinweise*) which formulated aims and a provisional description of content.

LER's general objective was as follows: 'It is the objective of the subject area LER to promote human Life Skills with special attention to the ethical domain and to different world-views and religions' (BB MBJS, 1994: 'Hinweise zum Unterricht im Modellversuch Lernbereich L-E-R', p. 51).

Target competences (self, social, ethical, interpretative) were defined; subject areas and thematic routes were laid out; methods and media were discussed (breathing techniques for relaxation, brainstorming, conflict resolution exercises, collages, posters, music and dance, as well as the more orthodox chalk and talk). Learning Theme 5 of the Guidelines dealt with People and their Religions, World-Views and Cultures. It paid attention to a wide variety of phenomena: for example, the Golden Mean as minimal consensus, the dangers of indoctrination, male and female values, the Enlightenment, secularisation. individualisation and pluralism in modern society, religious sects and the New Age movement. In Section 6, the notional syllabus for Evangelische Religion was specified. Here existential problems were related where appropriate to Christian scriptures and history: living with foreigners ('I was a stranger and you took me in'); reverence for life and nature (Albert Schweitzer, St. Francis of Assisi); the church in the Third Reich and in the GDR; astrology and soothsaying; unemployment and its potential to devalue human beings; humans as creators (gene manipulation and surrogate mothers); the search for God (Martin Luther, Mahatma Gandhi). It would be true to say that LER tried to promote tolerance and mutual understanding. It was not 'merely' directed at the pupils' cognitive capacities but was an 'Aid to Living the Good Life' (see Treml's second pedagogical concept above).

One hundred teachers from the state system were involved and were given special training at the Brandenburg Institute for In-Service Teacher Education and Training (PLIB). Religion was taught by church staff both in the integrated and in the differentiated phase. Referring to Buddhism or Islam or other religions, attempts were made to bring the pupils face to face with 'authentic representatives' of religion, so that they could begin to discover what it meant to live one's faith. These encounters were more easily available to urban than to rural pupils, and sometimes took place during excursions to churches, mosques and synagogues. Most teachers of Religion were seconded by the Protestant Churches, and were clergymen, clergy-women and catechists who came into the schools to teach on the under-standing that there was to be close cooperation between them and the state teachers. According to a formal agreement of 6 July 1993 (BB EK, 6.7.93), they were to be involved in planning content and organisation, even in the integrated phase, but the overall coordination was the responsibility of the permanent mainstream teachers employed by the state. For RE to be taught in its full-blooded form as denominational Protestant Religion, there had to be a group of at least twelve pupils wishing to participate; this happened in only four schools in 1993/94, although such lessons were given in an additional five schools to classes below the quota of twelve (BB MBJS, 1.2.96:14). Significantly the number of pupils participating in the overall experiment increased year by year, whereas the number of church staff decreased, as shown in Table 4.7.

Table 4.7 Numbers of Pupils and Church Workers Involved in LER

	1992/93	1993/94	1994/95
No. of Pupils	5,250	6,700	7,000
Church Workers	12	29	23

Source: BB MBJS, 1.2.96:14.

Relations between Church and state teachers became strained, leading to the eventual erosion of the Church staff and their partial withdrawal from the scheme. In the last year of the project, it became difficult to replace those Church participants who left the project, and the motiva-tion of those remaining sank to a low level (ibid.). There were a number of reasons for this conflict, some personal, some historical and some struc-turally determined.

- The clergy and catechists were variable in quality: sometimes excel-lent but sometimes not robust enough to handle full classes of not always docile pupils, some of whom were sceptical about the sub-ject matter.

- The fact that there were no marks for the subject caused difficulties. There was a tension between teaching for depth and teaching for pupil enjoyment, and this was exacerbated by the decision not to assess the pupils' work. At the cognitive level, the lack of marks made it difficult to attain academic rigour, and cognitive content was rather neglected in favour of social relationships and general communication. A few of the Religion teachers hailed from West Germany where the position of Religion in the curriculum was well established. Such teachers found it hard to come to terms with the fact that there were no marks to use as sanctions or as a mode of imposing discipline – everything seemed to depend on the students' goodwill, which of course fluctuated. They felt that a full academic subject needs marks if it is to command respect and motivate hard work, and a number of East German teachers agreed with them – though opinions on the issue varied widely (ibid.:34–36).

- There was a power and status differential between state-employed and Church teachers. The state teachers had the formal responsibility for the delivery of LER and this gave them a higher standing than the Church workers. The two groups were inexperienced in collaborative planning (ibid.:38). The 'authentic representatives of religion' from the Churches who came to communicate to pupils what it meant to have a living faith were easily marginalised.

- The formation of RE groups depended on pupils choosing to opt for Religious Education in the differentiated phase; since this choice was not made until term began, it was impossible for the Church staff to prepare their work in advance during the summer (ibid.:27–28).

- The Churches really wanted Religious Education to become a normal school subject. Although about half of the state teachers came from Christian households, the Churches perhaps had an interest in magnifying conflict so that they could win the right to run RE as a normal full school subject (ibid.:37). The legal definition of a 'normal full school subject' (*ordentliches Lehrfach*) is not quite clear but a Churchman (Steinert, 12.12.1996:21) gives an indication of some points which militate against such status. Religious Education is not a normal full school subject if (a) it is marginalised in the timetable by being taught before school begins or after it ends; (b) the supervision and responsibility for RE reside solely with the Churches ; (c) the teachers of religion are Church teachers, not teachers of the school, and are thus not integrated into the appropriate school committee structure.

- Both the Brandenburg Ministry and the Church agreed on this point: there was too much emphasis on Life Skills and not enough on Religion. It was not until forms 9 and 10 that children became spontaneously interested in the ethical and the religious (BB MBJS, 1.2.96:18, 29).

- The Church was afraid of losing its own Christian Instruction classes, so painfully built up and maintained under socialism. Such instruction bound the faithful into their Christian communities and the Churches were deeply unhappy about the prospect of losing their hold on it. It seemed unrealistic to expect that young people would go to Religious Education in school and still attend Christian Instruction at Church. Subsequently, however, an investigation by the Comenius Institute itself showed that numbers taking Christian Instruction did not seem to be suffering unduly (Degen, 3.4.95).

- On the grounds of its historical experience, the Church was basically suspicious of cooperating with the state in the area of Religious Education and was wary of any state intervention in religious matters. Church officials were mistrustful of the state and reluctant to see it in a sense usurping their distinctive functions. In a paper of April 1990, the Conference of Protestant Church Leaders took up this issue. It was clear to them that RE in the Federal Republic emanated from a residual concept of the Volkskirche which antedated the Weimar Republic. During the four decades of the GDR's existence, secularisation had taken place, and under these circumstances there seemed little need for the introduction of Religious Education in schools (BB MBJS, 1.2.96:8). In many ways, therefore, Lutherans in the New Bundesländer would have preferred a separation of Church and state.

- Perhaps, however, the biggest problem was a mismatch of expectations between what the Church expected of the whole experiment and what the reality turned out to be. Church officials had perhaps anticipated something akin to Christian Instruction, but in practice the offering was closer to Life Skills and Religious Knowledge with an emphasis on world religions and pluralism. The difference could be characterised as that between Religion as a living faith and cognitive knowledge about Religion. However, knowledge about religion does not necessarily result in religious faith, and the Church discovered to its chagrin that it could not expect to use LER as a forum to promote faith, devotion and worship. The viability of the differentiated phase was uncertain and tenuous, since it depended on pupil choice of the RE option, hence there had been only a limited opportunity for the Church to teach Religion in the context of the project as a whole.

It is evident that many structural and political problems were connected with LER; yet almost in contradiction of all that has been said above, the pupils liked LER. According to a survey conducted by the Project Group at

PLIB in April/May 1994 (PLIB, April 1995), 83.7 per cent were positively disposed towards the subject, and welcomed the opportunity to be able to discuss problems and existential questions without pressure for achievement and high performance (p. 149 ff.); 82.8 per cent rejected the prospect of marks, and the PLIB Group recommended that pupils be assessed only in forms 9 and 10. In GDR times, it would not have been possible to discuss individual problems and religious faith in class, and this was seen as a clear advantage of LER. Parents too approved; 86.6 per cent of them found the LER course important or very important, while only 2.5 per cent found it quite unimportant. What the parents most valued, however, was the social dimension which 94 per cent found important or very important; 75 per cent of them gave similarly high ratings to 'Mediating knowledge of life questions, ethics, world-views and religions'.

Teachers working on LER had been to in-service training courses and these, combined with their classroom experience, changed their classroom behaviour and pedagogy. Most teachers had entered the LER project altruistically for the well-being of their pupils: they felt responsible for the new generation, wanted to offer them help for their lives, and thought it important to treat the themes of Life Skills, Ethics and Religion with their pupils (PLIB, 1995:78–79). Their role became that of moderator, discussion partner and advisor, and their classes became more pupil-centred than they had been accustomed to. Teachers became much more flexible and versatile in their teaching methodology, moving fluently between individual, partner, small group and project work; in short, their self-perception and behaviour as educators were transformed (p. 172–3). The following comments cited by PLIB (1995:121) show teachers' appreciation of the project and of the training received.

> I am annoyed that such experiences used to be withheld from us; I would probably have had far more self-assurance and less nervous stress.

> I think I used to see things in black or white; now I understand my pupils better.

> I am really glad that I decided to participate in the Pilot Study; colleagues envy me because of it.

The PLIB Project Group in its summary and recommendations took the view that the Pilot Study had been a considerable success. However, the differentiated phase had not proved viable, nor had the participation of Church staff in the integrated phase. The development of teachers, both personally and pedagogically had been admirable, as was their long-standing commitment to the project, despite its uncertain future. The support of in-service education had helped them to shoulder the LER burden professionally, and PLIB believed that the programme should be extended.

The Guidelines (Hinweise) provided by the Ministry were helpful and 'should be further developed'.

Political conflict overshadowed the independent research work of Professor Leschinsky's group; through no fault of their own, there was not enough time to begin and broaden the study in a satisfying way. At the request of the Ministry, the report was submitted early (three months before the end of the school year and of the pilot study) and was used to legitimise the Ministry's decision. The main points of Leschinsky's report were as follows (Leschinsky, 1996, Ch. 11):

- The LER experiment was and is significant for the entire Federal Republic, in view of the increasing secularisation of modern society, the long schooling period to which modern youth is subjected, and the weakening of the family's educational influence. Considering these factors, it is not appropriate to regard religious or ethical convictions as purely a private matter which has nothing to do with Church or state. It is a legitimate task of the school to make up for deficits in socialisation, education and knowledge. The Brandenburg Pilot Study is highly significant and deserves widespread recognition. It is a real attempt to come to terms with the legacy of the GDR past.
- The conflict between Church and state manifested itself in the lack of coordination between the integrated and the differentiated phases of the Pilot Study, and in the lack of harmonious relations between state and Church teachers. The success of school policies should not be subject to personal vagaries of this nature.
- Too much had been expected from LER. It cannot cure all the ills of society (especially with only two lessons a week).
- The Pilot Study was underresourced and had to improvise. The Guidelines came too late (in the last year), and it was expecting a great deal of three PLIB staff to support one hundred teachers. The curriculum had been underdeveloped and underdetermined.
- LER had conceptual weaknesses. In the importance which it accorded to this aspect of the Pilot Study, the Leschinsky group differed from the PLIB group which was more concerned with how well LER 'worked' with pupils and teachers. LER, said Leschinsky, had begun as a response to the difficulties caused by German unification, but as normalisation set in it would have to address itself not to crisis management but rather to the problems of a modern pluralistic society. Its tendency to turn the school into an agent for psychotherapy was not in keeping with legal judgements in the Federal Republic emphasising parental rights and protection of pupils' privacy. LER had an anticognitive streak: the Ethics element tended to be subordinated to

the Life Skills. Moreover, there was no clear conceptual model of Ethics. In essence, the aim was to teach pupils what was 'right', but this smacked of indoctrination. There was a strong sentiment in the early position papers that harmony and unity were to be valued highly, but this was in tension with the involvement of religious denominations. The non-denominational element of LER did not do justice to Religion.

In more concrete terms, the Land Brandenburg should now

- build upon LER by developing a school subject suitable for those without any religion;
- deepen the developmental work in selected schools;
- even out the conceptual shortcomings of LER;
- involve the University of Potsdam in teacher education for LER;
- seek to overcome the divisions between Church and state which impeded the interaction of ethics, philosophy and religion.

The Protestant Church, too, drew up and submitted a report on the Pilot Study (EK, 9.6.95) in which it complained that

- Religious Education was relegated to a subordinate position;
- the integrated phase was not used to prepare for the differentiated phase;
- collegial cooperation between Church and school teachers was lacking;
- in some schools there was only an integrated phase and no differentiated phase;
- the costs of the Church staff's participation in the integrated phase were not always reimbursed or subsidised by the state;
- in short, the continued collaboration of the Protestant Church was contingent on Religious Education and Life Skills/ Ethics becoming regular school subjects with equal rights.

The Brandenburg Ministry of Education, Youth and Sport was not short of opinions and evidence on which to base its judgement. It was able to come to a clear and unequivocal decision about the future of LER: Brandenburg would keep LER as a subject and would teach it to all pupils as a non-denominational subject without a differentiated phase. The Churches could teach Religious Education on school premises if they wished, though it was not to be a 'full normal school subject'. Values education, however, was now to be the task of all teachers – not just Church people – and normal class teachers were encouraged to treat questions of religion and faith in their lessons (BB MBJS, 1.2.96). A new Land School Law (BB MBJS 12.4.96, para. 11) was passed in which LER was instated as an official subject for all pupils with effect from 1996/97. The last word of the LER cluster, however, was now changed to *Religionskunde* (Religious Knowledge) or *Religionen* rather than *Religion*, thus emphasising its educational rather than devotional purpose. It was intended to mediate knowledge about every significant religion in the world. An attitude of openness and tolerance was to be displayed towards religious and other world-views. Curiously, though, paragraph 141 added that pupils could be released from LER on application of their parents, 'if justified by an important reason'. From the age of fourteen onwards, students could do this on their own authority. Such opt-out provisions as these were usually applied to Religious Education, giving rise to the suspicion in some quarters that LER was a covert form of RE after all. New Guidelines (*Unterrichtsvorgaben*) were issued in preparation for the new school year (BB MBJS, 25.6.96). Notably, they omitted any mention of a differentiated phase, eroding the opportunity for the denominations to make a curricular contribution.

It was not long before the battle lines were drawn. Cardinal Sterzinsky declared that Catholic children would not participate in LER. Protestant Bishop Wolfgang Huber of Berlin-Brandenburg argued that in championing LER the state was attempting to mediate values and that this was a dangerous course of action (*Frankfurter Rundschau*, 26.12.96). He said that Ethics with RE tacked on was no adequate substitute for real Religious Education. It was a contradiction in terms to argue simultaneously that LER was 'value neutral', yet that it should somehow also 'mediate values'. If Religion is marginalised as a full normal school subject, then the supposedly neutral LER in effect asserts exclusivity in the realm of values orientation – a dangerous stance. The state should enable values education to take place but should not play a major role in determining its content. The present arrangements, says Huber, are in conflict with the duty of the state to maintain a distance in questions of religion and world-view. The Churches have a public responsibility in the ethical-religious dimension – to which they clung tenaciously in GDR times – and since this is such an integral part of education, they cannot abandon their involvement. 'To deny the Churches this involvement or to reduce it to a lower level in comparison with other educational offerings would be a break with an important element of the German Constitutional tradition' (Huber, n.d.:16).

The Brandenburg Minister of Education, then Angelika Peter, was accused of arbitrary exercise of power in the best GDR tradition. Nevertheless, she strongly defended the introduction of LER as a common school subject for all young people, and could see no reason why the Churches should have a monopoly on moral questions. She found it frankly 'inadvisable' for a New Bundesland like Brandenburg to take over Religious Education as it existed in the Old Bundesländer (*Frankfurter Rundschau*, 15.2.96). After all, the Ministry had faced up honestly to the need to fill the values vacuum left by the discrediting of Marxism-Leninism, and had mounted a carefully evaluated trial of LER before introducing it on a Land-wide basis. Moreover, it had used currents of thought and elements from the pre-Wende reformist GDR tradition which were likely to be congenial to Brandenburg. The argument was also put that LER was distinctive and good for the identity of the New Bundesländer because it was a genuine East German cultural product.

The following quotations (taken from *Deutsche Lehrerzeitung*, 49/50, 12.12.96:22) give a flavour of the debate's emotionalism:

Against LER

Prepare to arm yourselves for the fight. The children have no chance to talk about faith. The supposedly 'non-denominational instruction' is Religious Knowledge without God. The really significant questions cannot be posed; for example: 'What is your greatest consolation in life and death ...?' (Bishop Huber, 'L-E-R methods, just like in GDR military knowledge instruction', *Bild*, 2.4.96. See note for an agreement which he negotiated on Religious Education.[3])

In a scandalous agreement, the Brandenburg SPD and PDS lay the axe to the Christian roots of our society. The aim is the imposition of the state's neutral world-view. (CSU General Secretary Protzner, *Wochenpost*, 3.4.96)

Whoever looks round attentively will see the way in which the threshold [of resistance] against the PDS is systematically being lowered from the red-green side. This is especially the case yet again in Brandenburg: Religious Education is being taken out of the schools there. We have been through this once already in Germany. We know the consequences. And I consider that there are far too few voices raised against this scandal. We must communicate this to people: we have experienced it twice in this century, in a brown and in a red dictatorship. We desire, in accordance with our understanding of the Constitution, that children in German schools should receive instruction in faith in God, if they and their parents so wish. (Helmut Kohl, Report to the 8th Party Day of the CDU, 20 October 1996)

For LER

A modern multicultural society must finally free itself from all state-Church relics and establish the strict separation of Church and state. As a professing Christian and a Protestant free church pastor, I do not mean to support the unbeliever: quite the contrary. The strict separation of Church and state would hopefully lead to the so-called great Churches becoming more conscious of their distinctive task, and using their influence to teach about and mediate experience of Jesus Christ in a more committed and convincing manner. (Bernhard Storek, Pastor from Barßel, *Die Welt*, 11.4.1996)

3. In 1997, Bishop Huber reached an agreement with Minister Peter about the teaching of Evangelische Religion in Brandenburg schools (BB MBJS, 11.2.1997). The subject could be (but did not have to be) offered, and would be taught by persons to whom the Church entrusted the task. The Ministry undertook to make a recommendation to parents' committees

Once again, the Churches do not recognise the signs of the times which require common instruction for all pupils in values education, as in the other school subjects. I refer to Learning to Live Together in school as an educational question of society concerned with peace, ethics and thus with basic religious values. That is the declared aim of L-E-R. All arguments to the contrary are moth-eaten remnants of former world-views which must be overcome for the sake of peace. The Working Group of Halle once again welcomes the introduction of the full normal subject Life Skills, Ethics, Religions (L-E-R) for all pupils in all state schools of the Land of Brandenburg ... and calls upon the Churches to work constructively for whatever improvements may still be necessary in this future-oriented subject. (Catholic Action Circle Halle (AKH), *Die Kirche,* 34/96, 25.8.1996)

Another approach to learning and teaching could be adopted, if that which the school at present neglects could only unfold: integration of experience [a free translation of *Ganzheitlichkeit*]. A form of teaching could be developed whereby life is integrated into school and the school into life. The debate up to the present has become bogged down, petty and bigoted. L-E-R must be given the chance to prove itself; perhaps it could provide lessons for the other Bundesländer instead of putting the curb on Brandenburg from the start. (Friedrich Schorlemmer, SPD, clergyman, *Potsdamer Neueste Nachrichten*, 20.3.1996)

Soon the Ministry was faced with complaints to the Constitutional Court at Karlsruhe from the two great Christian Churches (*inter alia*). There were two main questions in this controversy.

1. Whether Church supporters can insist that Religion must indeed be treated as a full normal school subject in the sense specified by Article 7 (3) of the Basic Law. The demand is that Religious Education and LER should have equal status and equal legal position in Brandenburg. There is no question of getting rid of LER.
2. Whether Brandenburg is indeed entitled to make its own special provision under Article 141 of the Basic Law. To be able to use this provision successfully, Brandenburg needs to be able to argue Constitutional continuity between the present Land and the Land which predated the Soviet Zone of Occupation. In other words, it needs to be able to prove that it is the legal descendant of the Brandenburg which existed before 1949.

---

that a representative of the Church could be invited to provide information about the subject. Teachers of Religion had the right to provide such information both orally and in writing, and if so desired this could take place in tandem with the school's information about LER. Religious Education was to be offered during the main teaching schedule and not marginalised to before or after school hours. Teachers of RE could take part in school committees in an advisory capacity. The agreement was valid for 1996/97, and was to be prolonged for one further year, unless terminated with three months' notice by either party.

In practice, the two issues are interrelated and raise profound constitutional questions. If Religious Education is to be taught as a normal school subject, the state takes responsibility for it. This, however, runs contrary to (a) the principle of the separation of Church and state and (b) the principle of the religious neutrality of Church and state. However, state support for Religious Education does not necessarily contravene the Constitution because in the Basic Law of the Federal Republic, Church and state are not clearly separated. For historical reasons, they are *res mixtae*. When the Federal Republic was established, elements of the Weimar Constitution were incorporated into the Basic Law. The Weimar Republic was supposed to be a modern secular state, but strong conservative forces existed without which the Weimar Constitution could not have come into being. Certain denominational elements of the Weimar Constitution (later imported into the Basic Law) were justified by popular support for religion in the interwar period (Renck, 12.12.1996). However, concessions to Christianity represent exceptions to the principle of state neutrality which is thus in contradiction to the Constitution. This blurring of the Church-state boundaries was once justified, but the consensual basis for the religious compromise incorporated in the Weimar and the Bonn Constitutions has become strongly attenuated in the New Bundesländer. To a lesser extent, this is true too in the Old Bundesländer. Renck (1996), a judge in the Bavarian Administrative Court, opines that

> The theory of Constitutional change states that if the factual conditions of a Constitutional rule and/or the evaluation of such a rule in the population undergoes significant change, then the obligatory quality of the Constitution vanishes. The Constitutional norm in question automatically forfeits its validity or at least changes its significance according to modifications in circumstances or their evaluation.… The rules of denominational Constitutional law, contrary to principle but based on a predominantly Church-going population, become minority privileges no longer democratically justified. The contraventions of the neutrality principle appear neither practically nor legally justified under present conditions.

If Renck is correct in his judgement, then the pro-religious elements in the Constitution would give way to the principle of the state's neutrality – if not now, then at some time in the more distant future. Denominational Religious Education would be taken out of state control and become purely a matter for the Churches. This would affect all the Bundesländer, not just those in the former GDR. In view of the fact that East German Church people already had reservations about instituting Religion as a full school subject after the fall of the Wall, such a change might prove more upsetting to Western than to Eastern Länder. In any event, it looks as if Brandenburg's attempt to deliver values education and to marginalise Religious Education may have far-reaching consequences. The transfer of West German RE conventions to East Germany after the latter's forty years of atheism has created considerable problems and raised major questions. From the point of view of the Churches, both Protestant and Catholic, the most powerful actions which they could take to extend their influence would seem to be (a) to continue to develop and support their networks of schools, and (b) to do the same regarding their own Christian Instruction given in their parishes.

Chapter 5

TRAINING FOR THE WORLD OF WORK

The GDR Tradition of Vocational Education

Historically speaking, German vocational education had its roots in the Middle Ages' structure of 'apprentice–journeyman–master', and involved imitation, learning on the job and building up working habits. That traditional model was almost destroyed during the Industrial Revolution with its emphasis on division of labour, separation of head and hand, and disjunction between school and work; nevertheless, it was during that period that the origins of the so-called Dual System evolved sufficiently to be resuscitated and later developed. As a way of combating the proletarianisation of young people, continuation schools were established to carry on where the elementary school left off, and although they were a means for the ruling class to exert power over the socialisation processes of workers – and were thus in a way paternalistic – they were the precursors of the future vocational schools (Kell, 1995:372). The notion that practical instruction, observation and imitation on the part of the apprentice needed to be supplemented by systematic instruction on the part of the master or firm gained currency at a relatively early stage of economic modernisation in Germany; the concept arose that instruction for apprentices should be a contribution to their trade or craft as well as to their general education (conceived predominantly as religious education). The so-called 'Dual System' developed in its modern form in the late nineteenth/early twentieth century when the prototype of the present-day 'vocational school' developed and was enshrined in the Imperial School Law of 1938. Less hidebound by tradition and less permeated by state politics and pedagogical theory than German higher education, the Dual System adapted more readily to changing circumstances. Educational thinkers like Georg Ker-schensteiner (1884–1932) and Eduard Spranger (1882–1963) helped to raise the prestige of vocational education by providing it with an explicit ideology. The central tenet of this liberal thinking was a rejection of the supposed antagonism between general and vocational education in favour of the concept that apprentices' trade and training can be the carrier of education and humane values (MPI, 1994:559–61).

Despite their common historical roots, there were certain differences of balance and structure between the FRG and the GDR vocational systems. When the partition of Germany was introduced after the Second World War, the ethos of vocational education in the GDR was reinterpreted in keeping with socialism. Whereas Wilhelm von Humboldt had eschewed the notion of education for the purpose of merely earning one's bread, Marx and Engels wanted to give workers the possibility of dominating the whole process of production, and they viewed people simultaneously as creatures of theory and of practice. This was the rationale underlying *Polytechnik.* The principles on which GDR vocational education was organised were:

- education and upbringing to be state-organised, planned and unified;
- theory and practice to be integrated;
- good general, basic education to coexist with vocational specialisation;
- vocational education to be directly linked to production. (Autsch, 1995:16)

The GDR vocational education sector had its own Ministry and a Central Research Institute of Vocational Training in East Berlin, and through the Education Law of 1965, it was formally declared part of the unified social-ist education system. Interestingly, despite its strong orientation towards the world of work, theory was more strongly emphasised in the GDR than in the FRG. On average, it amounted to 33 per cent of the course content, but could vary between 25 per cent and 50 per cent. The final examinations at the end of an apprenticeship gave equal weighting to theory and practice, and over 98 per cent of apprentices succeeded – 50 per cent with 'good' or 'very good' marks (Schäfer, 1990b:314). Whereas the curriculum in East Germany was very much based on a socialist ethos, in West Germany it was based on a pluralistic world-view, in which private enterprise played an important role alongside state power. Whereas the East German vocational model was based on a unified school system and a centralised Ministry, the Western one was linked to a tripartite school-based vocational education system and a federal governmental training system, thereby making it diffi-cult to realise a homogeneous vocational structure.

In West Germany, the 'dualism' of the Dual System is real in both a phys-ical and a legal sense. Most apprentices are trained in firms and educated in vocational schools; the whole process thus takes place in two locations and is controlled according to two jurisdictions (Bund and Land). These two sectors are subject to different types of law: the firm to civil law and the school to public service law. The trainee – as a user of a state institution (the school) who is also contractually involved with private enterprise – is therefore subject to two legal systems. He or she works on a mixed pattern of funding: private financing from the firm and public financing from the school. Many apprentices in the FRG are trained in firms with fewer than fifty employees. Since small firms naturally have a limited range of facilities, free-standing Training Centres (*Überbetriebliche Ausbildungsstätten* (ÜBS)) with an enriched curriculum and a wider range of equipment have been set up so as to even out any deficiencies in the apprenticeships offered. They are provided by public finance, Chambers, Mutual Associations or limited companies, and their existence makes it easier for small firms to participate in training since they did not have to provide all the resources regarding master-craftsmen and curricula (though they have to pay for the ÜBS). These ÜBS were in effect a third place of learning, in addition to the firm and the vocational school, and have led some observers (e.g. Kell, 1995:380) to suggest that the addition of the ÜBS to the 'Dual System' makes it a triadic or pluralistic system with the ÜBS as a possible alternative to the two locations traditionally associated with the Dual System. These Training Centres receive financial support from the Bund, the Chambers and Guilds, and are financially better supported than vocational schools with the result that teachers' associations and unions often feel threatened by the possibility of a triadic system (Münch, 1990:324).

In the former GDR, 'dualism' of the Western type did not exist. Vocational education and training were both based mainly on the firm or business rather than being split between them and the school sector. For more than 70 per cent of apprentices, theory and practice were mediated in the same physical location, namely the firm-based school (*Betriebsberufsschule*) (Hörner, 1990a:19). From the year 1948 onwards, the development of these establishments was pursued until they completely predominated over communal vocational schools. Table 5.1 shows the increasing percentage share of training provision which they represented.

Table 5.1 Percentage of Training Done in Betriebsberufsschulen

1950	1960	1980	1989
49	54	74	80

Source: Autsch, 1995:16.

This emphasis on the firm-based school was in keeping with the ideological goals of the Party. Since the SED and the working class were supposed to be seen as a unity, priority was given to building up vocational education where the influence of the Party was at its strongest, namely in large firms which eventually formed *Kombinate* owned by the people. The Kombinate had an important role in determining the training course syllabuses which were supposed to be based on extensive job analysis. In the GDR, 37 per cent of all employees with a completed apprenticeship had been trained in a firm with more than five hundred employees, whereas this applied to only 11 per cent in the FRG (MPI, 1994:581). The average large GDR firm trained about seventy apprentices who formed a clearly defined subgroup within it. Large businesses took in apprentices and trained them for other firms (*Fremdausbildung*), as well as for their own needs.

Psychologically, each apprentice underwent a group rather than an individual experience, and this was intensified by the fact that many apprentices lived in residential accommodation. Because the firms were so large, apprentices had to be drawn into them from a wide catchment area, and needed to have living quarters arranged for them. By 1987, there were 1,310 hostels that housed about one-third of all apprentices (Schäfer, 1990b:312). Small independent businesses (*Handwerksbetriebe*) were unpopular with the Party because they were run by artisans for private gain and were thus incompatible with the spirit of socialism. The number of apprentices trained in such businesses was systematically reduced: in 1950, it had been 80 per cent and in 1989, just before the fall of the Wall, it was only 3 per cent. By contrast, it was and remains true that in West Germany about two-thirds of employees with completed apprenticeships have been trained in small and medium-sized concerns. However, the East/West differential in the sheer size of training establishments began to narrow somewhat towards the end of the 1980s; between 1980 and 1989 a demographic decline in the GDR caused a fall of about 40 per cent in numbers entering the vocational system, and this necessitated the setting up of small vocational schools taking about two hundred apprentices. To sustain all of the behemoth, firm-based, Training Centres would have involved making apprentices 'queue' for acceptance into them and constructing more residential hostels; hence the authorities decided on an alternative strategy (ibid.).

The East German emphasis on productive work and the manufacturing industry permeated not only the training sector but also the school sector, which became strongly vocationalised in keeping with Marx's and Engels's philosophy. In effect, the school was made to anticipate and contribute to later vocational education, and this tight relationship between school and work reflects the fact that the FRG and the GDR had different concepts of 'youth' in the life cycle. In the West of Germany it has become a very protracted phase which can extend even to the third decade of life, whereas in the East, the transition phase from childhood to adulthood was much shorter: by the age of twenty, young people had adult status and many of them were already rearing their own families (MPI, 1994:544).

In the late 1950s and early 1960s there was a tendency to integrate training into the general school curriculum, and in 1959, it was decided to import basic apprenticeships into the ninth and tenth years of the POS and the eleventh and twelfth years of the EOS. This school-based training – which was unique in German educational history – led to a shortening of the total training period by one year for the POS pupils; between 1962 and 1967, EOS pupils who performed satisfactorily were awarded a certificate of completed apprenticeship along with their Abitur. These school apprenticeships were, however, in tension with the need to professionalise training and make it adequate for the demands of the modern technological revolution. By the mid-1960s, the tendency to develop an out-of-school vocational sector had reasserted itself, and was consolidated in the 1970s and 1980s. The development of GDR vocational education at school level, which was far from linear (Schäfer, 1990c:282–4), was thus characterised by policy changes reflecting the demands of generalism and specialism, theory and practice.

In 1958, the subject Polytechnic Instruction was introduced into general education on the basis of a concept elaborated by Heinz Frankiewicz: production was reinterpreted as 'Technik' and as creative action, thereby modernising it and linking it with knowledge. In fact, the school and production were regarded almost as a unity. The new subject was intended to promote the very close relationship which the Party believed should exist between schools and the world of work. It was different from an apprenticeship, and aimed

- to provide the future worker with an induction into working life;
- to contribute to general education;
- to promote character formation, especially work-related virtues and socialist attitudes.

In the lowest school forms, this was accomplished through subjects such as School Gardening, while in the more senior forms it was mediated through Technical Drawing and Introduction to Socialist Production. Practical work was done in firms, thus eliminating the need to set up and equip school workshops with expensive apparatus.[1]

The GDR vocational system was intended to produce qualifications quickly (Anweiler, 1990:19), and the Polytechnische Oberschule was expected

---

1. In the Federal Republic, *Arbeitslehre*, a similar subject to Polytechnic Instruction, was introduced in general secondary schools but not in grammar schools.

to contribute to this drive for speed. By the 1980s, the POS was required to take more account of the typical demands made of a future skilled worker and had become for the majority of young people a stage preliminary to vocational education. Offering Polytechnic Instruction in the POS made it possible to reduce the duration of apprenticeships because school-leavers had already completed some of the work at school. The young people were well qualified to undertake their training courses: by 1988 only 11 per cent of new apprentices were without the leaving certificate from the tenth form. The pupils who were not doing well at school had the option to leave the general school after the eighth form and learn a trade. Those who had not even completed the eighth year successfully could train for restricted areas of skilled worker jobs (Hörner, 1990a:14). About sixty-two training categories were especially reserved for low achievers – a necessary measure in a state where all citizens had the right to work. The valid classification of training categories was resolutely reduced in number during the course of several decades, and prior to the fall of the Wall it contained 238 formally designated skilled jobs, including some which would have been *Angestellte* jobs in the FRG.

The GDR commitment to vocationalism was manifested in a vocational leaving certificate called Vocational Training with Associated Abitur which lasted three years and was open to about 6 per cent of sixteen-year-olds completing form 10 successfully. Although this double qualification was formally part of the vocational rather than the general sector of education, the theoretical component in it amounted to more than fifty per cent. In the years leading up to the Wende, about one-third of all Abitur holders attained their qualification by the vocational route and two-thirds by the general (EOS) route. Eighty-six skilled jobs, according to the last classification, were intended for the three-year Vocational Training with Associated Abitur (*Berufsbildung mit Abitur* (BMA)). The double qualification was intended especially for those going on to higher education in engineering subjects, but many people took up other programmes of study, so it did not fulfil this objective very well. Empirical studies showed that the vocational Abitur was as good a preparation for higher education as the more generalist EOS-based Abitur (Hörner, 1990a:20).

Vocational education and training were supposed to enjoy parity of esteem with the general education track. Efforts were made to enable ordinary people to enter higher education, and in 1949 special pre-degree 'Workers' and Peasants' Faculties' were attached to higher education institutions. Apprentices who did well in their first year could participate in Abitur courses which led to matriculation within two years, and even those who left the EOS early could also take preparatory courses towards university entry (Schäfer, 1990b:314). The way to higher education was by no means barred to skilled workers without Abitur: special one-year pro-paedeutic courses were provided for them and these, together with distance and continuing education, opened up higher education perspectives. The GDR was thus much more successful than the FRG in broadening access to third-level education (MPI, 1994:184, 581), though the overall percentage of those allowed to enter was smaller.

At upper secondary and tertiary level, institutions specific to the GDR widened the palette of choice in vocational education. There existed Specialist Colleges known as *Fachschulen* which had their roots in the eighteenth and nineteenth centuries. Developed in Soviet-occupied Germany after 1945, they were less theoretical than universities or other forms of general higher education. They were of two main types, one third level and one not: Type 2 did not assume prior completed vocational training, whereas Type 1, which took about 60 per cent of all Fachschule students, did (Schäfer, 1990e).

TYPE 1. Over 90 per cent of Type 1 Specialist Colleges were of tertiary level, though they also produced some engineers, agronomists, etc. at sub-university level. This Type 1 College was part of an older education genus which the GDR retained into the 1980s but which the FRG abandoned when it upgraded its Engineering Colleges to *Fachhochschulen* under the pressure of EC legislation in the mid-1980s. In 1988, there were ninety-six engineer and agronomist Specialist Colleges and nine commercial Colleges; also four Colleges for training instructors in vocational education and three for applied art (Hörner, 1990a:23).

TYPE 2. Type 2 Specialist Colleges encompassed paramedical, educational and artistic activities, and took in students who had completed form 10 of the Polytechnische Oberschule (and thus were without Abitur). Such Colleges did not give entry into higher education. In 1988, there were sixty-two Specialist Colleges for paramedical courses, and six Colleges for the visual arts (drama, ballet, dance, etc.). It is important to note that teachers of young children (primary and kindergarten) were trained in Institutes for Teacher Education (*Institute für Lehrerbildung* (IfL)); in 1988, forty-six such education colleges existed (ibid.). These Type 2 Colleges were good for young women's upward mobility.

Shortcomings in the GDR Model of Vocational Education

Most apprentices entered their training with good qualifications from school. From the 1950s onwards, the skill level of the GDR working population steadily increased: in 1955, 69.9 per cent of workers were unskilled; by 1985, this proportion had sunk to about 15 per cent. By the beginning of the 1990s, only 5 to 6 per cent of GDR twenty-five- to twenty-nine-year-olds were without a vocational qualification certificate, whereas the figure for the FRG was 15 per cent (MPI, 1994:553). There was continuous assessment from the beginning of the training onwards. Good marks enabled candidates to progress faster through the system to the termination of their apprenticeship and the award of the title 'skilled worker'. Unfortunately, because teachers were penalised for their pupils' failure, high marks were sometimes awarded too easily and without being fully deserved. This negated the notion of merit. The relationship between achievement and reward was anything but transparent and on occasion the state apparently functioned to protect the weak or incompetent. Trades, for example, were under an obligation to offer apprentices a job, even if they did not pass their examinations or had terminated their apprenticeship. This contributed to full employment and possibly to social justice but must have appeared *personally* unfair to some employers saddled with inadequate workers.

If employers lacked choice, so did employees, despite the fact that according to the Constitution, they had the right to free choice of trade or profession. All jobs were the object of central planning and had to fit within the structure of socialist society. The means of reconciling the potential conflict between the needs of the individual and those of society was a system of vocational advice which had the function of 'guiding' pupils into socially necessary jobs or training courses, even if these seemed for the moment unattractive to the young person in question. Local authority councils had offices for vocational education and vocational guidance, including a Register of Apprenticeships which monitored local needs. The advisory centres were responsible to these offices and conducted the vocational counselling process in collaboration with schools. Each centre had about four full-time workers, usually former teachers with postgraduate education (Hörner, 1990a:14). From form 6 onwards, pupils' job aspirations were systematically collected and transmitted to the advisory centres so that they could be matched up with actual needs. Schools were informed of discrepancies so that they could help pupils to adapt to the planners' needs even if this meant moving to second or third choices. Polytechnic Instruction was especially important in inducing pupils to take on workers' jobs because it mediated contact with the world of work. State planning resulted in a lack of freedom for both individuals and firms. Many apprentices were denied their top career preference, and if they could not settle to the job into which they had been directed, many of them later did a second course of training with corresponding sacrifice of time and money (Autsch, 1995:20). Firms were not allowed to decide on the number and sectoral placement of apprentices and had very limited possibilities of influencing the content of state plans and curriculum. In fulfilling the state Plan, they lacked the power to take decisions in matters which closely concerned them.

Despite lack of freedom, the GDR system successfully enskilled people and ensured that they were provided with employment. However, the apparently solid skills level of the population did not necessarily produce the high level of success which one might assume. A major problem was that the infrastructure was not sufficiently well developed to make maximum use of workers' qualifications. When workers' competences outstripped the infrastructure's capacity to deploy them productively, they were said to have an 'anticipatory function' – presumably anticipating societal progress to be made at some future time in the larger society. The mismatch between qualifications and infrastructure meant that young workers suffered from low levels of motivation and job satisfaction. Moreover, the way in which training places were distributed across sectors lacked modernity and flexibility. The employment sectors were differently distributed in East and West Germany, with service industries being less strongly represented in the East than in the West (MPI, 1994:581). The relative proportions of the apprentices entering different training sectors in the GDR were as follows: 42 per cent in industry; 16 per cent in the building trade; 11 per cent in forestry, land and food industries; the remainder in trade, manual occupations or in the service sector (Hörner, 1990a:20).

The concentration on agronomics and on the manufacturing industry to the detriment of services constituted a handicap. During the lifetime of the GDR, it became imperative to respond to the growth of computers and Informatics. This was an ideological as well as a practical challenge, because the Information Revolution did not easily fit into the conceptual and political schemata of a country whose traditional emphasis was on the working class and peasantry, the manufacturing industry and collective agriculture. Schäfer (1990d:326) points out that the SED was rather slow in adjusting to technological advances and made some wrong prognoses which were difficult to reverse in the short term (this notwithstanding Honecker's boasts about computers in the GDR during his meeting with Gorbachev in 1989). Hörner (1990b:222–4) shows how certain problems arose when pupils experienced the interface between industry and school. One was the sheer monotony and boredom of the production process which seemed at times to be in crass contradiction to the ideal picture of socialist society as portrayed by the school. Frankiewicz, developer of Polytechnic Instruction, called this a dialectic and conceptualised it as a 'challenge' to workers' morale. Another difficulty was that the heavy, closely packed school curriculum left little room for the incursion of unstructured experience from the 'real' world of work. In order to get through syllabuses, teachers often had to evade problems raised by pupils and concentrate on more mechanical activities like imitation and reproduction. Schurer (1990) shows that in the GDR, there was a concept of a linear, largely problem-free causal relationship between social progress and technological development. Personal development was subordinated to the postulate of societal usefulness, and the 'activity principle' in education was subordinated to a rigid political line leaving little scope for innovation or for a genuinely learner-centred curriculum.

After the fall of the Wall, during the brief interval before West German structures were imposed, the East German government sought to change its own vocational educational system. In a ministerial decree of April 1990 it emphasised the necessity of mastering the new technologies and drew up syllabuses for 'Bases of Automation' and 'Information Technology'. It wished to retain Vocational Training with Associated Abitur, entry to which was to be on the completion of the tenth year of the POS. On 19 July 1990, the East German government bound itself to try to achieve the equivalent of the West German Dual System. This meant accepting the state-recognised West German job categories; it also involved establishing vocational schools provided by the local governmental authorities, and taking theoretical instruction out of the firms and relocating it in the schools. Problems were anticipated, especially in the newly established private commercial sector. Many businesses were trying to divest themselves of training because of the expense and, to combat this, new financial measures were taken, especially so far as small and medium-sized businesses were concerned. They were bound by ministerial decree to keep to the existing agreements. Most of the Type 1 Fachschulen tried to model themselves on FRG structures, supported by partnership with West German Fachhochschulen, and indeed applied to change into Fachhochschulen themselves. The transitional government insisted on the principle of achievement (such as realistic marks and willingness to fail unsuitable or weak apprentices).

Introduction of the West German Dual System

Provision was made in the Unification Treaty for application of the West German Vocational Training Law (*Berufsbildungsgesetz* (BBiG)) to the New Bundesländer, and from 13 August 1990 onwards, this was implemented. By the end of October 1990, about 80 per cent of apprentices were being trained according to West German regulations, with the other 20 per cent (about 25,000 youths) being handled according to GDR structures for a transitional period (BMBW BBB 1991:2). A sum of DM 703 million was allocated to the NBL for vocational training in the financial year 1991 (BLK, 1993a:7). The qualifications of GDR workers achieved under the old structures were recognised as being valid in the new regime. In the

GDR, there had been 1,175 vocational schools (1990/91), of which 936 (about 80 per cent) were based in firms and 239 (about 20 per cent) belonged to the communes. The profusion of institutions in the GDR was due to the high degree of specialisation and the binding-in of schools and firms to the state Plan. With the introduction of the new BBiG Law, provision was made for all vocational schools to be transferred to different providers: supervision and funding of staff were to become the responsibility of the Länder, while the firm-based part of the duality was transferred to commercial concerns under the jurisdiction of the Bund. There was a certain amount of resistance on the part of the firms to losing their schools, and some continued to use them regardless of the new Law. Another problem was that there were too many small, free-standing vocational schools to be cost-effective (BLK, 1993a:25–26). It was frankly admitted in the Annual Report for Vocational Education (BMBW BBB, 1991) that many employers' knowledge of the Training Regulations was inadequate and that advice structures were poor. Moreover, there was a disparity between the demand and supply of in-plant placements which necessitated an immediate remedial programme of DM 300 million – the first of many special measures to come. The contribution of the economy and of employers was stressed, as was the need for the Dual System in the NBL to adapt to the demands of the social market. The objectives were that every school-leaver who wanted an apprenticeship should have one and that firms should not be left without a proper supply of skilled labour.

Apprenticeship programmes changed in number, structure and content: the canon of the GDR state-recognised training courses was discontinued and 377 officially designated Western courses were introduced. The new job descriptions did not always correspond to the old, and the problems of transition were especially onerous for those firms undertaking training for the first time, and for those training for new-style jobs characteristic of a free market economy (tax advisers, legal assistants, etc.). Such jobs had not existed in the old GDR and required a new approach (BLK, 1993a:21–22, 28). Frequently, firms had to acquire new equipment and provide new facilities to conform to the legal requirements for training apprentices (who had the right to free materials and equipment). The trainers themselves had to undertake supplementary courses in order to achieve official recognition; in this, they were sometimes supported by their partner Länder in the Old Bundesländer. In their vocational teaching role, they needed additional time for preparation, and found that the syllabus content had become more abstract, harder to transmit to trainees, more removed from action and practical experience. Most of them had been very well in control of their work under the old regime, and Kroymann and Lübke (1992:35) state that the trainers in the former GDR were perhaps educationally better prepared for their tasks than those in the former Federal Republic. Schwarz too (1993) defends the East German trainers, whose prestige seems unfortunately to have dipped under the new regime. She points out that they are well qualified and have valuable experience to offer. Deficits in areas of law, new pedagogies, new learning media, and work with foreign youngsters are being compensated by strong participation in continuing education courses. To this, Degen (1993) adds that some trainers are even mounting their own tailor-made courses, especially in the areas of commerce; they are very keen that training should continue to be led by East Germans rather than be taken over by Westerners.

The overall apprenticeship situation in East Germany was rendered more difficult to manage by some factors relating to the school structure. In all the new Länder (except for Berlin and Brandenburg), compulsory school ended after nine rather than ten years thus releasing pupils into the arena of training one year earlier and necessitating a longer training period. What had formerly been two years (usually) was now three to three-and-a-half – an extension of at least one year which required an increase in the capacity of the vocational education system (BLK, 1993a:5). The divided post-primary school system brought about a tendency towards high educational aspirations, sometimes causing a form of education inflation in the vocational sector. The Main School leaving certificate (Hauptschulabschluß) was unattractive to employers offering training places because they equated it with the GDR arrangements for weak pupils leaving school after form 8 of the old POS. Even the pupils themselves and their parents held the Main School leaving certificate in low esteem. As such, the qualification was hardly acceptable, and less able pupils found it very difficult to achieve entry onto the labour market (Autsch, 1995:26–27). An IAB (Institut für Arbeitsmarkt- und Berufsforschung der Bundesanstalt für Arbeit, November 1992 and 1993) survey shows that 48 per cent of all pupils in forms 9 and 10 were aiming for Abitur, and 47 per cent for a Realschule leaving certificate. Only 5 per cent wanted a Hauptschule leaving certificate. The strong desire to achieve Abitur reflects a wish to be competitive in the new society, and this is most especially true for young women, 55 per cent of whom believe that without Abitur they have no chance on the labour market (as against 48 per cent of young men) (Schober, 1995:49, 54–56).

The Vocational Training with Associated Abitur looked initially as if its chances of survival were good, and the transitional East German government certainly wished to retain it. Even after the Unification Treaty had come into force, it would still have been possible, in principle, to keep it, but this option was lost because of resistance on the part of the Chambers. They were critical of the qualification for several reasons. They would have liked it to contain more practice and had a strong preference for training which was in-plant rather than school-based. (Some young people took a school preparatory year when they had failed to find an apprenticeship, and firms regarded this as an inferior option to a fully developed Dual System of training.) They felt that in accepting Vocational Training with Associated Abitur, they were perhaps helping to support the academic side of training which was not really their responsibility. The Chambers' member firms were subject to the new market economy and they felt obliged to divest themselves of anything which would increase their costs (Berger, 1995: 30–32). In the end, they were unwilling to register a qualification which included the Abitur. With hindsight, however, many people think that this attractive combination of general and vocational education was too easily abandoned. Because of the difficulty of persuading the firms to offer apprenticeships, the Vocational Training with Associated Abitur was a model which would have suited the New Bundesländer very well and should probably have been retained.

Major changes were made to the Fachschulen. Those which gave initial qualifications were transformed into Vocational Fachschulen (*Berufsfachschulen*), except for those which did teacher training. In this case, it was decided that teachers were to be trained in universities, or in Colleges of Education. The Fachschulen were not allowed to become Fachhochschulen. It was, however, agreed that parts of them might be suitable for integration into an FHS, but Fachschule qualifications were not recognised as equivalent to Fachhochschule qualifications. Teachers in vocational education who were teaching at schools on the basis of only a Fachschule qualification were regarded as underqualified and could only be retained in their capacity as practitioners rather than as trainers. They were thus downwardly mobile. Those Fachschulen (especially numerous in Saxony and Saxony-Anhalt) which trained people for unusual skilled jobs (*Unikate*) were to be retained only if a clear need for such workers could be demonstrated (BLK, 1993a:56–57).

Economic Stringency and Its Impact on the Dual System

Since the East and West German systems of vocational training had common roots, it was hoped that they could be integrated reasonably easily after the fall of the Wall. This proved more difficult than anticipated partly because the differences in the political systems had widened the distances between the training systems, and partly because economic factors caused widespread unemployment, stagnation and economic decline in East Germany. The free market, a competitive capitalistic system characterised by concern for profit, was superimposed on a socialist system characterised by a desire to protect the largest possible number of people by offering them secure, universal employment regardless of their productivity rates.

The introduction of the Western Dual System was followed by a number of macroeconomic developments making it difficult for such a system to flourish in the New Bundesländer. Prior to unification, the West German economy had been characterised by low inflation, a good growth rate, high wages (wealth), high employment and a good trade surplus; this buoyancy fed through into the training sector. The 1990 Annual Report for Vocational Education stated that the 1988/89 apprenticeship situation was the most favourable since the introduction of statistical records in 1976. The supply of placements had outstripped the demand by over 11 per cent (BMBW BBB, 1990:1). In February 1990, a decision was made to introduce German monetary union according to West German procedures and fiscal discipline, on the basis that these had worked well in the past. As was pointed out in Chapter 1, one of the most important voices dissenting from this policy was that of Otto Pöhl, President of the Bundesbank, who stated publicly his fears that overvaluation of the Ostmark would cause the collapse of large areas of East German industry. He predicted an ensuing need for substantial subsidies from the West and stated his preference for a gradual rapprochement of the two German states rather than fast-track unitary merger. Nevertheless, in July 1990 monetary union was implemented on a one-for-one basis: one Ostmark was rated equivalent to one Deutschmark. The reasons for this decision were political rather than economic. It was believed that differing currency rates in Old and New Bundesländer would intensify high out-migration from the NBL. Easterners were already migrating westwards at the rate of about 2,000 a day (Marsh, 1994:69) in search of economic prosperity, and if the Ostmark had been valued at what it was worth – about 20 pfennigs, according to Marsh (1994:55) – there would have been no way of stemming this flow of disaffected people. The Easterners chanted a slogan on the streets: 'Kommt die D-Mark, bleiben wir. Kommt sie nicht, geh'n wir zu ihr' (If the D-Mark comes, we stay here. If it doesn't come, we'll go to the D-Mark) (Marsh, 1994:70).

In the early months of 1990, the effects of the one-to-one currency conversion were themselves disastrous, subjecting the fragile East German industry to a sudden and massive currency revaluation of 400 per cent which made it uncompetitive. Chancellor Kohl believed that introducing the Deutschmark into the New Bundesländer would provide the same economic boost that resulted from the currency reform of June 1948; when the Allies substituted the Deutschmark for the Reichsmark in the western zones of occupied Germany, German industry was revitalised. Yet the circumstances in 1948 were very different from those in 1990. At the end of the War, *many* European countries were in more or less similar states of ruin and disorder and so started off from the same baseline. In 1990, however, East Germany was at a great disadvantage compared to West Germany; it had to adapt overnight to an economic system in which the West had had decades of experience. In the first six months of monetary union, East Germany's industrial production *fell* 50 per cent, whereas in 1948, industrial production in the western zones of Germany had *risen* 50 per cent (Marsh, 1994:68–69). Initially the Westerners were not well informed about the East German economy and had overestimated its strength, believing that about two-thirds of it would survive. In the event, however, about two-thirds disappeared. East Germany's markets with the COMECON trading system crumbled, and in 1990–91 COMECON itself disintegrated in face of competition from Western markets and the switch to world market prices. Prior to unification, trade with socialist countries had constituted 60 per cent of sales for East Germany, so the collapse of these markets was a body blow (Flockton, 1993:315).

The currency conversion in the East gave some people money to pay for consumer goods, but for many others it led to unemployment, which rose relentlessly and was often long term. Prior to unification, the East German unemployment rate had been officially almost zero, and in 1989, the labour force had consisted of 10 million people; by 1992, this had contracted to 6 million, of whom many were on special job creation schemes or on short-time (Marsh, 1994:82). Investment that would help to create jobs was painfully slow in coming, and by the end of 1993, only DM 14.2 billion had been put into East German businesses by the investors who bought the former GDR state-owned companies; this contrasted with the Treuhand promises of over DM 200 billion (Prützel-Thomas, 1995:123). The decision that property in the East should be restored to its former owners where that property had changed hands after 1945 (or between 1933 and 1945) came into conflict with the need to promote investment in East Germany (Southern, 1993). The real rate of unemployment was much higher than the official rate, and there were considerable regional disparities in people's labour market chances, with the thinly populated agricultural regions of Northern Germany being particularly badly hit. The agricultural sector declined by 28 per cent between November 1989 and November 1993. There were also drastic declines in mining, metal, electronic and manufacturing industries. If the numbers of people working in West rather than East Germany and those taking premature retirement are taken into consideration, then by June 1994 unemployment in East Germany was more in the nature of 25 per cent to 31 per cent than the official 16 per cent which was already more than double that of West Germany (Brinkmann, 1995:18).

The long-term prognosis for improvement of the East German economic situation is not favourable. It has been estimated that despite the infusion of Western money, the economic performance of the NBL has been approximately 40 per cent lower than it was in 1989 (Goldberger, 1993: 304). Hughes Hallett and Ma (1993) applied the IMF's MULTIMOD economic model to the NBL, and on the basis of the results, they predict that for many years to come East Germany will remain a 'mezzogiorno' problem. Fiscal expenditures in the East are three or four times larger than expected (DM 180 billion as opposed to the government's 1990 forecast of DM 25–50 billion). High interest rates, low productivity and rapid wage increases have limited the flow of investment from West to East, implying lower growth in the future and a continuing necessity for Western fiscal transfers which unfortunately is at variance with the need for greater fiscal discipline. If convergence is ever to take place, productivity levels must be equalised and East German labour costs reduced relative to the West. If Western productivity continues to grow at 2 per cent per annum, and if the East starts with productivity at 26 per cent of the Western level, then the relationship between growth and productivity will be as shown in Table 5.2.

Table 5.2 Relationship between Productivity Growth and NBL Economic Catch-Up

Productivity Prognosis for NBL	No. of Years Required for NBL to Catch Up with OBL Based on That Prognosis
9.1%	20
6.7%	30
5.5%	49

Source: Hughes Hallett and Ma (1993:417–8).

'Rapid convergence', state Hughes Hallett and Ma (ibid.:418) '… looks unlikely. Especially when it is recognised that the rapid development of West Germany under the Marshall Plan, or of the East Asian NICs [Newly Industrialised Countries] since the 1960s, produced sustained productivity growth rates averaging 6 to 7 per cent *at most*.' They believe that it will take thirty to forty years to achieve complete integration without a mezzogiorno problem, thus making the official prediction of five to ten years look hopelessly optimistic. On the basis of current policies, the catch-up after fifteen years will be around 50 to 60 per cent, although 70 per cent is also possible with some policy changes. Fiscal transfers and a fiscal deficit will continue for as long as productivity in the East lags behind that in the West. The unification process would be accelerated if Eastern wages were restrained relative to Western wages or taxes were increased. But the same effects can be obtained more effectively with a self-eliminating employment subsidy in the East (ibid.:427). The cruel paradox is that private sector investment in plant and machinery is necessary to help reduce the productivity gap, yet because this productivity gap exists, it is difficult to attract private investors in sufficient numbers to reduce unemployment. State subsidies, which seem so necessary for social reasons, may encourage uneconomic production and make the goal of self-sustaining economic recovery more elusive than ever. Some even accuse Bonn of re-creating a second version of the old GDR economy – a gibe which was made against the government in 1993 by Tyll Necker of the Federation of German Industry (Marsh, 1994:113).

Sensitive to macroeconomic factors, the West German Dual System has to be seen in the context of the labour market, society, the economy and employment policies. From what has been said above, it will be obvious that the circumstances in East Germany conspired to create a very difficult environment for vocational training. The experience of the typical East German apprentice changed: whereas previously training had taken place in very large industrial plants, it was now located in rather small businesses, and as such moved closer to the Western pattern. The East German economy had been characterised by very large state-owned businesses, both in the industrial and in the agricultural sectors. After the Wende, these concerns were disaggregated to form medium-sized and small businesses, and the prospects of finding apprenticeships in industry and agriculture deteriorated. A shift took place in the sectors most involved in training. The industrial sector, formerly the most heavily involved, gave way to the small artisan sector (*Handwerk*); by November 1993, the proportion of apprentices in Handwerk was about 50 per cent with only 18 per cent in industry (Schober, 1995:43). This represented a shift from very large concerns to medium- and small-sized ones which by 1993 were training 37 per cent of the total (having formerly trained only 9 per cent). The large businesses which had had one-third of all apprentices now had only 12 per cent. Small businesses tended to prefer those who were retraining rather than those who were undertaking their first apprenticeships, partly because this was said to be 'cheaper' (because they were publicly funded, the firm didn't have to pay for them), and partly because the retrainees were already experienced and could adapt more quickly to their job situation (Schober, 1995:48).

It became difficult to obtain a suitable training place, and in attempting to achieve one, individuals were very much thrown back on their own resources. Formerly, the state had done all the necessary work of placing people and running the training system. It had also maintained an elaborate advice service, the purpose of which was to harmonise the personal interests of the individual with the requirements of the country (Schäfer, 1990a:300). After the Wende, individuals – both apprentices and employers – had to assume much greater responsibility for these tasks themselves by learning about and implementing the regulatory, organisational and funding mechanisms. Local organisations helped them but there was no single central agency to do so. With unification, the old mechanisms for matching apprentices to the needs of the planned economy broke down. The central Register of Apprentices was discontinued and the advisory centres were linked up with the newly created West German-style Labour Offices; it was felt that with increasing unemployment, it would be preferable to correlate the advisory and the job-finding functions. The link between schools and advisory centres was broken, and the educational dimension of the advisory process was lost or forced into the background. Kroymann and Lübke (1993:43–47) are critical of the advisers whose purpose is to monitor the training process and to help young people, but Schober (personal communication, 9.6. 1997; Nürnberg) points out that the Labour Offices with their integrated vocational counselling services were quite rapidly established after the Wende and takes the view that compared to other authorities they functioned quite well from the beginning. Most of the advisers took over the staff of the former advisory services of the communes and did a very good job in acquiring training opportunities both in firms and in out-of-firm training establishments. The acceptance of vocational counselling among young Easterners was actually very high.

At first, there were plenty of firms offering training opportunities to apprentices in the NBL. At the end of September 1991, there were only 2,421 unplaced applicants with 6,608 unoccupied training places to choose from (BLK, 1993a:4). Within two years of the Wende, however, the number of indentures had dropped by one-third, and by the end of 1994, the ratio of supply to demand for apprenticeships was 1:2 (Schober, 1995: 39–40). It became difficult to obtain an apprenticeship, especially in certain regions and if one was female. Employers reacted to the unfavourable economic situation by withholding their cooperation in the training process. In the circumstances of economic stringency, it is not surprising that some firms were reluctant to accept apprentices at all. Yet the work of Bardeleben et al. (1994) shows that it is short-sighted of employers to refuse to train apprentices. In a survey designed to measure the benefit of training for a company, they conclude that the cost-benefit relationship for firms undertaking training works out to the benefit of the employer in the end. A company that trains and subsequently offers employment to a young person saves the cost of personnel recruiting (newspaper advertisements, interviews and travelling expenses) and gains a worker who knows the firm's specific requirements and who in turn is known to the firm; he or she is therefore 'low risk' compared with an outside candidate who may turn out to be the wrong person. A company that does not provide training can only recruit qualified specialists from other companies by offering higher wages and salaries; moreover, a non-training company's image, though non-quantifiable, is likely to be lower than that of a training company. For all these reasons, Bardeleben et al. believe that it is economically worthwhile for companies to undertake training, even if the costs during the training period are not balanced out by the trainees' production performance.

Notwithstanding all the arguments and research, the market was tight after the Wende for young would-be apprentices to break into, and this was most especially true for young females. The level of female training and employment had been much higher in the GDR than in the FRG: in 1989, 70 per cent of women in employment in the FRG had a formal vocational qualification, whereas this was the case for over 85 per cent of GDR women. Moreover, the employment rate for women was 20 per cent higher in the GDR than in the FRG, and a smaller percentage of female workers were part-time in the GDR than in the FRG (GDR 26 per cent; FRG 40 per cent in 1989/90) (Damm-Rüger, 1993:4). In GDR days, there had been quotas for women; once these were abolished and the economic system changed, women suffered disproportionately. Yet young East German women very much *want* to work and have clearly internalised the 'working-woman' ethos of the GDR. According to Beer-Kern's survey of two thousand school-leavers (1995:154), women are slightly *less* prepared than their male counterparts to give up work temporarily for family reasons (28 per cent females (F) compared with 31 per cent males (M)). They do not want to work short-time hours (44 per cent F; 55 per cent M), and fewer of them can envisage leaving work altogether and setting up an alternative lifestyle (13 per cent F; 19 per cent M). A higher percentage of females than of males cannot imagine a life without work (22 per cent F; 19 per cent M); moreover, they seem more persevering in their job search than the men, 28 per cent of whom had given up looking for an apprenticeship compared with 15 per cent of females. Women are more prepared to move elsewhere in search of a training opportunity, but are less successful in achieving one. They have to make almost twice as many applications for apprenticeships (eight on average) to achieve an offer as the young men (five on average) (Beer-Kern, 1995:151).

East German women have less chance of getting a job than men, stand less chance of being re-employed if they lose their jobs and are more in danger of being unemployed in the long term. If females take premature retirement, they have half as much chance of finding another job as men. If they have a job, it is less secure than that of a man. In 1991, 64 per cent of jobless were women, and they had been out of work for a period of forty-four weeks in comparison with an average of thirty-two weeks for men (Damm-Rüger, 1993:6). In November 1992, almost three-fourths of males who had been in employment twelve months in 1989 were still employed, whereas this was the case with only 60 per cent of females (Brinkmann, 1995:19).

Women are very much specialised in particular apprenticeships for which the gender-typing is stronger in the New than in the Old Bundesländer: administration, office work, the retail trade, banks, insurance and hairdressing. In 1993 the quantitative and structural breakdown of apprenticeships was especially detrimental to the life opportunities of young women since they had only a 30 per cent share of training places in business (Schober, 1995:45) and only a 37 per cent share overall. They were less able to key into an informal, inside-track network than young men and more obliged to resort to formal agencies such as the Federal Labour Board. Beer-Kern's survey (1995:150, 153) shows that 76 per cent of males were trained in-plant (much better for future employment prospects), compared with only 54 per cent of females, and that 46 per cent of males against only 35 per cent of females relied on the assistance of family and acquaintances in their search. Females clearly had more difficulty than males in finding work, once 'out of their time' (Schober, 1995:67).

Because it was difficult to persuade firms to accept trainees, the traditional West German Dual System structure began to assume a different configuration. In the classical model, the apprentice was given vocational training in a firm or business, and vocational education in a school. In the inclement economic environment of East Germany, the planned duality began to break down, and faced with the possibility of mass emigration and/or mass unemployment, the authorities partially retreated from the duality and established free-standing Training Centres (*Außerbetriebliche Ausbildungsstätten* (ABS)) in which both theory and practice were mediated. These institutions were a continuation of para. 40, section 4, of a GDR Law for the Promotion of Work, the limited continuance of which was permitted in the Unification Treaty (Krekel-Eiben and Ulrich, 1993: 15). They were particularly useful for the disadvantaged, the handicapped and those who for various reasons could not compete on the open market, but job prospects for their apprentices were not as good as for those who had been trained in-plant under the Dual System. Nevertheless, the Training Centres were important in preserving the skills level of the East German population and ensuring that the young were given a reasonable start in life – even if some critics did discern in them a certain similarity to the old East German monotypical school-and-firm training establishments!

The number of Training Centres (TCs) varied according to regions and reflected the quality of the traffic infrastructure and the degree of industrial and commercial development (or lack of it) in the various New Bundesländer. Broadly speaking, the better the infrastructure, the less the need for TCs; conversely the more depressed the area, the greater the need for TCs. Table 5.3 shows the proportions of TC apprentices in the different NBL by 1995. The reason for the smaller percentage in Saxony was a delay in implementing the 1995 Community Initiative which was designed to establish Training Centres. Further subregional variations in proportions of TCs existed within each NBL, and in 1995 Neubrandenburg in Mecklenburg-Vorpommern had TC provision of almost 40 per cent.

Table 5.3 Proportions of Apprentices in Training Centres in NBL

New Bundesländer	Percentage
Mecklenburg-Vorpommern	30
East Berlin	20
Brandenburg	20
Saxony-Anhalt	18
Thuringia	16
Saxony	6

Source: BMBW BBB, 1996:6

From the earliest stages of unification, the authorities had expressed regret about the need to establish the TCs on such an extensive scale, but admitted that they were necessary, for example to provide facilities for young people placed in firms having suffered bankruptcy. They stated, however, that 'Everything possible must be done – not least for financial reasons – to transform the free-standing Training Centres into firm-based centres. Priority must be given to training under the Dual System' (BMBW BBB 1992:4). By 1993/93, however, the difficult economic situation caused by unification had begun to affect the Old and well as the New Bundesländer, and the willingness of the OBL employers to train apprentices had decreased markedly. The authors of the Annual Report for Vocational Education made the following grave statement:

> If this tendency towards decreasing involvement in training continues, the danger exists that an outstanding advantage of Germany as an economic location, that is to say the high degree of social and subject competence of its skilled workers, will not be sustained. In the long term, this would lead to a continuing weakening and destabilisation of the Dual System as a whole with serious negative economic consequences. This cannot be compensated by an increasing number of third-level education graduates.... 'Lean production' can scarcely be achieved with 'small qualifications'. (BMBW BBB, 1994)

The situation in the NBL had in fact stabilised somewhat: the small artisan sector (Handwerk) was offering more apprenticeships than before, but the free enterprise sector (*freie Berufe*) was still below average. There were insufficient offers of in-plant apprenticeship, however, to satisfy demand, and in face of this shortfall the authorities set up Community Initiative East (*Gemeinschaftsinitiative Ost*). The European Social Fund, the Bund and the New Länder contributed money in the ratio of 2:1:1 to create up to ten thousand Training Centre places for those who could not find placements in firms. This formed a satisfactory solution in the short term but the trouble was that it involved the use of public funds, and so was not in keeping with the long-term policy objective of making the East German training system self-sustaining. By 1995, 65 per cent of new indentures in the NBL were financed with public money (BMBW BBB, 1996:6) and the trend looked set to continue. The difficulties of young Easterners in finding apprenticeships in the fragile East German economy point to the need for continuing subsidisation of the Dual System.

Certainly, public funds were deployed on a massive scale both to induce employers to accept apprentices and to mitigate unemployment. The European Community was an important source of financial subsidy to encourage training in the New Bundesländer, and for the period 1991–93 the EC granted DM 6.2 billion for this purpose. The EC Social Fund gave DM 1.85 billion to help solve structural problems, create new permanent posts, combat long-term unemployment and help young people get into the labour market. Despite the fact that it was very difficult to predict regional trends and needs, the EC Regional Fund gave another DM 226 million (BLK, 1993a:13–14). So-called work creation programmes were used to promote projects rather than individuals, and were a palliative concealing the real extent of unemployment (Brinkmann, 1995:25).

Employers were given government cash subsidies to encourage them to accept trainees. The amounts of money involved varied according to Land and were relatively modest – usually between about DM 700 and DM 10,000—with an additional monthly allowance available in Berlin for firms accepting female apprentices, the less able, and *Konkurslehrlinge* (apprentices whose firms had suffered bankruptcy) (BMBW BBB, 1992:3). These subsidies, which were certainly not enough to cover all of the employers' expenses, were intended as an inducement to encourage firms to accept trainees. There were problems, however, in ensuring that the subsidies achieved their desired effect. It would not have been cost-effective to set up administrative machinery to verify whether all of those who accepted subsidies did in fact undertake training, but government officials were well aware from their personal observation and knowledge of the system that, unfortunately, some employers took the money without real commitment to accept trainees, or else played a rather cynical game of brinkmanship with the authorities: 'No subsidy, no trainees accepted.'

The difficulty of achieving an apprenticeship made many young people think of going West, because there were surplus training places in the Old Bundesländer (Degen and Walden, 1995:75). In the first year after unification, over 40 per cent of those seeking apprenticeships stated that they would at least consider accepting an indenture in the West, but this readiness to move subsequently sank to about one quarter (Schober, 1995:61). The Annual Report for Vocational Education (1995) showed a falling trend for the years 1992–94, as illustrated in Table 5.4.

Table 5.4 Numbers and Percentages of NBL Apprentices Being Trained in OBL, 1992–1994

Year	No. of NBL Trainees Being Trained in OBL	Percentage of Total Trainees
1992	19,393	3.9
1993	16,504	3.5
1994	13,704	3.0

Source: Calculated from BMBW BBB, 1995.

Many young people commuted or took temporary accommodation rather than moving altogether. The 1993 Vocational Report notes that about 57 per cent of those apprenticed in the OBL were daily commuters and wanted their parents' home to be within easy reach (BMBW BBB, 1993:10). The tightness of the apprenticeship situation led young women, especially, to be mobile and seek a placement in the West, if necessary; of the 1994 NBL citizens training in the OBL, 59 per cent were female. The major reasons for such a decision were the greater likelihood of achieving an apprenticeship, better payment and having friends or relations there in the West (Schober, 1995:64). Ulrich and Westhoff (1995:138) show that those working in the West were indeed better paid than those in East German firms. The fear of the planners is that the strong pull of the West makes emigration quite likely, thereby reducing the youth population of East Germany. However, from the Annual Reports it would seem that young Easterners have a strong regional loyalty. This is favourable to the New Bundesländer, and everything possible should be done to consolidate and build upon it. Kloas (1993) notes that those young people who are best qualified are most likely to want to go to the OBL and that those who already have a family or live with a partner rather than with their parents are much less likely to go West. He makes a requirements for retaining the NBL young which include: job security, good prospects, chances for continuing education, contact with modern technical equipment, improvement in status of NBL jobs, and better living accommodation.

The need for quasi-permanent subsidies caused resentments and tensions between the citizens of the Old and the New Bundesländer. The people of West Germany had been led to believe that unification could be achieved with minimal increases in the tax burden, and were resentful when it became obvious that sacrifices were necessary. For a brief initial period, unification gave an impetus to West German growth: high demand for Western products helped produce a GDP of 5.7 per cent in 1990, but this expansion only lasted until 1992 (Marsh, 1994:83). Thereafter, there were big increases in taxation. Wage increases in both East and West Germany ran ahead of productivity making the 1992–93 recession worse. In Berlin, where Easterners and Westerners lived in close proximity to each other, tensions were especially evident, and it was sometimes the Westerners who felt particularly hard done-by. They had been accustomed to the special Berlin allowance which had been paid to help them cope with the disadvantages and hardships of living in a divided city. After unification, this was withdrawn, leaving West Berliners with less money in their pockets. They feared that the Easterners were being accorded too much positive discrimination by the state, and they resented competition from them on the labour market. Because East Germans had been used to full employment and were so keen to get jobs, they persevered in their job searches, tending to accept whatever came up even if it was not quite what they wanted, and sometimes beat West Berliners in the race. Moreover, the whole employment situation in Berlin could be problematic enough: Berlin was expensive as an industrial location, and firms were drawn out of the centre of Berlin into the suburbs or even into Brandenburg. There came a time when unemployment was higher in West than in East Berlin, and some West Berliners talked of re-erecting the Wall to keep the Easterners out.

It had been hoped that privatisation would become a panacea for the ills of the economy but this turned out not to be the case. In January 1990 at the inception of the *Treuhand* agency (THA), which was appointed to privatise much of East German industry, the THA's assets were valued at DM 1,000 billion and indeed secured DM 184 billion in investment guarantees. In early 1991, the head of the THA, Detlev Rohwedder – subsequently murdered and replaced by Birgit Breuel – valued the THA's assets at DM 300–500 billion (Flockton, 1993:322). Eventually the 'assets' left DM 270 billion in debts to be taken over by the state (Marsh, 1994:193). Treuhand privatised 7,838 of 12,246 companies and liquidated 3,196. Only 37 per cent of the original jobs were saved and 85 per cent of sales were to West Germans. By 1 January 1994, the total value of sales amounted to only DM 45 billion (Flockton, 1994). Treuhand enterprises had 200,000 apprentices in 1990, but by 1994, this number had fallen to 5,000 in Treuhand businesses and a further 48,000 in privatised Treuhand enterprises (IAB, 1993; Schober, 1995:42). In August 1991, THA insisted that apprenticeships begun in firms under its managements must be continued and that suitable alternative arrangements must be made for trainees whose firms became bankrupt. It was not legal to dissolve the indenture agreement, but out of ignorance of the law many young trainees did not receive the support to which they had a legal right and were left to flounder. It became obvious as the crisis continued that the free labour market was not a sufficient solution to the problems of the New Bundesländer. In the face of widespread unemployment, the authorities discovered a need to relate their production of woman- and manpower to the needs of the country, and planning was rediscovered to an extent unknown in West Germany (Brinkmann, 1995:18). The discreditation of the GDR planning orthodoxy after the fall of the Wall was thus only temporary.

Seventy per cent of East German training was done in about one thousand firms which were taken over by Treuhand (Kroymann and Lübke, 1992;21). The collapse of many such firms due to bankruptcy left trainees with disrupted apprenticeships and incompleted training programmes. Sometimes the difficulties were more subtle and arose from the confrontation between older-style GDR-oriented expectations and attitudes, and those of the newer-style post-unification Germany. The following short 'slice of life' provides an example of the psychological problems faced by a young East German both during her training process and in the initial stages of employment.

Case Study: The Goldsmith

Gabriele is the daughter of a clergyman in Brandenburg. She always wanted to become a goldsmith but was hindered from entering on her formal apprenticeship during the GDR regime because of discrimination against clergy families. She did, however, work informally at goldsmithing and in doing so built up her skill and consolidated her motivation to pursue that particular career. After the fall of the Wall, new opportunities opened up to her: she immediately began her serious training in West Berlin and, being talented, made rapid progress. Because the start of her training had been delayed, she was in her mid-twenties at that stage, so rather older than the typical apprentice. In her first firm, she found that the commercial pressures in the new entrepreneurial society put a premium on speed of work. Though she produced work of very high quality, she eventually left that training firm because of the tension between her drive to produce fine work and the speed of output required to survive commercially.

She then moved to another firm, and here – coming from a society of scarce resources – she was almost overwhelmed by the wealth of some of the customers and the value of the materials with which she routinely worked. For example, shortly after joining this West Berlin firm, she helped design and produce a high-carat gold necklace studded with diamonds. She had never seen or handled such rich materials before. The successful completion of such assignments was a great responsibility and, like all such burdens, brought with it nervous tension. Gabriele stayed with the firm until she completed training, and in due course took up employment there. Her job was stressful, but at a certain level enjoyable. She was good at what she did, and good at managing people. The firm, however, constantly tottered on the brink of bankruptcy and this led to a tense atmosphere within it. The boss was under great pressure and was often explosive and bad-tempered. Gabriele, a gentle pretty young woman with good communication skills, could have moved elsewhere, but although she suffered from the unpleasant atmosphere in work, she discovered in herself a capacity to endure aggression and sometimes to defuse unpleasantness. Being a Christian, she felt that for the time being she was 'meant' to serve in this firm and to bear witness to her faith. This she did, and in the process built up a solid relationship with her colleagues and her mercurial, explosive employer, and quietly contributed to improving the business climate and the day-to-day communication within the firm.

✿ ✿ ✿

This case study illustrates a number of factors: the conflict – sometimes intolerable – between a perfectionist, quality-oriented craftswoman and the more pressurised *modus vivendi* of the entrepreneur who has to survive in a competitive world. It is a dilemma faced by young West Germans as well as Easterners. Gabriele's West German firm makes its own demands for quality; it routinely puts its employees in contact with valuable gold and precious stones and offers very interesting opportunities for professional development, but suffers from a whole series of market-induced pressures and tensions which would have been alien to East Germany and which are not easy for a young ex-GDR citizen to cope with.

A case study gives a qualitative impression of individual experience, but it is important to examine quantitative data too. The attitudes and experiences of young East Germans have been systematically explored by the Federal Institute for Vocational Education (BiBB) (Beer et al., 1995) in a survey involving 1,986 subjects in 1992/93 and 1,046 in 1993/94. The authors explored trainees' level of satisfaction with their apprenticeships and the following findings emerged:

- Most people enjoyed their apprenticeships, the girls even more than the boys; 79 per cent male and female respondents were satisfied with their lives and most were optimistic about the future (72 per cent M; 68 per cent F). Yet young females especially cannot imagine a life without work (76 per cent F; 66 per cent M), and are prepared to move house in order to find some. Those who were at first negative subsequently became more positive, while those who had begun with superpositive attitudes moderated these somewhat in the second phase of the survey. The more extreme attitudes evened out over time. Those in the public services and in the free enterprise sector (freie Berufe) were more enthusiastic than those in industry. The trainees generally were more enthusiastic about their work in the firm or plant than in the vocational school.

- Those in small businesses had to do hard physical labour more often than those in large businesses and this made them feel like cheap labour. The factors which seriously perturbed the young trainees were 'being treated like cheap labour' (28 per cent), 'firm and vocational school not collaborating properly' (23 per cent), and 'low chances of being taken on' (22 per cent). The young people are prepared to accept many inconveniences and negative experiences without being seriously annoyed by them, but the issue of overriding importance to them is to obtain employment.

- The size of the firm in which the training took place had an important influence on the trainees' level of satisfaction. The bigger the business, the less often the trainees would make exactly the same choice again. In small firms with up to nine employees, 60 per cent of the trainees were quite satisfied, whereas in those with up to one thousand the percentage dropped to 50 per cent. Beer at al. (1995:16) believe that this difference is because the chances of being taken on permanently on completion of apprenticeship are lower in large business; for many of these firms, their continuing existence is in doubt, and their staff are threatened with redundancies and downsizing. Such problems have a negative impact on apprentices' experience.

- Trainees in free-standing Training Centres were significantly less satisfied than those working in a genuine 'Dual System' of school and firm. Here again, it was clear that attitudes were very much coloured by trainees' assessment of how likely they were to find employment. Statistically, the chances of those emerging from Training Centres were lower than those of young people who had a chance to build up a close 'insider' relationship with a firm.

- The young East Germans were not keen to go West; 87 per cent of them stated that they did not want to go to the Old Bundesländer to live and work, but 16 per cent would be willing to do so in order to get work. If obliged to uproot themselves for economic reasons, few of them wished to take up residence in East European states; they would rather go to a West European state or to West Germany (which in some cases seemed just as foreign to them as 'abroad').

- In summary, Beer et al. (1995:29) conclude: 'The high professional motivation of young people, their strong work ethic, their achievement motivation and desire to "get on" show that the trainees in the New Bundesländer are certainly not characterised by a "Null-Bock" (layabout) mentality, nor do they regard earning their living as a necessary evil to pay for out-of-work activities or leisure pursuits. The type of person who is only interested in his or her job for the money scarcely exists. Quite the contrary: young people in training hold work and jobs in high esteem.'

Conclusion

The positive picture of young East Germans' values and attitudes to work is reassuring: the majority of apprentices in this NBL survey want to work and want to stay in East Germany if they possibly can. Their strong work ethic is a precious heritage from GDR days and needs to be put to good use. Yet mass unemployment and the failure of firms to offer apprenticeships call up the spectres of possible depopulation and xenophobia. If young people cannot find apprenticeships and jobs, there is a risk of them becoming disaffected, dropping out, and turning to violence and political extremism, or else sinking into apathy. All of these dark possibilities carry with them potential danger for democracy. A survey carried out by Detlev Oesterreich (1993) shortly after the Wende found that pupils in vocational schools were significantly more authoritarian than those in grammar schools, and that East Berlin pupils were twice as apprehensive as their Western counterparts about a political Right-wing polarisation. The success of the newly democratised political culture in post-Wende East Germany cannot be dissociated from the success of the vocational education system, because that system is entrusted with the responsibility of socialising the majority of the nation's children into work and binding them into a common culture. It is enormously important for the distribution of life chances.

The Dual System was already showing signs of strain in the Old Bundesländer at the point when it was extended to the New Bundesländer (Pritchard, 1992; Casey, 1992). Scholars like Mertens (1988) argued that training was too often confined to mere procedures whilst neglecting deeper-level problem-solving, which is so important in the long run. Women were less well served by the system than men. The average age of apprentices was increasing, and a whole cohort of people qualified to enter higher education took up apprenticeships, thus offering stiff competition to school-leavers of lesser ability who had fewer career options. Trainees were becoming more and more heterogeneous. There were tensions between

Bund and Länder, between the schools and the firms, between economic and educational values. The functioning of the entire Dual System was subject to the vagaries of the general economic situation, and many employers were unwilling to provide apprenticeships. Expenditure on students in the vocational schools was much lower than for grammar schools, lower even than for mainstream schools in general. Klemm and Pfeiffer (1990) argue that these negative factors hit working-class children (42.9 per cent of seventeen- to eighteen-year-old trainees in 1987) especially hard, and that vocational schools were neglected, weak and increasingly irrelevant 'poor relations'. They discern signs of an incipient new type of 'Duality'. The first part of the duad consists of powerful, well-equipped firms which supersede the schools and conduct both education and training themselves; the second part of the duad consists of small firms still working with local vocational schools, often in thinly populated regions, and generally in an increasingly deprived and unsatisfactory partnership. In other words, it is a duad of the 'haves' and 'have-nots'. Waterkamp (1995:4), in a discussion of the woes of the German training system goes so far as to speak of '… a crisis in vocational education that in the long run cannot be mastered within established patterns'.

All of these problems were evident well before unification took place and were exported to East Germany where they are exacerbated by economic crisis. Goldberger (1993:297) demonstrates that the dominance of Germany has been sharply challenged by unification, and that in less than two years the costs of unification have taken it from being Europe's largest net exporter to its greatest net importer. The trend towards apparently chronic reliance on public subsidies for training is cause for dismay, but Davids (1993) for one believes that if they are withdrawn, a large number of young adults will be socially excluded and alienated. Skrypietz (1994) lists a number of neo-Nazi organisations which are more popular in East than in West Germany, and shows that the links between skinheads and right-extremist groups are considerably stronger in the former GDR. The difficulty is that in view of the parlous state of the NBL economy, the Dual System seems very far from being able to sustain itself, and social objectives seem to run counter to economic balancing of the accounts. A possible solution to the problem of shortage of apprenticeships would perhaps be to do as Waterkamp (1995:8) suggests, and take a leaf out of another nation's book: in France, all enterprises make a contribution to vocational education irrespective of whether they themselves train or not. Since Germany is 'locked into high-skill, high valued-added production' (Steedman, 1993), this might be in the long-term greatest interests of the greatest numbers of people, but it would be important to have a sliding scale of contributions so as to ensure that already shaky East (and West) German firms would not be further disabled.

The development of free-standing Training Centres in East Germany is regarded in some quarters as a symptom of the 'breakup' of the Dual System proper, but this may be an unnecessarily negative view. Kell (1995) poses the question of whether there is a dual, triple or plural vocational system, and implies that a de facto plurality already exists. The Training Centres constitute one way of overcoming the threatened adverse social effects of firms being unwilling or unable to provide training. As such, they are harbingers of the future and should not be negatively regarded, even if in some limited ways they recall the GDR Betriebsberufsschulen. The experience of East Germany provides the Dual System (if it is indeed still appropriate to call it 'Dual') with an economic context which throws the System's pre-existing problems into sharper focus than ever before, and has forced urgent trials of various solutions. Some – perhaps many – of the new structures may be useful in the West as well as in the East. One thing is sure: new combinations and new patterns of financing are necessary if Germany's vocational system is to be as successful in the future as it has been in the past.

Before unification, there had been a parliamentary agreement between the training authorities in East and West about collaboration; the German Bund and Länder had in place excellent systems of reporting, research and information-gathering about their vocational education system which proved vital after August 1990 when the Dual System was introduced to the NBL. The authorities were able to say, for example, that by December 1992, all those desiring apprenticeships in the NBL had been placed, with the exception of 333 (BMBW BBB, 1993:10). Such detailed knowledge enabled them to make provision for almost everyone, including those with special needs. Herculean efforts – both organisational and financial – were made to ensure that everyone had a training placement, and these endeavours largely succeeded, though at the cost of much greater public expenditure than originally anticipated. The authorities were well aware that women were at a disadvantage, and tried to do something about it, like giving enhanced subsidies to firms which would take females. They liaised actively with businesses: their questionnaires indicated that companies not yet involved in training needed advice and help in how to go about the process much more than they needed cash subsidies (72 per cent in favour of the former as opposed to 12 per cent for the latter) (BMBW BBB, 1996:9). Active attempts were therefore made to encourage and persuade firms to participate in training, and the so-called 'May Beetle Action' of 1995 entailed visits to 36,000 firms resulting in 7,900 offers of training placements. 'School/Economy' (*Schule/Wirtschaft*) working groups were set up at the interface between school and business so as to smooth the pupils' transition from secondary education to training when compulsory education was finished (ibid.:2). Many millions of Deutschmarks were spent creating and sustaining apprenticeships.

The efforts made to create a skilled workforce for East Germany were – and are – impressive. Yet they are rendered ineffectual if there are insufficient jobs for qualified skilled workers to enter. This is a central problem so far as training in East Germany is concerned. To quote Hughes Hallett (1996:520,539) once again:

> To state the dilemma in a nutshell: if wage catch-up must continue, eastern unemployment will stay high for very long; while if wage discipline is introduced, the gap between eastern and western wages will widen for just as long, and either route increases the potential for migration.
>
> … Every pfennig of public support for eastern output seems to have been allocated to labour. Nevertheless, whatever effect these subsidies may have had in funding capital directly, it has been offset by transfers from capital to labour in the east in support of inefficient levels of employment. Hence any proposals for further subsidies to employment would simply be aiming at the wrong target.

Unemployment is, as we have seen, associated with inadequate productivity. Both of these in turn are linked to decisions made in 1990 about the currency union, complicated by the issue of property restitution. At that point, few questions were asked and the imperative for immediate one-to-one currency conversion seemed compelling. Initial calculations of the fiscal support needed from West to East turned out to be gross underestimates. The results of the policies carried out after the Wende are far-reaching. It is likely that the profitability of Germany relative to other countries will decline; furthermore, the plight of Germany will make it much more difficult for European Monetary Union to be carried out – which is ironic since it was a project dear to the heart of Chancellor Kohl. Within Germany, either the social security and tax burden for those in work must increase in order to pay for unemployment benefit, or else the government must cut benefits and throw individuals back even more on their own resources. Inequality within East Germany has increased and will continue to do so. If the economists' economic models are right, then unemployment in Germany is now structural, and as everyone knows, unemployment *may* constitute a danger to democracy – though it does not *necessarily* do so. One thing is sure, though it is now a truism: the dilemmas confronting those who devise and implement vocational education policies for East Germany are nothing short of excruciating.

≫ Chapter 6 ≪

RENEWING THE TEACHING
PROFESSION AND
HIGHER EDUCATION

Teachers and Their Universities before Unification

Teachers in the GDR were entrusted with the special responsibility of inculcating socialism in the new generation, particularly during the first two decades of the GDR's existence (1949-69). The SED believed in the omnipotence of education, and teachers were sworn to uphold and promote the establishment of socialism and the leading role of the Party. One of its major objectives was to break the influence of Nazism and fascism, and this necessitated the replacement of a large number of the existing teachers. In 1946–47, 28,000 new teachers (*Neulehrer*) trained on short crash courses were put into position; by the end of the 1940s, this figure had risen to about 40,000 (Schreier, 1991:36). The anti-fascist post-war cull prefigured a second cull – this time anti-socialist – after the fall of the Wall.

A second and more important objective in the long term was to break the educational privilege of the dominant classes. Lenin had stated that property owners use education as a means of exploitation to keep the majority in slavery, and it was widely believed that the 'exploiting classes' try to influence higher education with a view to perpetuation of their class dominance (Köhler, 1989). The German Education Administration (Deutsche Verwaltung für Volksbildung (DVV)) set out to create a new intelligentsia based on a much broader student intake to higher education than heretofore. (This had actually been an objective in the Weimar Republic too.) Command Number 50 of the Soviet Military Administration gave special attention to the question of abolishing the privileges of certain social strata, and in 'Basic Ground Rules for Admission to Study and Universities' (12

December 1945) the conditions were set up for admitting students without Abitur to higher education. Pre-Study Institutions (*Vorstudienanstalten*) were formed to give young workers and peasants the equivalent of Abitur and were regarded as a 'ladder' to help them storm the bastion of higher education, in short as a means of upward mobility. In general terms, the policy objective was to make the composition of the student body match the social class distribution of the population as a whole.

The new admissions regulations quickly became a steering mechanism for producing politically well-adapted conformist students. The selection boards had more representatives from public life than from academe (Olbertz, 1996:29), which seemed to indicate that the ideological rather that the academic element was of paramount importance. In December 1947, the Pre-Study Institutions were declared a constituent part of the universities. The preparatory students were deemed to possess the same rights and duties as matriculated students and were able to become members of the Student Council. They did not have to pay entry or examination fees, and their preferential situation caused many rows and political struggles at Halle and Jena (Lammel, 1989:26). By 1949, arrangements had been made for the transformation of the Pre-Study Institutions into nine Workers' and Peasants' Faculties (subsequently extended to fifteen), and by 1955, the proportion of students in this social grouping in higher education overall had exceeded 50 per cent. The Faculties' existence was declared to be indissolubly bound up with that of the GDR. There is impressive evidence (Schneider, 1995) that the purpose of these new Faculties went beyond the honourable one of ensuring equality of opportunity and eliminating social disadvantage. By the late 1940s, the aim was to recruit an academic elite loyal to the system and suitable for the formation of a socialist cadre. The Workers and Peasants were expected to demonstrate 'correct' attitudes, socialist consciousness and an acceptable level of political reliability.

The teacher training sector assumed great dominance in the GDR, and trainee teachers formed a larger proportion of the total cohort of university students in East than in West Germany: in 1988 22 per cent in the GDR as opposed to 8 per cent in the FRG. This was reflected in a low staff-pupil ratio. In 1989, there were approximately 167,000 teachers and almost 2.1 million pupils in the general school system – a staff to student ratio of 1 to 12.5 (Schreier, 1991:38), though Kiel (1996:161) cites a ratio of 1:9. Teachers in the GDR did not always work within the school system; there were positions for them in administration, recreation and other sectors. Teacher training was, however, separated from other disciplines – almost ghettoised – and was strongly vocational in nature. Institutionally, it was somewhat hierarchical in that the nine Pädagogische Hochschulen (Colleges of Education) were isolated and were under the control of the Ministerium für

Volksbildung (Ministry for Education), whereas the universities were under the control of the higher-level Ministerium für Hoch- und Fachschulwesen (Ministry for Higher and Specialist Education) (MPI, 1994:700).

There was a serious lack of freedom at all levels in all educational institutions. Although Berlin was the place where Wilhelm von Humboldt had developed his seminal ideas of academic freedom, the dominance of the Party and of Marxist-Leninist ideology undermined the traditional Humboldtian ethos and divided East from West (though paradoxically it was the East which possessed the 'Humboldt University'). From 1951 onwards, due to the advent of the Second Reform of Higher Education, all students, especially trainee teachers, had to study Marxism-Leninism at college or university, typically for about 20 per cent of the available curriculum time (MPI, 1994:653). The M-L course – intended to propagate SED state doctrine – extended over six semesters and had to be passed if the final qualification was to be awarded. Most dissident professors had fled to the West, and the remaining teacher trainers were required to be especially 'loyal' to the socialist regime; they were 'watched' for political unreliability and were discouraged from developing contacts abroad (WR, 1991). Many of them felt themselves to be the scapegoats of society.

The Stasi was very active within universities. Christian students, being engaged in 'hostile ideology', were the particular object of surveillance, and Stasi employees made reports on lectures, on their own so-called operational personnel monitoring, on contacts with the West and on contact with the enemy. Both Protestant and Catholic communities were regarded with suspicion because they provided free space for uncontrolled discussions, 'true freedom' and 'a model for democracy' (Straube, 1996: 80). 'Existing love relations', whether Christian or not, were monitored so that friendships between Easterners and Westerners – possibly leading to applications for resettlement in the West – could be nipped in the bud (ibid.: 77). Assistant deans were regarded as 'social collaborators' without even having been recruited to the Stasi. Lecturers who insisted on teaching in an objective way without political bias were sometimes threatened with disciplinary procedures in an effort to make them educate students in the spirit of the SED state (ibid.:78). The Stasi 'thus made a specific contribution to the undermining of the independence of the universities and colleges, and to impeding an efficient development of students, scientists and scholarly activity itself' (ibid.:81; see also Geißler and Wiegmann, 1996).

Yet East Germany had been the place which in the nineteenth century had provided an inspirational model for a modern university system: the University of Berlin. Notwithstanding the traditional Humboldtian commitment to the unity of teaching and research, the SED to a considerable extent took research out of the universities and placed it in academies or other institutions. Varying estimates exist of the proportion of research which was carried on within the universities: Buck-Bechler (1994:24) puts it at 11 per cent and Klemm et al. (1992:126) put it nearer to 8 per cent. It is certainly impossible to give a precise figure but there is agreement that the proportion was very small. The bulk of the nation's research in Education was assigned to the Academy of Sciences (Akademie der Wissenschaften (AdW)), an immensely powerful body which had sixty institutes, 23,750 workers and a budget of 1.4 billion Ostmarks. Among its other functions, it developed syllabuses for the whole GDR but, unlike the universities, did not even make a pretence of independence. The Academy of Educational Sciences (Akademie der Pädagogischen Wissenschaften (APW)) was part of the Academy of Sciences. The APW's immediate predecessor was the Deutsches Pädagogisches Zentralinstitut (DPZI) which was led by Hans Siebert. The Academy of Educational Sciences was established on 15 September 1970 very much on the model of the Russian equivalent founded in 1943 (Eichler and Uhlig, 1993:117). The fact that the most significant basic research took place in Academies and not in universities weakened the creativity and self-assurance of universities and rendered any claims to academic freedom unconvincing.

By the time of the Wende, East German universities had reached a stage where they could be described by Schiedermair (1996:92) as 'a desert almost devoid of oases'. Pasternak (1997), the East German founder of the journal 'hochschule ost' (sic), notes with a touch of irony that Westerners' admission that the supposed 'desert' of East German research contained at least *some* oases still perpetuates the insulting 'desert' metaphor! The GDR Third Reform of Higher Education (1968) was in large measure responsible for the miserable state of universities. The aim of this law was to subordinate universities and their pursuit of knowledge to the control of the Party. Its enforcement was rigorously implemented by the SED, which set up a 'cadre system' whereby leadership functions were entrusted to those who demonstrated political conformity and reliability rather than academic excellence. Instead of Faculties, it introduced 'Sections' that were subject to ministerial instructions and had to act in accordance with SED decisions. The Sections were based on single subjects or on very limited subject combinations; their effect was to cut the disciplines off from each other thus alienating the GDR university from its traditional Humboldtian principle of the unity of knowledge. As Schiedermair (1996:95) puts it:

> It was a matter of isolating the academic disciplines in ever-increasing specialisation in order to gain distance from the original idea of a university organised to preserve a spirit of unity amidst the multiplicity of disciplines. The Sections were meant to produce highly qualified skilled workers with a strong socialist class consciousness, able and willing to bring about high achievement on the

basis of Marxism-Leninism and the socialist community of workers (GBl. der DDR 1970, Teil II). They were thus strongly politicised and instrumentalised.

It was not only the Sections which were narrow and isolated. The whole of higher education was split up into specialist institutions, all of which had tasks and functions specified by the Party according to the demands of the Plan. In addition to its universities, six in number, East Germany had its Specialist Colleges (Fachschulen) concentrating on subjects like agriculture, economics, forestry and engineering. These institutions were viable only within a planned economy which sought to allocate almost every individual a place in the state's occupational system (Krull, 1994:210ff.). Some of the specialist institutions had the right to award doctorates (as did the Academy of Sciences). The intellectual fragmentation of GDR universities reduced opportunities for the creative insights that arise in cross-disciplinary work, thus diminishing the performance of East German universities. The ethos of so much specialisation ran deeply counter to the value placed in West German universities on having a full range of subjects (*Fächerspektrum*); hence, the Specialist Colleges fared badly after the Wende.

It was just as difficult for schoolteachers as for university staff to preserve independence inwardly whilst *not* asserting it outwardly. In class and in public, they were required to conform strictly to the Party line. Those displaying signs of political heresy could be reported by their pupils to the authorities, with unpleasant consequences for the staff member concerned. Teachers were expected to inculcate in the young the belief that Erich Honecker was 'a good person' and to interest boys in careers in the armed forces which would protect the fatherland against its ideological enemies. The curriculum was handed down from on high and, as we have seen, was very one-sided, especially in subjects like History. In pedagogy, detailed and strict guidelines were given, even to the extent of suggesting blackboard layouts. It was part of teachers' function to indoctrinate and, according to the Wissenschaftsrat (1991:87), this tendency survived the end of the GDR state. School principals almost without exception were members of the SED, and teachers were routinely expected to carry out political functions and tasks which made them subservient to the regime.

Although education was regarded as of supreme significance in sustaining and promoting socialist society and values, this did not mean that commensurate importance was accorded to teachers – either collectively as a profession or individually as professionals. On the contrary, they suffered from low status and pay. Indeed, teachers were paid less than skilled workers and in some schools less even than the school caretaker. This was regarded as appropriate in a workers' state in which power had to be wrested away from the bourgeoisie. The status of teaching in the GDR was not helped by teachers' obvious lack of independence compared historically, for example, with doctors' free-standing professionalism (Bauer and Burkhard, 1992: 207). Nor was it improved by the feminisation of the teaching body, which by 1988 exceeded 77 per cent (Fischer, 1992:75).[1] There was also a widespread tendency to scapegoat teachers for the ills of society. In 1989, the author Christa Wolf published an article in the *Wochenpost* (No. 43) accusing teachers of having educated the nation's children 'to untruthfulness', and of having damaged their character. The article touched such a nerve that it elicited a response of about three hundred letters (edited by Gruner, 1990), many of which agreed with Wolf's castigation of the profession.

Teachers in the GDR were, therefore, simultaneously the tools of state power and the disseminators of socialist ideology. Expected to bear the major responsibility for both the education and upbringing of youth, they were supposed to equip their most able pupils to fulfil their potential, yet were also held accountable for the failure of the least able in the same mixed-ability class. Teachers were responsible for working cooperatively with youth organisations, with parents, with the world of work and with the central political and education authorities. However, the society in which they functioned was less homogeneous than state authorities wished to acknowledge, and the interests of families, business and the Party often clashed. Teachers were relatively powerless to use their own initiative in confronting these problems, restricted as they were by tight accountability to the Party and watched as they were by the Secret Police. They were thus exposed to many conflicts and tensions – with consequences for their own health and personal well-being. Schmidt (1990:535) states: 'Studies in the GDR have demonstrated that the teaching body is one of the occupational groups which bears a heavy burden physically and above all psychologically….'

The Students and Student Life

The internal organisation of teacher training courses and certain characteristics of student life contributed further to undermining intellectual freedom and independence. The curriculum was so tightly constructed and clearly specified that there was little opportunity to follow individual interests or to choose options. Since the education ethos was strongly vocational, the proportion of workshops, practical exercises and seminars was supposed to equal the proportion of lectures. Students worked in stable seminar groups analogous to school classes that consisted of twenty to

---

1. 'Feminisation', however, is not necessarily to be equated with poor standards, and Schmidt (1990:529) points out that male entrants to teaching typically had Abitur scores which were inferior to those of females.

thirty students carried over from one year to the next. Within these groups the students mutually cooperated, especially in helping the less able and those with special problems. A generous staff-student ratio in higher education resulted in good personal contacts between those who taught and those who learned. The tight course structure, the low staff-student ratio and mutual assistance between students resulted in high pass rates: in the 1980s between 79 per cent and 86 per cent according to subject area (Buck-Bechler, 1994:23). It is difficult to cite comparable figures for West Germany, but the Max Planck Institute estimates that the wastage rate at the end of the 1980s was between 25 and 30 per cent – which was somewhat higher than in East Germany (MPI, 1994:641). The difficulty in establishing exact records of student numbers in West German universities highlights the contrast in ethos between East and West before the fall of the Wall. 'Phantom students' in the West are officially registered but do not actively pursue their studies; some use their student pass to obtain cheap food and transport, while others wait until the first serious job offer before finally taking their last exams. Some of the least well-off are obliged to spend most of their time in wage-earning employment before they can continue; some change universities or go to the local Fachhochschule. Interestingly – and understandably! – the phantom student syndrome is tacitly tolerated by university authorities because resources tend to follow high student numbers.

It is often alleged that the East German higher education system 'spoon-fed' its students and fostered in them a culture of dependence. (An old gibe of the Easterners about their own system was: 'Ultimately, no student is allowed to escape getting his degree.') No doubt these accusations seem justified when judged according to the Western perspective. The 'clannishness' of students in East German higher education institutions was intensified by the fact that about two-thirds of them lived in student halls of residence (*Wohnheime*) compared with only about 12 per cent of West German students in 1991 (MPI, 1994:648). This fact tended to consolidate East German students' social networks and feed their mutual dependence. Their close affiliative bonds also, however, helped to protect them against the attempts of state organs and FDJ to 'educate' them (that is, make them ideologically conformist) in return for the high degree of social security which they were offered (Buck-Bechler, 1987:362/5). Close relationships between students helped build up an anti-competitive ethos which the trainee teachers later in their turn cultivated in their own pupils. The teachers, having been raised in a protected environment themselves, were nurturant of their pupils to an extent which was (and is) striking to a Western observer. A West German official in the Thuringian Ministry of Education recounted to the author how, after the fall of the Wall, he happened to witness a pupil demonstration in one of the schools for which he had responsibility. The East German teachers' major priority was primarily not to defuse the protest but rather to ensure that no pupil was hustled, traumatised or physically hurt in road traffic.

One of the most important advantages of the East German higher education system was that students rarely exceeded the expected number of semesters for their course. Normally, the GDR programmes lasted four to five years, whereas the typical West German university students took 6.8 years (MPI, 1994:640). There was a variety of reasons for the more rapid progress of the GDR students, the most significant of which was undoubtedly the tight specification and delivery of course content. Moreover, living in student hostel dormitories – though not without its positive side, as pointed out above – gave students an incentive to move on as rapidly as possible to the next phase in their lives, which they hoped might be in more comfortable circumstances. Even according to GDR standards, buildings and equipment in higher education were in a poor state – neither technically nor physically up to the task of supporting teaching and research. Authorities estimated that only about one-third of building stock was in good condition and 12 per cent was seriously deficient (Buck-Bechler, 1994:27). Most East German students had domestic responsibilities: by the end of their courses, the majority were married and over half of these had offspring (Schmidt, 1990:531). Indeed, the undergraduate period was regarded as especially favourable for starting a family, and the level of state support was such that few students with babies underachieved or had to drop out of their courses (Klemm et al., 1992:140). Naturally, parenthood fuelled their motivation to complete their studies promptly, though in fairness it should be said that student-parents *did* receive enhanced grants from the state. At the time of the Wende, about 88 per cent of the East Germans were receiving state maintenance grants, whereas only 28 per cent of West Germans were using the equivalent interest-free loan system (BAföG) (MPI, 1994:635). The GDR state authorities for their part had a vested interest in students not exceeding the normal course duration. If they were to fulfil the national Plan, predictability in terms of student output was needed; this meant that any delay in students entering the job market in a particular year was unwelcome. The students were state-sponsored and the state wanted a rapid return on its investment.

Access to higher education in the GDR was not merely a matter of obtaining good marks, nor was it driven by demography. Criteria such as gender, social background (the ideal being good working class or peasant stock), political activity and the performance of military service all played a role (MPI, 1994:647). Since 85 per cent of those who applied were in fact offered university places (21 per cent of them for teaching), the real selection point for higher education was actually at school after form 10 – the end of compulsory education – when people sought to enter the EOS to do Abitur. Only 10 to 15 per cent of the age cohort were admitted to the EOS (Klemm et al., 1992:135), and failure to gain entry to the EOS was usually tantamount to failure to gain access to university, especially for clergy's children who were unpopular with the regime. There were, however, ways of getting around blocked entry to the EOS, for example by doing a three-year apprenticeship with Abitur or a preparatory course for skilled workers. GDR middle-class parents, like those the world over, tried to outsmart the system and quite often succeeded. From the 1970s onwards, the proportion of young people in higher education (HE) whose parents had also undergone HE was far in excess of the percentage of graduates in the population. Due to the dominance of Party cadres, workers and peasants became underrepresented, and this was such an embarrassment to the GDR authorities that after the end of the 1960s they no longer published data about the social origins of students. When social origin *did* have to be specified, authorities naturally chose the parent with the lower qualification (Klemm et al., 1992:133).

The record of the SED/GDR regarding higher education for women was by no means as positive as one might have thought. Lothar Mertens (1996) chronicles the milestones for GDR students and finds the situation depressing. After the partition of Germany, attempts were made to change the social composition of academe, but the participation rate of women continued to sink, and by 1952 it was a mere 27.2 per cent. The chronic shortage of labour in the 1950s led to attempts to integrate women into the labour force, and by the mid-1960s, they were dropping out of their courses five times more often as men. The East Germans did not wish to devise gender-specific policies (Kühn, 1995), but it was a problem to them that the academic strata seemed to self-recruit and that there was a strong correlation between fathers' and daughters' achievement (Mertens, 1996:105). In 1970, a special programme was introduced for women with children, and in ensuing years grants were given to help retain female student-parents. Despite these endeavours, by the time of the Wende employment patterns in Education had become strongly polarised. In 1965, 55 per cent of teachers had been female, and this figure rose to 80 per cent by 1989. In East German universities, only 5 per cent of professors were women, and only 3 per cent were top management like Rectors or Pro-Rectors (ibid.:113).

All this having been said, it must be remembered that the monetary rewards for higher education were poor, and this is a reason for the great emphasis that East German academics and intellectuals placed on titles and honorific – a fact which was frequently noted by West Germans after the fall of the Wall. Because salary differentials were slight, there were correspondingly few opportunities to use money as a mark of status – hence titles such as Doctor and Professor were all the more cherished and all the more actively deployed.

In West Germany, an important part of academic freedom was the right to choose the area of study which one wanted. The Constitution (Art. 5 (3)) stated that 'Art and Science, Research and Teaching, are free', and if restrictions such as the *numerus clausus* were to be imposed, then careful legal safeguards were needed. In East Germany, the freedom of the individual to choose had to be subjected to the imperatives of the Collective and the planned economy. The realisation of the latter was assisted by a very active system of careers advice calculated to match people's personal aspirations to the needs of the nation. It is estimated that only about two-thirds of those embarking on higher education were able to take their preferred subject while the others had to change direction (Buck-Bechler, 1994:21). Regionally, the provision of higher education was uneven with a strong concentration in Berlin, Leipzig/Halle, Dresden and Karl-Marx-Stadt/ Zwickau; approximately 42 per cent of students and 38 per cent of staff in the GDR were in the south. Brandenburg was underprovided with higher education because the GDR government wished to keep youth *on* the land so as to promote socialist agriculture (Reiche, 1997). Consequently, many students from elsewhere in the GDR had to study away from home, giving rise to regional inequalities. There was a multiplicity of specialised institutions and only the largest universities such as Berlin, Leipzig and Dresden offered a broad subject range (Buck-Bechler, 1994:18). By the time unification came about, participation in higher education was about 12 to 13 per cent of the age cohort in the GDR and 23 per cent in the FRG (WR, 6.7.1990:13).

The Wende

The Federal Republic was not really ready for unification and had no concrete plan for that contingency, but all the same before the fall of the Wall there had been a contract between the two Germanys to promote academic and technical cooperation. The GDR authorities eventually became conscious that many factors reduced teachers' professional room for manoeuvre and hampered their effectiveness; they resolved, just prior to the fall of the Wall, that some reform was necessary to empower teachers and improve the climate between the various partners in the education process (Schmidt, 1990:536–7). The reform urge extended to higher education and just before German unity took place, Dr H.J. Meyer, the last GDR Minister for

Education and Science, made the government pass a Provisional Higher Education Decree (Vorläufige Hochschulordnung) to facilitate the transition to the West German system of higher education. The Decree remained in force from 18 September 1990 to 30 June 1991 and was closely modelled on Western legislation. Indeed, it caused something of a sensation in the GDR as it guaranteed the longed-for academic freedom of research, teaching and study (Hall, 1994:166).

Early in 1990, a common commission was formed between the GDR and the FRG to define the characteristics of the future amalgamation. The Bundesministerium für Bildung und Wissenschaft (later merged with Higher Education to become the Bundesministerium für Bildung, Wissenschaft, Forschung und Technologie) put in millions of Deutschmarks of special funds to promote cooperation during the first half of 1990. The last government of the GDR in the person of Minister Frank Terpe explicitly asked for the help of the Higher Education Council (Wissenschaftsrat (WR)). This led to the formulation of Article 38 of the Unity Treaty and to the evaluation of all research institutions and a number of universities, resulting in the 'winding up' (*Abwicklung*) of some institutions or parts of institutions. The Unity Treaty, notably in Article 13 and in an Annex, set out how those employees in public service were to be handled if their jobs were adversely affected by unification. If the place where they worked was closed, they were put into a kind of limbo for six months (nine for those over age fifty) during which they were paid 70 per cent of their average income during the previous half-year. At the end of this period, if no possibility of further employment had been identified, the employment was terminated. In higher education establishments, however, existing students still needed to be taught, and in order to sustain this commitment, a number of HE teachers were given fixed-term contracts which ran alongside their 'Waiting-Period Money' (Tüffers, 1991:20). After unification, education became the responsibility of the New Länder which were given until 3 October 1993 to bring in Länder laws for higher education which were in keeping with the Federal Framework Law (Hochschulrahmengesetz (HRG)) of the Federal Republic. The application of the HRG caused great insecurity and anxiety among the academic staff (WR, 1991:117).

One of the most important actors in the reform of higher education was the Wissenschaftsrat (WR) which tendered advice to Bund and Länder in all matters pertaining to higher education. It carried out a selective evaluative survey of higher education institutions in the GDR and within eighteen months had appraised many academic institutions and made recommendations about their future. This process gave rise to 'initial irritation' on the part of those being evaluated, but was eventually accepted (BMFT, 1993: 11). The WR also proposed the setting up of Commissions on the Structure of Higher Education (Hochschulstrukturkommissionen (HSKs)) which were established at the level of the New Länder between autumn 1990 and early summer 1991. They had a wide remit: they advised on new or changed higher education institutions, on the development of new subjects and the restructuring of existing ones, on investment in higher education and on appointment to Chairs. The effectiveness of the Commissions depended to a large extent on whether the Länder were or were not disposed to pay attention to them, and this in turn was bound up with local politics and personalities. In Mecklenburg-Vorpommern, the Commissions had little or no impact, whereas in Saxony-Anhalt and Brandenburg, they were quite influential. Amazingly, there was no proper mechanism for liaison between the Commissions and the Wissenschaftsrat (Teichler, 1994:246), an example of a general weakness in the restructuring process. The plethora of advisory bodies all proffering advice and recommendations, sometimes contradictory, militated against coherence, and their work was sometimes vitiated by the power which the Länder exercised as of right over education matters. Systematic coordination between Bund and Land was missing; the legal structures which emerged were complex, existed at many different levels and were sometimes incompatible – a state of affairs which tended to encourage appeals to a higher level such as the Constitutional Court (see Klemm et al., 1992:152–8 for a closer analysis).

Members of the Wissenschaftsrat produced an entire volume (WR, 1991) on teacher training which recommended a two-phase model of education and training and called for most Colleges of Education to be integrated into the universities. It saw no need to ape West German practices and structures so far as staff and curriculum were concerned; indeed, it expressed admiration for the GDR practice of involving the higher education institutions (HEIs) in the practical aspects of teacher training (for example, school visits), and wanted to see them contributing to the second phase within a reformed structure (ibid.:114). A very great problem was the fall in the birth rate which reduced the need for teachers. Although about ten thousand teachers would have to be 'lost' by the latter half of the 1990s, the WR insisted that in order to maintain morale in the teacher training institutions and vitality within the schools, some newly trained teachers must be recruited every year.

In the end, the decisions were taken by politicians but the Wissenschaftsrat provided informed judgement and principles on which those decisions could be based. In its 'Twelve Recommendations' (WR, 6.7.90), it analysed the shortcomings in the infrastructure of East German higher education: lack of Western literature, outmoded research and Information Technology equipment, supply difficulties with consumables, poorly maintained building stock. The global figure needed to remedy matters was estimated at DM

6.5 billion: this was to purchase books, computers, calculators and laboratory equipment; to help train the up-and-coming young academics of the future; to bring guest professors into East Germany; and to promote its international relationships. The WR aimed to promote freedom of research and teaching – indeed, to promote academic freedom generally. It found the East German university sector underdeveloped and its strong preference was to ensure that research, including basic research, would be done *within* higher education institutions rather than outside them, for example in specialist institutions. Both competition and cooperation between HEIs and non-university HE institutions were to be welcomed.

The Higher Education Special Programmes (Hochschulsonderprogramme (HSP)) became the most powerful financial instrument for the reform of third-level education in East Germany. They had their genesis at the end of the 1980s in the Federal Republic's Bund-Länder agreement based on Article 91b of the Basic Law. On 10 March 1989, the chief representatives of FRG Bund and Länder launched HSP 1 which was intended to remove entrance restrictions on crowded courses.[2] On 2 October, one day before German Unity Day, HSP II was ratified[3] in the awareness that special measures would be necessary to help the New Länder during unification. Its purpose was to promote the education of new academics and female academics, and to develop the Fachhochschulen and the European dimension in HE. On 11 July 1991, the Higher Education Renewal Programme (*Hochschulerneuerungsprogramm* (HEP)) for the NBL was approved with a period of validity up to 31 December 1996. The objectives of HEP were to help implement the recommendations of the Wissenschaftsrat and restructure the non-university research institutions, as well as to help women towards success.[4] HSP II was evaluated in 1995 and replaced by HSP III which was intended to implement measures in both OBL and NBL, including the further expansion of the Fachhochschulen and the maintenance of German higher education's competitiveness and innovatory potential.[5] HSP III is to extend until 31 December 2000 with funding of DM 3.6 billion of which the Bund-Länder ratio is 57.67 per cent to 42.33

2. HSP I: Bund-Länder-Kommission, Drs 96.36, Hochschulprogramm I: Ausgaben und durchgeführte Maßnahmen im Jahr 1995, Bonn, 17.9.1996.

3. HSP II: Bund-Länder-Kommission, Drs 96.37, Hochschulprogramm II: Ausgaben und durchgeführte Maßnahmen im Jahr 1995, Bonn, 17.9.1996.

4. Förderung von Frauen im Rahmen des Hochschulerneuerungsprogramms (HEP) (BLK, 1993c).

5. HSP III: Bund-Länder-Kommission, Drs 96.27, Hochschulprogramm III: Gemeinsames Hochschulprogramm III (HSP III), Bonn, 9.9.1996. Also Vereinbarung zwischen Bund und Ländern nach Artikel 91B des Grundgesetzes über ein Gemeinsames Hochschulsonderprogramm III (HSP III) vom 2. September 1996. The HSP III was made retrospective to 1 January 1996 and superseded HSP I and II.

per cent.[6] A distinctive subprogramme was created to integrate research groups and individuals from the Academies into the mainstream HEIs. As part of this Academic Integration Programme (*Wissenschaftler-Integrations-Programm* (WIP)), 1,920 academics were assisted (BMFT, 1993:4). It was decided to prolong WIP to 1996 and to increase the budget to DM 600 million. Some (e.g. Simon, 1995) sneered at the scheme as mere up-market 'job creation' designed by Bonn to head off the danger of unrest or latent rebellion on the part of thousands of unemployed academics. Those non-university HEIs which were retained were developed in their own right and the Ministry in its report to the Bundestag (BMFT, 1993) stated that research in this sector had proved to be the most stable and the best ordered in East Germany (ibid.:15). In the summary at the end of this document, there is a note of unmistakable pride in what has been achieved:

> The restructured and newly established research institutions are ... a gain for the whole of Germany. That is true of subjects, of structures and most especially of people. German research has been complemented, extended and enriched by the institutions and potential of the New Länder.... The building up of the new research scenario in East Germany and the ensuing new qualities now occasion a comprehensive review of the whole of German research and research policy, as called for by the Wissenschaftsrat, in order to assess the structures, priorities, the strategies for promotion and the location of research centres all over Germany with a view to devising new research areas and tasks.

The said Wissenschaftsrat was, however, not quite so sanguine about what had been achieved. It had reservations about the soundness of the West German model which had been exported to the East. In 1993, the WR published a 63–page working paper entitled 'Ten Theses on Higher Education Politics'. This is a tough, radical document which calls in question many time-honoured German university values and structures. The Wissenschaftsrat (WR, 1993:10) produced figures to show quantitative changes in higher education in the Federal Republic between 1977 and 1990:

- The number of students entering HE had increased by 73 per cent.
- The time taken to complete a programme of study increased by 48 per cent.
- The number of students exceeding the recommended duration for a study programme increased by 106 per cent.
- The number of those completing their courses increased by 20 per cent.
- Expenditure on HE increased in real terms by 12 per cent.

---

6. I am grateful to Dr Wolfgang Mönikes of the Bundesministerium für Bildung, Wissenschaft, Forschung und Technologie, Bonn, for helping me to disentangle the complexities of all these special programmes.

- The research grants distributed by the German Society for Research increased by 18 per cent.

Clearly, these figures are indicative of an underresourced system with a high wastage rate and excessive degree completion periods. The WR went on to describe the problems in more detail. The management structure is outdated; there is too great a disparity between the size of the university (large) and the Fachhochschule sector (much smaller); student recruitment is spiralling out of control; many institutions are large, soulless and impersonal; achievements in teaching are not recognised; there is no systematic evaluation of HE teaching and no career incentive to improve it.

The Wissenschaftsrat called for a greater diversification of the higher education system (though narrow specialisation was to be avoided). The pretence that it was homogeneous could no longer be sustained in a modern industrial society. The Fachhochschulen had been created in the late 1960s and early 1970s out of the earlier engineering colleges; their courses were more applied and more tightly structured than university courses (Rotenhan, 1980). This sector was to be expanded – in the long term even to the point where the Fachhochschulen would take more students than the universities. Deficits in their staffing and equipment were to be eliminated and their graduates were no longer to be disadvantaged relative to those from universities in terms of salary scales and civil service categories. There must be greatly increased mutual recognition between universities and Fachhochschulen; for example, FHS graduates should be able to go on to universities to do doctorates. Of course, says the WR, the expansion of the FHS sector is contingent on obtaining an increased share of the national budget; if this proves impossible, further limits on student access must be introduced. Indeed, it is altogether an illusion to think that anyone or everyone with the basic qualification for entry to HE can be admitted; here too entry restrictions must be considered (WR, 1993:30).

Teaching must be given a much higher status; university teachers should be evaluated by their students and such assessments should be publicised so as to lead to greater openness. Not all subjects necessarily need to be taught by supremely highly qualified experts. The basic elements of statistics and foreign languages, for example, could quite adequately be taught by instructors rather than professors or assistants; such personnel could perhaps do service teaching alongside other employment and should be offered a competitive fee and reasonable status for doing so. Tutorials should be offered in conjunction with lectures during the foundation semesters of degree programmes, and consideration should be given to employing graduate students for this purpose. Retired professors could be offered part-time teaching positions and could continue to be involved in supervising dissertations. Professional courses like Law, Administration and Management could be restructured advantageously on the principle of the Dual System whereby students would learn on the job as well as in higher education. In the Humanities, many subjects would benefit from tighter organisation and more compulsory core content (ibid.:37). Only a tiny proportion of students are interested in being trained as researchers; hence the purpose of higher education ought not to be conceived as an induction into research – traditionally an all too prevalent model. Even for university staff, the link between research and teaching needs to be re-examined. In previous decades, all university staff were resourced to do research, but this situation had already begun to change in the 1970s. In view of shrinking resources, surely the duty to do research needs to be reviewed (WR, 1993:17).

The bottom line in the Wissenschaftsrat's 'Ten Theses' document is that a fundamental reform of higher education is necessary all over Germany. It is, says the WR, not reasonable to insist that a higher education system suitable for an age participation rate (APR) of 5 per cent of the population could or should be suitable for an APR of 30 per cent. Teaching, research, management, governance, financing, course structures and evaluation (or rather the lack thereof) all need to be examined critically and reformed to make them serve the needs of modern-day Germany.

However, by the time of the WR's writing – 1993 – at the cost of much effort, money, time and sacrifice, East Germany had been given the same higher education structures as West Germany – and with them some of the same problems.

Restructuring and 'Cleansing' of University and School Staff

A major drive on the part of the West German reformers was to increase academic freedom and to purge the universities of Marxism-Leninism. Most of those outside the GDR HEIs and even some of those within felt that they were incapable of reforming themselves autonomously. The Halle scholar Johannes Mehlig uttered the rather moving words: 'We will go to enormous trouble to achieve renewal. But we cannot manage to pull ourselves out of the mire alone. You must help us' (Schiedermair, 1996:103). Certain subjects within higher education such as History, Economics and Law were ideologically loaded – after all, they had been used to legitimise the GDR (WR, 1991:100). Even Mathematics was taught in a very authoritarian way and could be used to achieve the sort of socialisation process welcomed by the SED regime. Education was *par excellence* a carrier of M-L ideology, whereas the hard sciences were much less vulnerable to politicisation.

Higher education staff in the New Bundesländer would now be required to profess loyalty to the Basic Law of the Federal Republic, though recently they had professed loyalty to a very different constitution. The assessors were of the opinion that a large proportion of the GDR teacher educators – both the subject teachers and the pedagogues – would have to be replaced, and the legal basis for doing so was provided by Article 13 of the Unity Treaty. The staff-student ratios were so excessively generous by Western standards that it was impossible to keep all existing employees on the payroll, and it was assumed by the West German side that the Easterners would not tolerate the retention of anyone with a tainted political record.

Staff were subjected to an evaluative process which began by investigating their personal and political integrity and went on in a second stage to assess their academic competence. (See Appendix II for the translation of a questionnaire used to evaluate teachers.) This screening process could make or break employees' reputation, professional future and financial security. For dismissal to take place, close and continuous association with the SED and its regime had to be proved; there had to be proof of a violation of the General Declaration of Human Rights of 10 December 1948 or the International Pact of Civil and Political Rights of 16 December 1966. Mere membership of a political Party was an insufficient cause for dismissal: 'The customary loyalty and cooperation necessary to maintain oneself and to progress in the public service [was] not, in itself, according to the Unity Treaty, sufficient grounds to establish personal unsuitability' (Huber, P.M., n.d.).

The cleansing process aroused much fear and resentment among those assessed; feelings of injustice abounded. The race for jobs had a strong element of competition and the Wissenschaftsrat had not only endorsed the competitive ethos but had insisted that the standards must be those of international scholarship in a particular discipline (WR, 6.7.90:21). Actually, the Federal Ministry (BMFT 1993:12) had acknowledged that East German research was often of high quality – especially in scientific disciplines – but the problem was that conditions were basically unequal between Easterners and Westerners (Hartmer, 1991). Easterners felt that those assessing academic excellence made little allowance for vital practical factors in the former GDR: lack of paper which inhibited work in all subjects; uncertain or rationed supply of electricity which affected experimentation in the Natural Sciences; modern linguists' lack of contact with the country of their target language due to travel restrictions; lack of teamwork and interaction, even in the Humanities; the fact that the 'subordinates' of top professors had to have professorial permission to publish, which could be denied arbitrarily.

Maier and Wenske (1993) describe how at Rostock University the subject assessors rarely even interviewed the staff; many of the assessors were not personally known to those being evaluated and none of them were from East Germany; great weight was attached to publication in refereed journals but little account was taken of the fact that for certain subjects no refereed journals existed in the GDR, and basic research – the most prestigious – had long been allocated to the academies, not to the universities; it was simply impossible for Easterners to be familiar with Western literature because it had never been available to them; and of course given the travel restrictions it was impossible to give papers at international conferences. In the end, about 40 per cent of university staff were judged 'not suitable' at Rostock University. For those who remained, the third stage was that of actually obtaining a post. Lists of job vacancies were posted up within the institution and applicants had fourteen days to apply. There were often more than eight internal applicants for each post, and in the Land as a whole the number of redundancies ran into thousands. The authors admit that although formally the procedures were carried out correctly,

> ... from the point of view of those concerned, the enduring impression after the completion of the transfer procedure was that the staff renewal described above was perceived as a questionable and arbitrary act of discrimination against academics and recognised lecturers and as a devaluation of research, some of which was of international significance.... A large number of higher education teachers felt themselves unfairly judged by strangers in a process which was dubious and difficult to understand. (Maier and Wenske, 1993)

This was the way many people felt, but when the matter was contested in court, the Federal Constitutional Court in a judgement of 24 April 1991 declared that the ending of employment in public institutions being closed was not contrary to the Constitution, and a complaint against the 'waiting period' procedure was also rejected. The uncomfortable fact was that the East German universities had been grossly overstaffed in comparison to those in the West; there was a drive to make the staff-student ratio in the East correspond more closely to Western norms, not just for ideological but also for financial reasons. There were a number of important respects in which higher education staff structure differed in East and West Germany. In both, there existed a layer of staff called the *Mittelbau* (middle level) which was positioned below the full-fledged professoriate. In West Germany, most of these staff were preparing their post-doctoral theses in the hope of being appointed to university Chairs. Many of them exercised teaching functions but did so on temporary contracts – sometimes strung out over many years. The average age at which the post-doctoral thesis was successfully completed was almost forty (Grund- und Strukturdaten, 1994/95), but even with this high-powered qualification there was no certainty of appointment to a Chair. The seemingly endless waiting and hoping was often nerve-wracking and debilitating, especially for those with young families to support. Through their research and publications, the West German Mittelbau contributed in a major way to the prestige and productivity of German academe but many, if not most, of its members did so without any secure long-term prospects on which to plan their lives. In East Germany, the majority of the Mittelbau were on permanent contracts and contributed regularly to teaching and research within their institutions; their posts were regarded as valid in their own right rather than as stepping stones to professorships. In Colleges of Education about 95 per cent of the teaching was done by non-professorial assistants (WR, 1991). Such people were useful members of staff whose employment improved the staff-student ratio and enhanced the academic environment for the students by providing face-to-face contact and personal attention.

All members of the NBL higher education staff were evaluated for both subject competence and political soundness. In the latter process, specially constituted Boards made recommendations, and the HEI itself applied to the appropriate body, the Gauck Authority, to have the records of the Secret Police checked. It is not possible to present precise figures about the number of academics who lost their jobs in the restructuring because the GDR kept aggregate rather than individual figures about higher education staffing (Burkhardt and Scherer, 1997:329). Nevertheless, the following can be stated:

- Between 1989 and 1994, when the restructuring process was largely completed, there was a reduction in academic staff posts by 13,300 to 24,500 (ibid.:323). This represents about one-third of the staffing which existed in the former GDR, and applied exclusively to Academic Assistantships.
- Twenty thousand academics left their jobs involuntarily during the course of restructuring. Of these, five thousand were professors. The reduction predominantly affected universities, where staffing was halved, but some of these staff (mostly professors) were redeployed to Fachhochschulen. The Mittelbau suffered disproportionately more than professors.
- Eight thousand full-time academics were made redundant because their jobs no longer existed due to the closure of their subject areas or entire institutions. Of these, 61 per cent were in Law, Economics and the Social Sciences, and 23 per cent in Languages and Arts. Mathematics, Engineering and Natural Sciences suffered only to a small extent (ibid.:332).
- Very few people were dismissed due to lack of competence in their subjects – only about 0.6 per cent of those evaluated (ibid.:335).
- Under 5 per cent of staff were judged guilty of political unsoundness. There were numerous legal cases of people suing against recommendations

for dismissal. About one-third of these accepted a settlement. According to the Gauck Authority, over 90 per cent of the academic staff were 'clean'. Only about 2,200 persons actually had to leave higher education because they were politically tainted, which in relation to the total number of staff in HEIs at the end of 1991 is a proportion of between 2 and 3 per cent. Most of those who with good reason believed that they would not get through the appraisal process did not wait to be dismissed; they left of their own accord (Mayntz, 1994a:303/4).

- The GDR ratio for permanent to fixed-term posts had been 80 to 20. By 1994, there were 10,000 fixed-term posts and only 7,000 permanent posts for middle- level academics which represented a considerable diminution of the more secure jobs and a reversal of the previous proportions. It is estimated (Burkhardt and Scherer, 1997:326) that 17,000 permanent posts at subprofessorial level were lost. It should, however, be pointed out that about one-third of new professors in the NBL were recruited from the Mittelbau of the ex-GDR.

- The New Bundesländer differed in their profiles as regards staff reduction. East Berlin and Saxony reduced academic staffing by 48 per cent and 44 per cent respectively; Mecklenburg-Vorpommern reduced by one-third, while Saxony-Anhalt and Thuringia reduced by about one-fourth each. Brandenburg, which had had an under-provision of higher education, expanded its staff by 20 per cent (ibid.:326).

- Women were strongly represented in the vulnerable subject areas such as Humanities and Social Sciences; in higher education (including art colleges), about 31 per cent of them were dismissed (ibid.:333).

- The new universities attracted Westerners in quite substantial numbers (see Table 6.1).

Table 6.1 Origins of Professors in the New Bundesländer

HEIs NBL	Professors from NBL	Professors from OBL
Universities	52	45
Colleges of Art	71	22
Fachhochschulen	58	41

Source: Burkhardt and Scherer, 1997:343.

The position of both non-professorial and professorial staff deteriorated considerably after unification. The typical reduction in the tenured Mittelbau was from 75 to 80 per cent to about 20 per cent: in Jena, the number of academic workers with tenure was reduced from 75 per cent of the staff to 20 per cent, while in Leipzig the number of lecturers was reduced from 302 in 1990 to 53 in 1994 (Huber, P.M., n.d.). The role of the Mittelbau changed; whereas earlier they had looked after the students, they now had to work predominantly to improve their own qualifications. Their status sank, as indeed the status of teaching sank in a culture which valued research over teaching. Many East German professors were downgraded from the top C4 to the second-highest C3 salary scale (Neidhardt, 1994). About 650 professors were not assimilated into the new conditions of service but remained in their existing jobs as 'Professors according to Old Law' with an ambiguous legal status and inferior conditions of service (Tüffers, 1995). Now East German academics were forced to live just as insecure lives as Westerners had long done. Professors from the closed Academy of Sciences applied for jobs in universities, thereby making the job market tighter than ever. The terror of joblessness made Easterners comply formally with Western values and practices, but this was often a process of forced adaptation through fear rather than through conviction. So much nervous energy was expended on the more dramatic aspects of 'staff renewal' (like cooperation with the Secret Police), that there was scarcely enough left for debates on educational topics like objectives, course structures and content. Brentjes (1997), discussing the University of Leipzig, says that participation in reforms was often ritualistic – a fact which prolonged typical GDR modes of behaviour. Opportunism was in her view the most successful survival strategy.

School teachers were also tested, and the onus of proof was on the employer to show that employees were *unsuitable* rather than on the teachers to show that they were suitable. The first stage in recognition of East German teachers was to establish whether or not they deserved to retain their jobs in the new Germany. As was pointed out above, the teaching profession in East Germany had been subjected to an anti-fascist cull after the Second World War. Now, after the fall of the Wall, it had to undergo a second one, this time to ensure as far as possible that no one who had damaged others by collaborating with the Secret Police retained his or her job. Compulsory redundancies sometimes boomeranged back on those who had created them, causing trouble, unpleasantness and, above all, expense. Some of the teachers who were dismissed appealed against the judgements of the Ministry of Education, first to the Labour Court, then to the Federal Labour Court (Bundesarbeitsgericht), and won their appeals by showing that the Ministry had made formal mistakes or had not produced sufficient evidence. It was of course difficult for the Ministry to obtain concrete documentation showing that a teacher had, for example, discriminated against middle-class pupils by not letting them enter the upper forms of the school or by blackening someone's reputation. Those who were able to win their appeals on technicalities had the right to be reinstated in their jobs, but unfortunately in some cases their staff colleagues knew for certain that despite their legal victories they were indeed guilty of the accusations with which they had been charged. Such cases, though exceptional, tended to bring the Rechtsstaat and the Law into disrepute and made innocent colleagues cynical and angry at the miscarriage of justice.

Restructuring of Higher Education Institutions

Closure of the Academy of Sciences and of the Academy of Educational Sciences

An important core value of West German academe was the unity of research and teaching in higher education: teacher educators were expected to do research. The East German structure violated this principle by placing fundamental research in specialist institutions outside the universities, for example in the Academy of Sciences (Akademie der Wissenschaften (AdW)), the Academy of Agricultural Sciences and the Academy of Building Sciences. Between them these three Academies employed almost 94 per cent of the research and development staff in the state sector. Renate Mayntz (1994b) of the Max Planck Institute has chronicled the history of the Academy of Sciences after the fall of the Wall and the unification of Germany. The Academy of Sciences was the most important of the three Academies, employing about 24,000 staff and by 1989 consisting of sixty institutes. Though basic research was important, it had a strong industrial steer. After the stagnation of the 1970s, a 'highly authoritarian solution' was adopted, and the decision was taken in 1985 that the majority of the Academy's research would be concerned with the large state manufacturing monopolies (Kombinate). About 15 per cent of the Academy's work was devoted to productive tasks like making equipment, publishing and various service activities; in fact by 1989, only about 64 per cent of the AdW's staff were classified as research and development personnel. The institutes were underresourced for what they had to do, and grossly overmanned by Western standards; they attempted to compensate with numbers of workers for what they lacked in resources (in 1989, about one-third of the AdW research equipment was judged below standard). The AdW was centrally controlled and oriented to the needs of the GDR's economy; nevertheless, despite its lack of academic freedom, it was privileged in comparison with the universities and the Kombinate (Mayntz, 1994b:42–46).

The Chair of the Wissenschaftsrat, Dieter Simon, was invited by the East German SPD minister, Dr Frank Terpe, to undertake an evaluation of the Academy. The task was a demanding one and differed from the WR's usual remit in that it transcended subject assessment; the WR was required to make a set of recommendations about the future of the powerful federation of AdW institutes and their thousands of staff. It proceeded pragmatically with quality as its over-riding criterion – but 'quality' was defined according to Western criteria. Judgements about excellence, efficiency and coherence were especially controversial in the Humanities and the Social Sciences because they were more closely involved with ideology than the hard sciences were. The institutes were convinced of their own merit and sent the WR literally kilograms of material to prove it. In direct personal contact with the Easterners, the WR usually tried to formulate things tactfully; if the formal judgement later turned out to be negative, this was experienced by the Easterners as a shock and a betrayal. The situation was of course stress-ridden, and Mayntz (1994b:156) quotes Dieter Simon's words revealing how difficult it was to strike the right manner in contact with the East Germans:

> The assessor ... must not be tactless. He must not grin in a superior way. He must not grin at all. He must not look grim but not too friendly either. He must not nod in approval, but neither must he look away in an uninterested way. He must concentrate on the matter in hand and avoid political questions. He must not make any promises. He must not come out with any threats. He should be silent about his impressions. He must keep recommendations and advice to himself. But he should be collegial. And human. In the end he merely stands before his irritated colleagues and chats about the weather.

Yet although there was a distinct feeling of 'them and us', the WR was not motivated by self-interest. It approached the transformation of the AdW as a problem-solving exercise rather than as a struggle between conflicting interests. The WR wanted a systematic restructuring without having any grand conceptual design as to how this should take place. The West German Ministry, the BMFT, did not have any very clear design either, other than to promote research and to avoid a proliferation of non-university research institutes. The WR had to find a solution which would work in practice, and undemanding goals were congenial, being naturally easier to realise than demanding goals. The AdW fought for its life. At first it tried to justify its right to survive more or less in its existing form as a federation of institutes though with severe downsizing of the order of 60 per cent (Mayntz, 1994b:84). The East German Ministry was the AdW's best advocate and Minister Frank Terpe was concerned to preserve jobs. The GDR government, however, was afraid of an imminent economic collapse and for this reason wanted to hasten the unification process; this weak negotiating position rather disarmed its defence of the AdW. In the Unity Treaty (EV, Article 38 (3)) a moratorium was granted guaranteeing funding to the AdW until 31 December 1991; the rate (not stated in the EV) was 900 million marks a year (Mayntz, 1994b:131). In October 1990, a decision to dissolve the AdW became law and between June 1990 and November 1991, the number of staff in the AdW was reduced from 24,249 to 15,836. This reduction was achieved through redundancies, premature retirements and re-deployment; some of the staff were taken into universities, others were employed in short-term jobs.

The Academy of Educational Sciences (APW), as part of the Academy of Sciences, suffered the same fate. At one time, it looked as if there might have been some hope for it. The Minister of Education and Science, Herr Meyer, had mounted a verbal undertaking to defend it and had praised its proposals for self-reform as a model for the possible reconstruction of other academic institutions (Kossakowski, 1992:95). However, the Wende revealed the splits within the APW: the 'Establishment' fended off change, while others wished it to come about. They had hoped for much from the Ninth Education Congress held in June 1989 just before the Wende: for example, less dogmatic syllabuses, less teacher-centredness, more flexible movement from one educational level to the next (ibid.:91). Unfortunately, only the President was allowed to speak at the Congress, and the voices of the would-be reformers went unheard. This was bad for the APW because it had serious problems which needed to be confronted, not hushed up. It was true that some of the research which went on there was excellent, but there was no real academic freedom. Publications could be, and were sometimes required to be, altered to fit in with the Party line, and scholars were on occasion forbidden to continue with certain lines of investigation which looked politically controversial. School reform was suffocated; scholars had become distanced from reality and even from theory, which was treated with suspicion. The standard way of dealing with pressure for change was to revise the syllabuses rather than the curriculum or the timetable; there was no attempt to address any of the deeper sources of tension in school life (Eichler and Uhlig, 1993:120). The APW, under the control of the GDR Ministry of Education, allowed itself to be used as the Ministry's tool.

In the autumn of 1990, the APW staff, of whom there were about six hundred, were told that it was not possible to carry out an evaluation on them; the GDR negotiator Professor Achtel blamed Herr Meyer who in turn blamed the Bonn Finance Ministry. Without an evaluation, there was no future for the APW, and the staff knew that they were doomed. From the first of January, work was to be stopped and distinguished professors qualified at post-doctoral level were advised to take part in retraining courses and to look for work. A number of project groups were formed using work-creation schemes but this only served to occupy a small fraction of the staff; in addition, this mode of funding was by its very nature unsuited to long-term research. Kossakowski (1992) who himself had been Director of the Institute of Psychology (1970–88) at the APW could see its shortcomings very well and acknowledged them freely. This insight still did not serve to dispel his emotions of anger and upset at the way the APW was treated.

> Acknowledging all the contradictions of the APW in connection with the over-lordship of the former GDR, the end of the APW still means the end of decades of committed and creative research and, at least for many of the research groups, the breaking off of many significant investigations. The indis-criminate *Abwicklung* of this research establishment cannot be justified in human, academic or financial terms; it can only be justified in political terms. (Kossakowski, 1992:99)

The AdW and with it the APW became defunct. The AdW had been unable to defend its interests effectively for reasons which related partly to its own intrinsic nature and partly to macropolitical factors.

- The academicians themselves had been slow in reacting to the new situation and tended to mark time rather than to innovate. Certainly, active innovators were in the minority. The AdW's leadership was weak and internally divided about the choice of a leader (Mayntz, 1994b:76ff.).
- Democratic decision-making was seen by AdW leaders as an attack on their authority. The Old Guard persisted and was re-elected. Per-haps people were afraid to change from the familiar in times of trou-ble, but so long as the Old Guard remained at the apex of the AdW, the old ideology still prevailed – a fact which made it unacceptable to the West Germans.
- At first the Federal Republic had been relatively non-interventionist about the AdW, and the Bonn BMFT refrained from the robust exer-cise of power in the New Bundesländer. There was, however, an intolerable tension between a centralistic Academy and the new-style political federalism. The Länder's control of education militated against an all-German Academy; once the Länder were established, the demise of the AdW was assured. So long as a confederation seemed a possibility, differences in research organisation between East and West could be tolerated. When integration on the basis of Article 23 was adopted, pressure mounted towards making the insti-tutional arrangements the same in East and West.
- Members of the Academy were not necessarily familiar with the implication of federalism for educational structures. This inexperi-ence made it all the more difficult for them to make a sound analysis of their situation and generate proposals which would be acceptable by West German standards (Mayntz, 1994b:82). Had members of the AdW had a place at the negotiating table, the decision to dissolve

the AdW and integrate most research into the NBL universities might not have been made.

- The AdW missed the chance to renew itself radically and could not convince outsiders that it had freed itself from the past.
- Defenders of the APW (e.g. Kossakowski, 1992:97) blamed its problems on the lack of an all-German Science Strategy and the Länder's financial uncertainty.

The then head of the Wissenschaftsrat, Dieter Simon, is on record as saying that the East German research scenario should not become a clone of the less-than-perfect West German system. However, if the strategy had been to create a research infrastructure which was different but equal in East and West Germany, then a plan and an ambitious set of objectives would have been necessary. As we have seen, these did not really exist. The WR, having taken an interventionist role which even extended to implementation, reverted to its usual advisory role when its main task was done. It did not become a planning body. As was almost unavoidable, the Easterners were left with a residual feeling of resentment at the evaluation process. They felt that if they were to be assessed, then it would be very proper to subject the West Germans to scrutiny, too. They asserted that the assessors had taken too little time over their work, did not know enough about the subjects involved, were arrogant and tactless, and did not make clear the reasons for their actions (Mayntz, 1994b:179). There were a number of long-term negative effects of the process. Those lost by out-migration to West Germany or foreign countries were predominantly the younger academics, resulting in a dilution of 'new blood' and a loss of research potential and intensity in the NBL. The industrial research base was eroded: Mayntz (1994b:265) argues that research and development were only 20 per cent in 1992 of what they had been in 1989. Above all, there was a pervading sense that East Germans even after the Wende were still being managed from above, and were relatively powerless to assume responsibility for their own fate. This was psychologically deleterious.

Changes in Third-Level Education Structures

In 1953, as the result of reform, a three-sector system of teacher training was established which continued up to the point of unification:

1. Primary school teachers (for the Unterstufe) were trained in Institutes for Teacher Training (Institute für Lehrerbildung (IfLs)). They entered the IfLs after ten years of school education at the age of sixteen or seventeen, having taken *Mittlere Reife* (the equivalent of GCSE in the United Kingdom) not Abitur, and having studied one subject for four

years. In 1989, their entry qualifications were thus inferior to those of primary teachers in the Federal Republic who had to have Abitur to enter their colleges or universities.

2. Teacher training institutes (*Pädagogische Institute*), which in the 1960s were transformed into Colleges of Teacher Education (*Pädagogische Hochschulen*), produced teachers for both the intermediate and the upper stages (classes 5 to 12).

3. Upper secondary teachers for classes 9 to 12 were trained at university, as were the staff of vocational schools and schools for the handicapped.

In 1988, the relative proportions of teachers receiving their qualifications from the different types of institution were as follows: IfL, 30 per cent; PH, 27 per cent; university, 43 per cent (Schreier, 1991:37)

With the reform of teacher training contingent on unification, those undergoing initial training were obliged to do both the First and the Second State Examinations. Those in Länder with strongly divided school systems (such as Mecklenburg-Vorpommern) could not simply train as *Grundschullehrer*, they had to undertake the Hauptschule training as well, contrary to the wishes of some of them. There was, however, firm and sensible action in abolishing the IfLs and in insisting that all entrants to teacher education should have Abitur as their entrance qualification. Those intending to be primary teachers now had to take two subjects instead of one. Colleges of Education were integrated, in part at least, into universities as follows.

The Integration of Colleges of Education into Universities

PH Dresden	Technical University of Dresden
PH Güstrow	University of Rostock
PH Halle	University of Halle
PH Leipzig	University of Leipzig
PH Neubrandenburg	University of Greifswald
PH Potsdam	University of Potsdam
PH Magdeburg	Technical University of Magdeburg
PH Zwickau	Technical University of Chemnitz

The nucleus of Erfurt University is to be located on the site of the Pädagogische Hochschule (Buck-Bechler et al., 1997:103).

Subject education for post-primary teachers was given in universities. Of the fifty-three HEIs, only twenty-three were taken over by the New Länder. Three new universities were established: at Cottbus, Frankfurt on the Oder and Erfurt. Table 6.2 shows the status of GDR HEIs after the Wende.

Table 6.2   Higher Education Institutions in the NBL Taken Over or Closed after the Wende

GDR HEIs	Number	Taken Over	Closed
Universities	9	9	0
Art Colleges	12	10	2
Technical HEIs	15	3	12
Colleges of Education	9	1 (Erfurt)	8
Other HEIs	8	0	8
Total	**53**	**23**	**30**

Source: Buck-Bechler et al. (1997:102).

The GDR had possessed a plethora of types of tertiary education institutions (Buck-Bechler et al., (1997:58) list 12) which was greatly reduced under the West German reforms. There was a strong move away from the specialist institutions of the GDR, the aim being to develop 'full universities' with a broad subject spectrum. An important innovation was the introduction of twenty-one Fachhochschulen which were set up at twenty-six locations. After only one year, they enrolled more than 20 per cent of all first-year students in the New Bundesländer, and by 1996 enrolled about 30 per cent of all beginners (Jahn, 1994:105). Actually, this type of HEI matched the GDR heritage very well because its courses were tightly structured, reasonably practical and well adapted to the needs of the economy. Also attractive to planners was the fact that students in the Fachhochschulen usually completed their studies within a set period of time. Although the reformers set out to uncouple the excessively close link that had existed between education and the employment system, they still sought to bring about a regional enrichment, for example through the Fachhochschulen. The FHS in Merseburg, situated in an area where the chemical industry was salient, concerned itself with the environment; the FHS in Leipzig continued to develop its ancient tradition of printing, publication and books; the FHS in Zwickau concerned itself with automobiles; and in Neubrandenburg with its rural catchment area of Northern Brandenburg and Southern Mecklenburg-Vorpommern, agriculture was emphasised (Jahn, 1993:259). It was obvious that new partnerships needed to be developed, some of them at a supraregional level ignoring the political boundaries of the Länder.

As a result of the reforms, the higher education system was made much more attractive for potential and actual students. In the former GDR, the limitation of access to HE had been both inefficient and unjust. In deference to an excessive orientation towards the Soviet Union, many specialist institutions had existed which were supposed to serve the planned economy but were so overspecialised that graduates had difficulty finding jobs corresponding to their qualifications; this was one reason for the Abwicklung of such institutions. Moreover, such overspecialisation seemed perverse to the Western eye because it did not do justice to the interests or gifts of the individual. Students are now able to choose from a much more varied and wider range of course offerings according to their own life plans and individual interests, and to enjoy freedom according to Article 12 of the Basic Law (free choice of profession, place of work and of education). This was facilitated through:

- a 50 per cent expansion in the capacity of higher education to accept students;
- a horizontal division of the higher education structure into university and Fachhochschule sectors;
- an improved regional network of higher education institutions;
- increased access in terms of the age participation rate;
- increased freedom of subject choice and institution.

A Reformed Teaching Profession

The Thorny Issues of Recognition and Pay

The most serious disparity between East and West Germany was in relation to Lower Level teachers. East German primary teachers did not have university degrees whereas those in West Germany did, giving rise to problems concerning recognition and salary scales.

The Greifswald Decisions (1994) promulgated by the Conference of Ministers of Education (Kultusministerkonferenz (KMK)) set out the salary groupings and the equivalence between qualifications in East and West Germany. The Ministry of the Interior proposed a lower salary scale for the Lower Level teachers. The hard-pressed Länder were inclined to be niggardly but the more liberally minded KMK pointed out that the Lower Level teachers possessed the only qualification which had been available to them in the GDR. Moreover, the group of teachers concerned was finite, shrinking and time-limited because all future teachers in the new Germany would henceforth be equipped with Western-style qualifications; one could thus afford to be a little more generous. The matter was debated in the Bundestag and the Bundesrat, and a decision was reached to take the Lower Level teachers out of the nationwide salary structure and turn the problem over to the New Länder for them to decide. The Ministry of the Interior was persuaded to withdraw its recommendation that the Lower Level teachers should be placed on a lower salary scale than primary teachers in West Germany.

Nevertheless, many of these GDR-trained teachers suffered unemployment because they had been Pioneer leaders and there was no call for such services in the New Germany. The Old Bundesländer refused to accept GDR-trained primary teachers because they were not as well qualified on paper as Western primary teachers. The comparison was done in a very formal way by examining input such as entrance qualifications and closely measured periods of study rather than looking at output criteria, for example how competent were these East German teachers at managing their classes, promoting learning and achieving results? The lack of recognition of Easterners' performance criteria constituted a serious barrier to East-West mobility which could be overcome only by further study and the passing of examinations – an onerous demand for those already carrying all the responsibilities of adult life.

University-educated GDR secondary school teachers at least had Abitur and had studied at universities, but even here there were problems. The GDR teachers had been trained in an integrated process of subject study and Education, including teaching practice, whereas the FRG teachers had been trained in two end-on phases. The difficult question was whether the Easterners were eligible to become civil servants (Beamte) without having done the Second State Examination as was required in the West. The solution reached was that the Second State Examination was to be replaced by four to five years of satisfactory service in the unified Germany – a performance criterion. As things turned out, however, despite this decision, the Easterners were still disadvantaged. One of the main differences which developed between teachers in East and West was in their formal employment category. The overwhelming majority of those in the Old Bundesländer were civil servants (Beamte) who could be dismissed only for good cause but otherwise had tenure; only 8.84 per cent were Angestellte (middle-level functionaries) who did not have tenure for life. In the New Bundesländer, however, the situation was reversed: 98.59 per cent were Angestellte (GEW, 12.11.94). In view of falling pupil enrolment, the Länder – understandably – did not want to lock themselves into a commitment to lifetime employment for teachers, many of whom would become surplus as supply came to exceed demand. Structural inequalities between East and West developed in conditions of employment, and for demographic and financial reasons there was little of a levelling upwards for the Easterners.

In fact, the opposite was true. A tendency arose towards levelling teachers (and many other categories of employee) *downwards* in the West: from Beamte to Angestellte. It was argued that this was necessary to increase flexibility in the labour market and to counteract the phenomenon of uncompetitive labour costs in Germany. Angestellte were paid according to different salary scales and had a slightly higher rate of payment than Beamte because their pension contributions had to be funded from salary. Beamte could become tenured after a relatively short probationary period (two or three years after full qualifications were obtained) whereas Angestelle reached this stage of secure employment only after fifteen years of satisfactory service. East Germans had, not unnaturally, hoped to become Beamte; after all, they had been accustomed to job security under the old regime. At first, shortly after the Wende, Berlin and Brandenburg made some teachers civil servants, but this trend stopped as soon as the difficult economic situation and falling birth rates became obvious. Not everyone believed that the overall tendency was negative. Otto (1996), for example, believed that it was no bad thing for teachers in both the NBL and the OBL *not* to be made Beamte because the rigidity of *Beamtentum* (a civil service employment category) could constitute an obstacle to reform, and the absence of Beamtentum might give greater freedom – for example to achieve increased teacher mobility between Länder which at present seem to erect walls around themselves.

The GEW leaders were not opposed in principle to the status of Angestellte for their new members, though naturally they demanded some basic ground rules and safeguards. They believed that the inclusion of teachers in the salary negotiations for Angestellte would give the GEW increased bargaining power. They even agreed that the law pertaining to Beamte status needed to be modernised, but they opposed any move to terminate the status of Beamte for those who already had it, arguing that this would be against the Constitution. In the long run, the GEW wanted to see a unified employment law for everyone. In the meantime, however, although East Germans were given less holiday money and a smaller allowance at Christmas than West Germans, their salaries were ratcheted up towards equivalence with Westerners over a period of several years.

Table 6.3   East German Teachers' Salaries as a Percentage of West German Teachers' Salaries

Date	Percentage
1 May 1992	70
1 December 1992	74
1 July 1993	80
1 October 1994	82
1 October 1995	84

Source: GEW, *Tarifrunde* as of 28 March 1996.

As has already been pointed out in the chapter on vocational education, salary harmonisation tended to fuel unemployment; on the other hand, low salaries made it difficult to attract good people – for example in the universities

– and some observers saw in the differentials a possible danger of East Germany becoming a substandard region with substandard teachers and academics. The case of Berlin was a special one since teachers were paid different rates in the Eastern and Western parts of the same city. This was invidious. If a West Berliner wished to change to a school in East Berlin, he or she had to take a drop in salary. Moreover, the Westerners had all lost their Berlin allowance after unification, so for different reasons, both East and West Berliners were disaffected: the Easterners because they were paid less than Westerners for the same work, and the Westerners because they had lost their special allowance and feared that Easterners would be favoured in employment. In October 1996, an agreement was therefore reached to equalise salaries at West German rates for all Berlin teachers – East and West. The aim of the GEW was that their East German members should eventually reach parity with West German salaries in all the New Bundesländer, an aim opposed by employers on grounds of cost. The union was criticised by the Easterners for not fighting harder to achieve parity, and by the Westerners for paying too much attention to the interests of the Easterners. The head of the GEW in the Berlin office received the following letter of resignation from a West German member:

> After many years of membership I wish my resignation to take effect at the earliest possible opportunity. Unfortunately, I no longer see the GEW pursuing progressive policies. I regret that the GEW is not committed to the employment opportunities of young West German teachers and has become a one-sided representative of East German colleagues. Obviously, a substantial increase in [subscription-] paying members is more important to the GEW [than representing West German teachers]; even Stasi teachers are accepted. I see no sign of any discussion about the educational aims of such teachers.

Such letters were not unusual, and similar missives were received from angry Easterners believing that their traditions and concerns were being neglected in favour of Westerners'. Being a representative of a teachers' union was a difficult and sometimes thankless task during the years after the fall of the Wall.

New Teacher Training Structures

The great difference between teacher training structures in East and West Germany was in the number of phases of the training programmes. The GDR operated a one-phase system in which a subject or subjects were studied concurrently with Education, and periods of teaching practice were integrated into the programme. The secondary school teachers who did degree-level studies took two subjects studied over five years, the fifth year having been introduced in 1982. In their last year, they did twenty-seven weeks of school teaching practice (Schmidt, 1990:531). Students then emerged with dual qualifications making them subject graduates and qualified teachers. This pattern ensured that the numbers of teachers who were going to be available for service could be identified a long time in advance, which facilitated state planning. The FRG, by contrast, operated a two-phase structure in which academic subjects and Education Theory were studied during the first phase at university or College of Teacher Education. In most Länder the theory was accompanied by some school-based work involving observation and a limited amount of practical teaching prior to the candidate taking the First State Examination. The second phase was conducted independently of the universities: *Seminare* (freely translated as Teacher Training Centres) offered a mixture of supervised or monitored school teaching practice and applied education theory which, if successfully completed, enabled the candidate to pass the Second State Examination.

In most Old Länder, clear divisions were made in teacher training according to the candidate's chosen school type. This had the effect of stratifying teachers in a hierarchy based on status, with the most academic – in the upper reaches of the grammar school – inevitably commanding the most prestige and the highest salaries. However, a more radical model existed, for example in North Rhine-Westphalia, whereby the differentiation was not so much according to school type but according to the age range of the children. A difference was made between intermediate and more advanced-level studies with the word *Stufe* used to indicate level or phase and the word *Stufenlehrer* to describe a teacher of a particular age range or academic phase (e.g. I or II).

In West Germany, a one-phase model of teacher training had actually been tried out in Oldenburg and Osnabrück as a special experiment within a system where the Two-Phase Model had operated for many years (see Pritchard, 1993; Ewert, 1981). The new model integrated practical teaching into the academic programme and inserted sufficient periods of teaching practice for candidates to emerge with the equivalent of passes in their First and Second State Examinations. The One-Phase Model had the advantages of keeping study periods relatively short, of integrating theory and practice, and of motivating students strongly. Subjects and Education were studied concurrently and in this respect it was similar to the traditional East German model. By the time unification had come about, the One-Phase Model had been discontinued in the Federal Republic and was no longer a possible education 'export' to the East.

The fact that it had not prevailed did not mean that it was a poor model: on the contrary, some of the main objections to it were of a mechanistic type, for example regarding the length and phasing of teaching practice. Interpersonal rivalries too played a role in the downfall of the One-Phase

Model. It involved professors and lecturers at university in a more practical role than was traditional in German Faculties or Schools of Education. This sometimes stimulated new creativity which has left a legacy reaching into the present. The University runs an annual Education Week which brings together in joint communication representatives from schools, higher education and administration. In Oldenburg, Professor Hilbert Meyer has become famous in educational circles all over Germany for his books – illustrated by his own witty drawings – which unite theory and practice, and his lectures which incorporate activities for the students. It was a feature of the new model that professors and lecturers journeyed to schools to visit and assess their students on teaching practice. These people were very highly qualified academically but their untraditional presence at the chalk-face stimulated the jealousy of teacher trainers in the Seminare who had spent many years in practical teaching and resented the incursion of the 'theoreticians' from the universities. Thus, the involvement of university staff – which at first seemed so praiseworthy – eventually came to be perceived negatively and was used as ammunition against the One-Phase Model's proponents. In addition, the Model suffered from legal difficulties: as always in Germany, it was very important to have a proper legal basis for an educational activity. The legal enabling machinery for the One-Phase Model came much too late to be effective. It was not possible to ensure that other West German Länder would accept teachers trained according to the One-Phase Model. Each Land had the right to decide what it would accept and what not. The unusual nature of the One-Phase Model proved to be a fatal handicap by making its graduates less professionally mobile than if they had been trained on the mainstream model. Yet when all was said and done, the One-Phase Model was one of the most effective ever devised for ensuring a close relationship between theory and practice and for cutting excessive study completion times. It would have suited the New Bundesländer well.

If there were already problems about mutual recognition of qualifications even within the Old Bundesländer, it was clear that the New Bundesländer would be seriously disadvantaged by adopting a model deviating from the West German norm. In any case, the Easterners themselves were inclined to try something new; at the point when the GDR broke up, De Maiziere had in fact been about to introduce the Two-Phase Model. The Wissenschaftsrat recommended that this Model be developed in the New Länder and the recommendation was implemented – with corresponding major effects on curriculum and staff in higher education. Compared with what it had been in the GDR, the practical element was greatly de-emphasised in the First Phase, reducing the need for university staff to supervise in schools and conduct practical studies. Lecturers feared for their jobs. The emphasis on teaching competence had been a marked feature of higher education in the GDR and had attracted the admiration of the Wissenschaftsrat (WR, 1991:104, 114). Under the influence of professors from the West, East German Education departments became much more theory oriented and the previous strong relationship between theory and practice was eroded. Even so, the East German structure was still too skills oriented for some of the West German professors, one of whom told the present author that such an approach was 'superficial' and suggested that the Fachhochschule rather than the university was the right place for those who wanted a skills-based course.

The content of the First Phase was broadly regulated by Study Ordinances but was not fine-tuned to prepare students for the Second Phase. East German staff of the newly established Seminare not unnaturally expected that the Education professors at the universities would gear their First Phase subject content to the needs of the Second Phase so that there would be a sound relationship between theory and practice, even though they were working with a consecutive rather than a concurrent model. West German staff at the Seminare knew better than to expect this: the (mostly West German) university professors asserted their right to academic freedom and continued to teach and research as they pleased, not as the Seminare felt would best serve the students as a preparation for the Second Phase. The disjunction between the phases, which was a shortcoming of West German teacher training, was thus perpetuated in the East. An observer who was executive secretary of the Commission on Teacher Training was not uncritical of the outcome of the reformed structures: 'One could criticize the Wissenschaftsrat's recommendations by saying that they do not bring forth any new ideas but rather fix the status quo of the West for the new states' (Schreier, 1991:38).

It is true that innovations were limited by the need for federal compatibility. However, one attempt to achieve some reform of teacher education is the Potsdam Model, which arose in the context of the German unification process. The blueprint, launched in July 1991 by Professor Wolfgang Edelstein of the Max Planck Institute in Berlin, is 'export oriented' in that it is intended to be influential in the whole of Germany (Jahnke, 1996:21). It is a two-phase model, as indeed it has to be if its graduates are to be acceptable outside Brandenburg, but it aims to bring the two phases closer together by linking subject study, Education and practical teaching experience, and by overlapping the courses taken by primary and secondary trainees. The following research centres have been established: an Interdisciplinary Centre for Research into Youth and Socialisation, an Interdisciplinary Centre of Research into Teaching and Learning, and an Interdisciplinary Centre for Research into Pedagogy and Teacher Training, which is to form the organisational core of the Model. Interestingly, one of its tasks is to analyse the subject LER critically as it develops. Subject methodology specialists carry the heavy responsibility of integrating the elements of the programme and linking academic subjects with education (ibid.:25). They are to be assisted by educationalists who work half of the time in schools and the other half at the University; also by guest professors who may local or from abroad. Practical Teaching Studies have a special integrative role in that they help coordinate content and Education. The aim is to mount a modular course which will help bridge the gap between the First and Second Phases, which will give an equal education to future teachers at various levels and in different school types, and which will do justice to the demands of the classroom and of academic excellence.

Jahnke (1996), himself a Westerner and a mathematician employed at the University of Potsdam, judges that the Potsdam Model works better for future primary than for post-primary teachers (ibid.:24). Most of the academics, when newly appointed, were enthusiastic about a reform model, but they brought with them their own preconditioning. After a certain period (typically about two years), their commitment tended to wane, and their old norms and experiences reasserted themselves. Subjects and Education diverged and seemed as divorced from each other as ever. The Practical Teaching Studies were supposed to be supervised by university personnel, but the highly qualified academics were sometimes reluctant to perform these service activities, and found it more beneficial in career terms to prioritise research. The Mittelbau were of course well placed to help supervise in schools, but they had a lower status and the University of Potsdam would have been stepping out of line by giving them too salient a role. Similar personnel-related problems had occurred in the Oldenburg/Osnabrück One-Phase experiment two decades previously, and it is difficult for any observer of German teacher training to disagree with Professor Klaus Ulich (1997) of the University of Munich when he writes:

> In the end, although I too am involved, I have to say that many shortcomings of teacher education arise from the qualifications of the higher education staff. If, as in Bavaria, personal experience of teaching is an entry requirement only for [professors of] Education and Subject Methodology, but not for other educationalists, subject specialists and psychologists, then it is inevitable that there will be a lack of vocational focus, to the disadvantage of the students. (p. 57)

Easterners Learn New School Law

East German teachers came to enjoy much greater freedom as a result of unification, but the price which they had to pay for this was an increased degree of insecurity. This existed on many different levels both inside and outside the classroom. The former tight, prescriptive guidelines were replaced by more general guidelines which left scope for the teachers' judgement and creativity but also sometimes left them feeling insecure as to whether they were acting correctly and in keeping with expectations within a Rechtsstaat (state based on the rule of Law) as understood and practised in the Federal Republic.

The legal tradition of the GDR had been rather nebulous. It did have a catalogue of basic rights but it was not possible to insist on them legally. The principal of a school was its sole and individual leader and exercised this leadership on the basis of the decisions of the SED Party. Pupils were not seen as individuals entitled to certain rights but rather as members of a Collective to be consolidated and developed. The FDJ and the Pioneers took the place of School Councils. The Parents' Committee was under the control of the school principal and members were elected in public rather than by secret ballot. After German unification, teachers had to make the transition to becoming citizens of a Rechtsstaat rather than subjects in a dictatorship, and had to learn how to promote democratic values so that their pupils could learn the interrelationships between basic values, rights and freedoms as propounded in the Western societal model (BFSFJ, 1994:207). The Institutes of Continuing Education, such as Pädagogisches Landesinstitut für Bildung (PLIB) at Ludwigsfelde in Brandenburg, ran courses which showed teachers how to interpret the Law and implement it in their everyday lives. They learned how to contextualise the new school law in a hierarchy ranging from everyday classroom life right up to the Constitutions of their Länder and the Basic Law of the state. They were taught to operate the committee organs of joint decision-making intended to inculcate democratic ways of thinking into the young. At PLIB, they were presented with case studies like the following (cases collected and interpreted by Weiland, 1995).

Case Study 1: Monika and the Miniskirt

Monika Meyer, form 10B, always comes to school dressed in the height of fashion. Especially this summer, she frequently appears in airy, short dresses and skirts. Her class teacher, Frau Lange, has often warned her that this sort of clothing is unsuitable for school. When Monika appears one day in a very short miniskirt, Frau Lange immediately sends her home, telling her that she must put on something suitable before she will be allowed to come back.

Case Study 2: Verena and the T-Shirt

Verena Lurz is very interested in politics. She is keeping a very critical eye on what is currently happening in the Bund and Länder. Before the elections to the Bundestag, she appears in school in a red T-shirt. On the front is printed 'Stop Kohl now!' The back is decorated with the Party slogan: 'Politics begins with opposition.' Her class teacher, Herr Schwarz, is of the opinion that this T-shirt is not in keeping with the principle of the political neutrality of the school. He therefore asks Verena to keep her jacket on during class and to come into school next day without the T-shirt.

The next morning, the School Principal, Herr Liedtke, asks Frau Lange and Herr Schwarz to come and see him in his office. He requires Frau Lange to apologise to Monika. Frau Lange is outraged by this and defends herself by saying that making young people dress appropriately is part of a decent school education. Herr Schwarz is instructed that the principle of political neutrality and reticence is not applicable to pupils; on the contrary, one of the most important tasks of the school is to encourage pupils to form political opinions. The class teacher objects that this is best achieved not by propagating a single opinion but by taking a broad political view.

Questions to the Teachers Doing an In-Service Course

1. To what Articles of the Basic Law or the Land Constitution can the participants appeal?
2. Make a judgement about the actions of Frau Lange, Herr Schwarz and Herr Liedtke. Is there a legal basis for their arguments?
3. What would you have done in these cases?

The Commentary

Monika can appeal to the general provisions of Article 2 (1) of the Basic Law in which the free development of the personality is guaranteed. The limits lie in the constitutional law of morality and the rights of others. In the decision as to whether the miniskirt can be tolerated or not, it must be remembered that the GDR would have been quite arbitrary. It sometimes happened that pupils who wore jeans or long hair were expelled from secondary school. There are examples of pupils wearing a crucifix being denied the right to sit Abitur.... The new rule of law is in contrast to this arbitrariness; it respects the personality and restricts the rights of the individual only in so far as absolutely necessary to keep inner peace. Especially in the New Bundesländer, Article 2 should be generously interpreted. The guiding principle is that human rights by their very nature are defensive rights of the citizen against his or her state (represented here by the school), a fundamental thought which permeates the whole of European and American constitutional history.

Verena Lurz can appeal to the right to free expression of opinion laid down in Article 5 of the Basic Law.... The school Law of the Land Brandenburg states in paragraph 13 that this Law is also valid in school in so far as the educational mission of the school is not jeopardised.

The Constitutional Court has made it clear in several verdicts that freedom of opinion is to be very highly valued. The possibility of making known one's opinion is absolutely essential for the preservation of a free democratic state. Politicians in particular must be prepared to put up with this. The right to the free expression of opinion is open to everyone, hence also to the schoolgirl Verena Lurz. Verena is not obliged to give reasons for her opinion since the freedom of opinion is protected. She would, however, be denied the right to wear a Party badge in school. This would be recruiting for a particular grouping and would be an offence against the principle of party-political neutrality. By contrast, a teacher would be allowed to wear the badge of his or her Union. This is directed at colleagues not at pupils....

The earlier view that schools are an institution in which pupils are subjected to a particular power relationship was no longer sustainable after the introduction of the Basic Law. Basic rights are valid in the school for staff and pupils;... it has taken some time for this legal interpretation to become commonly understood. The concept of the power of the institution has a long authoritarian tradition. Now the dominant idea is that school must be constituted according to principles based on the rule of law and democracy. Only then can it fulfil one of its most important tasks: the education of democratically minded, committed citizens. Without this, democracy has no chance of survival. School must make democracy a living reality.

Source: Jörg Weiland, Case Study Collection used at an in-service course for School Principals at PLIB, Ludwigsfelde (29.03.95) where the author was a participant observer; written commentary sent to the author (16.5.95) at her request.

✵ ✵ ✵

Courses such as these were systematically undertaken in the New Bundesländer and were appreciated because of their immediate relevance to practice and classroom reality. Participants were expected to disseminate knowledge gained from these courses within the schools where they worked. It was an unfamiliar thought to many of them that all persons, including teachers and pupils, are carriers of inalienable basic rights which they may seek to enforce by law; that these rights cannot be set aside in schools; that pupils and teachers cannot be handled in an arbitrary manner by the school administration; and that school committees have an important, indeed decisive, contribution to make to communal life. The complexities of the law were sometimes confusing to all concerned: Article 6 (2) of the Basic Law guarantees the educational right of the *parent*, while Article 7 (1) guarantees the educational right of the *state*. Thus different rights stand in conflict with one another. An example of the interplay of such influences can be seen in the vexed issue of secondary school choice. Officially, parents can choose which school type their child shall attend; the will of the child, too, has to be taken into consideration – progressively more so as she or he becomes older. The state, however, sets the admission requirements, and if the child is not academically in a position to benefit from the school type in question, the parents cannot force through attendance at the desired school type. At first sight, it looks as if the conflicting rights could become dead-locked, but the resolution of such impasses is the very stuff of democracy. As Weiland (1993) states:

> Without convinced democrats, democracy has no chance of survival. In a demo-
> cratic state, interests clash with one another. Conflicts arise. The regulation of
> interests and the solution of conflict by peaceful, legal means are part of the core
> of our democratic basic order. Our Constitution is so designed that power is bal-
> anced between government and parliament, between Bund and Länder. It is
> impossible for any single organ of state to arrogate all power to itself and to
> dominate the others. At the end of a conflict, compromise usually takes place; it
> makes everyone dissatisfied to a certain extent and it also affords everyone a cer-
> tain degree of satisfaction.

Teaching of this sort was an important part of West Germany's resocial-isation of the East German schools. There were of course many counter-vailing forces, such as the residual GDR traditions and the sheer pressure of economic stringency. In schools, the participation in school committees was sometimes disappointing, and once the novelty had worn off, apathy became a problem. This was, however, the case in the West as well as in the East. In essence, however, the study of the law was intended to help create citizens rather than subjects and to contribute towards a new ethos of human dignity and self-confidence. It is a pity that such study could not have been made more widely and systematically available in walks of life other than teaching.

The Aftermath

Human Relationships

As regards interpersonal relations within mixed East-West school and uni-versity staffs, it would perhaps be true to say that Easterners had more of an idea of how to get on with Westerners than vice versa. East Germans had exposure to Western culture through television whereas Westerners had no such exposure towards the East; this left them unsure of how to interpret behaviour patterns and situations. Sometimes the negativity of the East-erners was directed against the recently appointed West German professors who came to provide 'new blood'. Mayntz (1994a:303) wryly points out that left to themselves, the East Germans were capable of vigorous criticism of those who had misused power in the old regime but when confronted with an incursion of West Germans, they closed ranks. Many of the West-erners had children at school in the West as well as partners with jobs and pension schemes. Accommodation was expensive in the New Bundeslän-der and the deficit of suitable housing for those wishing to relocate from the West was acknowledged by the Wissenschaftsrat (6.7.90:16). Many Westerners were reluctant to uproot their families and so they commuted, some of them being nicknamed Di-Mi-Do (Tuesday-Wednesday-Thurs-day) professors. This gave rise to 'problems of acceptance' by Easterners (BWFT, 1993:7). Failure to take up permanent residence was interpreted as a lukewarm commitment to educational reconstruction in East Ger-many, or as financial greed for the (temporary) subsidy paid for working in the East – bitterly termed 'bush money' because East Germans felt their country was regarded by some as the equivalent of the African 'bush'. Con-versely, however, most Westerners who did decide to move lock, stock and barrel to the East were warmly welcomed because their action implied acceptance and commitment.

Many new West German professors had attained C4 (top-salary scale) posts in the New Bundesländer, whereas Easterners often had to make do with lesser posts (*Nature*, 1994). Some of these newcomers had never held Chairs before and were thus completely inexperienced. Why had these peo-ple not been able to attain Chairs at home? The suspicion was rife that the West was exporting its 'second-raters' to the East, thereby possibly condemn-ing the East German universities to second-class rank in the near future; and when these Westerners in due course retired, it was feared that the number of Easterners would be insufficient to replace them (Krull, 1994:213; WR, 1992, Part 1:25). It therefore looked as if the promotion blockage would last for many decades and keep Easterners from occupying the top positions in their own institutions. Ambitious young East German scholars and civil ser-vants were perplexed about the unwritten ground rules of the 'game' they were now playing. For example, it seemed obvious to many that it would be advantageous to join a political Party in order to advance professionally, but the difficulty was, which one? Resentment existed too about the very fact that institutions in East Germany had been subjected to evaluation. Teichler (1994) points out that the higher education culture of West Germany was relatively unfamiliar with assessment and performance indicators; there was a perceived inequity about applying these to the East when they had been so little used in the West. Moreover, the Wissenschaftsrat's style was sometimes negatively perceived. Teichler concludes: 'Despite existing, long-standing analyses of the shortcomings of the West German higher education system, in the end there was a lack of courage to undertake fundamental reforms.... Hence, one form of misery replaced another' (ibid.: 224).

Yet it would be facile to judge the Western contribution with unmitigated harshness. It was true that West German higher education was in much need of reform and precisely because it was so fossilised, many academics took up Chairs in the East. They hoped to be able to innovate and to create something better than had existed at home, and in this respect, they were idealists. Some took up posts in East Germany at considerable personal sacrifice and inconvenience, but in the firm belief that by doing so, they were serving their country. Distinguished staff came out of retirement and went to serve their stint in the New Länder. Hundreds of officials and civil servants from the de Maiziere era onwards regularly flew from Cologne/ Bonn to Berlin/Schönefeld in the so-called 'Beamtenbomber' to assist in the reconstruction of education in the NBL. Some professors were seconded or released for a period to serve as foundation Deans of Education, posts which were extremely onerous in their demands. To give one example drawn from the University of Leipzig, the tasks of the Founding Dean included overseeing the integration of the local College of Education into the University; deciding whether to take on any professors from the former GDR (he decided against this); appointing new professors; reviewing the library provision and obtaining new books (he describes the library he found on arrival as a 'poison cupboard'!); raising money from firms and from the Rotary Club to provide books and equipment; setting up new courses in initial and continuing education. Most of these duties were typical for all founding Deans. The Leipzig Dean had a personal weekly schedule which involved spending Monday, Tuesday and Wednesday in Leipzig, Thursday back at his home University cramming his week's lecturing there into one day, Friday doing his administration, Saturday and Sunday doing preparation for the following week. Not surprisingly, this man had a heart attack at the end of his three-year assignment, yet he still describes his time in the East with affection as 'eine schöne Zeit' and looks proudly upon the framed University of Leipzig tribute hanging in his study.

How Did Students Fare under the New Regime?

What about the students? They were at the receiving end of all this change and it had the potential to be either destructive or constructive in their lives. A considerable achievement of the reformers and the bureaucrats was that the education of the 100,000 young ex-GDR people in the system at the time of the Wende was *not* interrupted and could be successfully concluded. But to what extent, if at all, was the new higher education landscape perceived as an improvement on what it had been in the GDR?

An illuminating picture of what the changes in East German higher education mean to students is provided by the 14th Social Survey of the German Student Body conducted by the Higher Education Information System (HIS) for the German University Students' Social Welfare Organisation, financially supported for this purpose by the Federal Ministry of Education, Science, Research and Technology (Schnitzer, 1995). This survey of the social circumstances of German students ranges from politically sensitive issues such as participation in higher education right down to relatively mundane concerns about where students take their meals, what mode of transport they use to reach their place of study and what their health problems are. Such surveys have been carried out since 1951, recently at three-year intervals, and are regarded in Germany as an important aid to decision-making on social and higher education policy. This is the second such census which has been taken since German unification and as such naturally includes the New Bundesländer. Its central interest for the present work is that it provides high-quality data which enable the reader to discern trends and developments in higher education within the united Germany.

As we have seen above, access to higher education in the German Democratic Republic was limited to a small percentage of the age cohort. After unification, the authorities set out to increase participation rates (12 per cent to 13 per cent). By 1993, when the survey was carried out, the HE participation rate was 21.5 per cent in the New Bundesländer and 32.1 per cent in the Old Bundesländer. This represents considerable progress in increasing access to HE in East Germany. In the OBL, although there has been a rise in the participation of children of blue collar workers (primarily due to attendance at Fachhochschulen rather than universities), lower income families are still underrepresented in higher education: in 1994, only 14 per cent of all students came from lower social backgrounds in the OBL – a drop from 23 per cent over the past twelve years. In view of the great efforts made in the GDR to break the educational privilege of the 'exploiting classes', it may come as a surprise that for the New Bundesländer the figure was even smaller – only 10 per cent. The problem of underrepresentation of the working classes in higher education was already giving concern in the GDR (Fritsch and Rommel, 1987). Higher education is thus still inescapably socially selective: even in the erstwhile land of 'workers and peasants' over half the students came from academic families (Liscka, 1997:255). More of the students' parents in the NBL than in the OBL had the requisite qualification for entry into higher education: 43 per cent in the Old Länder and 61 per cent in the New Länder. It is therefore clear that there is a very strong syndrome of self-reproduction among the more highly educated, and that socialist policies have been unable to reverse this trend.

A feature of higher education in the GDR was that study times were shorter and students were on average younger than in West Germany. The age profile as revealed by the 14th Social Survey shows that although students in the New Bundesländer are still younger than in the Old Bundesländer, the mean age is increasing (see Table 6.4).

Table 6.4   Mean Age of Students in OBL and NBL, 1991 and 1994

	OBL	NBL
1991	24.9	22.5
1994	25.5	23.4

Source: Schnitzer, 1995.

However, East German students still want to get through their courses quickly and are much more successful at doing so than West German students. Seventy-four per cent in the NBL compared with only 44 per cent in the OBL universities complete studies in the required period (Buck-Bechler, Jahn and Lewin, 1997:515). The conditions in NBL universities are favourable enough to allow the Easterners to finish on schedule, and it is important for their competitiveness that they should continue to do so. The quality of the East German student experience is now very different to what it was in the GDR. In many disciplines they are exposed to lecturers from the West who have different expectations of them and whose teaching style is less 'pedagogical' than they are used to. Westerners' expectations of independence sometimes unnerve the Easterners, accustomed as they were to being carefully led through structured courses. The former year-cohort Seminare no longer exist and their friendly support is missed, but the erosion of support structures has not (or not yet) resulted in undue lengthening of the study period.

Rapid completion of study courses in the GDR was facilitated by state maintenance grants for students. The 14th Social Survey shows that nearly one out of two students is now commercially employed either during breaks or during the semester, and as a result there is an increasing tendency for 'job' time to increase at the expense of study time, though this is still less pronounced than in the Old Länder. In 1994, the job activity rate for the New Länder was 49 per cent as opposed to 66 per cent in the Old Länder. Average monthly income for the NBL students is DM 954 compared with DM 1,343 in the OBL; one-fourth of students in the New Bundesländer have maximum incomes of only DM 700 so it is obvious that student poverty is greater in the NBL where the student labour market is still less developed than in West Germany. Money for student maintenance is derived from several sources. Parents are students' most important source of income both in East and in West Germany (it is not perhaps widely realised internationally that German parents who support grown-up children are given family allowances until their offspring are twenty-seven). This is a big change in a country where students used to derive all maintenance from the state and so were independent of their parents. In the New Bundesländer, BAföG loan aid (under the Federal Training Assistance Act) is the second most important source of funds for students; it is claimed by 56.4 per cent in the NBL as opposed to only 30.4 per cent in the Old Bundesländer. Although East German students have had a long tradition of state grants, they are gradually reducing their dependence on state loans: the percentage of BAföG recipients actually fell by one-third in the NBL between 1991 and 1994. This mirrors a similar movement in the Western OBL where even moderately well-off parents usually try to ensure that their children will not emerge from university with a heavy burden of debt to pay off.

Rent is a substantial item in any student's budget. Students from East Germany traditionally lived in dormitories which were very cheap and 44 per cent of them, compared with only 12 per cent in West Germany, still live in such accommodation. The majority of them (54 per cent) share a room with one other person and 20 per cent share with three or even four roommates. Since 1991, the percentage of rooms with two or more beds has fallen – so living conditions have improved – but there are still major deficiencies in kitchen and bathroom facilities. In the Old Bundesländer most students would like to have their own flats and 22 per cent of them have actually achieved this in sole occupancy (compared with only 11 per cent in the New Bundesländer). Rent takes up a larger proportion of students' money in the West than in the East (one-third as opposed to one-fourth) but the structural condition of student housing in inferior in the East – though regional variation is lower.

A survey by Buck-Bechler, Jahn and Lewin (1995) corroborates the major findings of the HIS survey and adds some new insights about students' study choices and perceptions. East German students, confronted with the choice of studying in the New or the Old Bundesländer, typically decide on an institution in the New rather than in the Old Länder. Economic factors are vitally important in making this decision: it is, after all, much cheaper to study at a university near one's home. In addition, 90 per cent of young East Germans have been able to gain a place in the course of their choice (in West Germany the corresponding figure is 85 per cent), and thereafter are reluctant to change institutions. Indeed, after a short period (the first year of study) students have 'bonded' with their universities and only 4 per cent of those surveyed would not choose the same institution again (p. 50). East German students have a slightly different profile from West German students. They want to complete their studies rapidly and to this end, they welcome well-structured courses with an emphasis on achievement. The West Germans, however, some of whom come to the East to circumvent strict *numerus clausus* entry requirements or are 'lured' by special subject offerings, have a more free-and-easy attitude towards study and value critical exchange of academic opinion (p. 72). East Germans overwhelmingly feel that they are offered good conditions for study, even if some of the student accommodation is substandard. For the moment at least, universities in the NBL have not become excessively large and have not developed the same problems as in the West. For the first time in current history it is possible to escape from the constraints of the state Plan, and young people are free to choose courses of study according to their subject interest and their vocational aspirations. They come into higher education well equipped (with better Abitur results on average than in the West), they are highly motivated and they want to achieve high marks (p. 51). Faced with this freedom and favourable study conditions, East German students view the deterioration in financial support and their increased dependence on their parents as less than significant (p. 72).

Aulerich and Stein (1997) in an East-West survey of students (Dresden/Dortmund) endorse the positive findings of other researchers about the NBL studentship. Almost half of the Dresden students believed that the Wende has had a positive effect on the extent of their educational opportunities and choices. Admittedly, their financial circumstances were less than satisfactory and they disliked taking money from their parents, but few classified themselves as 'losers' as a result of the Wende. Instead, it was their parents who felt that their cultural capital had been diminished by the Wende. The authors conclude that the young Easterners are seizing their chance, and are well able to manage the social transition process to West German norms and institutions. It would be an error to suppose that their East German socialisation process has left them ill equipped to cope with ambivalent situations typical of restructuring. In fact, the GDR background of state doctrine on the one hand, and the protective nature of family life on the other, may combine to develop in them a special capacity for adequate adaptive social behaviour (ibid.:140).

In most respects, then, East German students are clearly better off after unification. They even have a new form of student representation called the Studentenrat (StuRa) which, though not strongly politicised, is gaining in power and might become a model for West German universities (Hörig and Schomann, 1997). The most positive development is the increased age participation rate in East Germany, though the small representation of lower social classes is still a problem, as it also is in the West. Before the

Wende, it was almost impossible to obtain passports and travel; now about 21 per cent of the NBL students spend study-related time abroad (HIS, 1995). Previously they were locked into courses which they had to finish expeditiously in order to fulfil the Plan but now they can switch subjects or institutions, though most do not exercise this option as often as their compatriots in the OBL. These are important aspects of academic freedom as conceived in the Federal Republic: free choice of subject and freedom of teaching and learning are guaranteed in the constitution, though in practice both are subject to certain constraints. The two surveys just discussed clearly show how these freedoms bring with them new problems for the Easterners: the strain of transferring economic responsibility from the state to individuals and their families, slightly longer study times and the need to become economically active in order to finance study. By and large, however, the students seem to feel that the advantages of the Wende far outweigh the disadvantages.

Change and Its Implications for Women Teachers, Students and Academics

The East German teaching profession, which was about 70 per cent female, faced mighty challenges in coping with unification. This was also true of female academics. In the GDR, socialist concepts of gender equality had resulted in measures to enable women to combine job and family duties with gainful employment and/or the pursuit of qualifications, as necessary. After the Wende, many of the support structures which they had enjoyed were removed or reduced; the social policies of the East were rolled back and teachers had to cope with circumstances of unprecedented difficulty without the resources to which they had been accustomed. School teachers' achievements in mastering professional change drew the attention and approval of many, including a West German official in the Ministry of Education in Saxony-Anhalt who, after joint school visits and discussions with the author, wrote to her as follows:

> The introduction of a new (federal German) school system has led to great changes in all domains of school life. Especially in Social Sciences and in Foreign Languages, new subject areas and indeed completely new subjects, had to be mastered in a short period of time. In vocational schools, the changes were such as to confront teachers with special burdens. In all domains, the new technology took teachers by storm and pupils suddenly had to be prepared for jobs which had never existed before in the GDR. New syllabuses had to be worked up and the methodology was different from that in the GDR. New school structures were introduced. In many places buildings had to be erected and specialist rooms equipped, often on the basis of local initiative. In addition to all of this, all staff had to undergo a wide variety of Further and Continuing Education

courses and even university in-service education. An additional difficulty was that for many young people and also for many adults the familiar structure of values and norms collapsed and they had to acquaint themselves with new democratic rules. Looming over them was the problem of very high unemployment – for GDR citizens a completely unknown phenomenon.

All this has been admirably worked through and mastered in the schools; it deserves the highest admiration. (Personal communication, Kultusministerium des Landes Sachsen-Anhalt, 11.05.95)

Despite all the difficulties and problems, few teachers really wanted to return to the old regime; they found many more advantages than disadvantages in the new order. Thus van Buer et al. (1995) found that in the sample they surveyed in 1992, teachers' levels of satisfaction remained constant, and the teachers looked on their burden as a potentially positive challenge. Döbert and Rudolf (1995) likewise came to the conclusion that East German teachers have – in their own opinion – coped well with the changes (though those in comprehensive schools have particular difficulties). However, the authors paint a subtle picture of a profession which is 'afraid of doing something wrong', and not yet able to make maximum use of the room for manoeuvre which is now available to them. Ex-GDR teachers (particularly female ones) tend to cling to what they know, that is to GDR pedagogy and practices of whose value they are firmly and deeply convinced (ibid.:193). Teachers who change schools are more critical in their judgement than those who remain put, as are teachers of Music, Art, Sport and practical subjects. Most teachers content themselves with minor modifications to their practical work and have not yet fully seized the magnitude of the conceptual and philosophical changes underlying the new system.

During a group interview with the present author (20.3.95), teachers of the Franz Friedrich Gymnasium in Parchim had an opportunity to outline their perceptions of the changes which had taken place since unification. They expressed relief at the removal of intense pressure to get through all of the syllabus by a specified time and enjoyed the opportunity to adapt material to the needs and interests of their pupils. They were able to be more pupil-centred and make use of games and creative strategies. The quality of their relationship with the children became more companionable and the possibility of a genuine exchange of opinions arose. It was pointed out that in the GDR, opinions could always be exchanged so long as they matched the official line! Teachers had been afraid of being betrayed by pupils or the FDJ for expressing dissident opinions, resulting in a bifurcation between their officially expressed and their personal opinions. The new freedom of self-expression was unreservedly welcomed, though it was admitted that it was sometimes associated with discipline difficulties in the classroom. The history teachers said that their personal knowledge of history had been dramatically transformed by the introduction of new textbooks and by in-service courses. In general, the new textbooks provided much stimulation and aroused enthusiasm in the pupils. Teachers were, however, sometimes at a loss to know how to handle them; this was partly because they were less prescriptive than in the GDR and partly because the language differed from that of the old textbooks which were full of the rhetoric of class antagonism. The teachers' relationship with parents had changed considerably, and although parents gained much more power after unification, they were not always sure how to behave at parent-teacher meetings. It took time for them to become more open and when they did, some brought many of their personal problems into the discussion.

Commitment and hard work brought success, and Händle (1996b) believes that this successful mastery of a difficult situation says much for the quality of East German teachers' GDR qualifications and for the skills which they were able to transfer from their personal to their professional lives. The teaching profession was primarily a female one, and competences such as child care transferred from family life could be redeployed to good effect in professional life. Händle adopts the concept of 'double qualification' to describe the mixture of personal and professional competencies particularly (though not exclusively) characteristic of women. Experientially derived knowledge is highly functional and those who possess it sometimes prefer it over formal qualifications. Händle (1993) illustrates this point in an earlier case study of a female teacher, Frau H., who actually gives up a retraining course in Mathematics because she feels that the subject knowledge peddled by the new regime is rather alien to classroom practice and not necessarily superior to her existing experiential knowledge. The retraining process is conducive to the new authorities asserting control, promoting competition and establishing a hierarchy which includes some and excludes others. In the end, Frau H. acquiesces in exclusion (meaning that she accepts that she will never rate highly in terms of West German salary and status). In the process she becomes a loser, but she does feel that she has supported her 'own side' and this is very important to her.

In East Germany it was taken for granted that job and family life could be combined. After the Wende, it became much more difficult to do so because most of the previous support structures (institutional child care, for example) were either removed or came with a greatly increased price tag. Some women students decided against starting families at all, and most thought that it had become much more difficult to bring up a child whilst at the same time completing one's studies. Händle (1996b) suggests that the decline of the birth rate in the NBL could be understood as a protest against how difficult it had become to combine child care and study or work. In the GDR, by the end of their time at university, most students were married and over half of those married had children. According to the 14th Social Survey discussed above, the percentage of married students in the NBL fell by half in the period from 1991 to 1994: by 1994 only 8 per cent of students were married in the NBL and 6 per cent in the OBL; only 7 per cent of all students in the Old and New Bundesländer had children. The dramatic fall in the rate of marriage among East German students is certainly a response to changed social climate and increased financial stringency. It is in keeping with a massive demographic crisis in East Germany as a whole where marriage rates are only half what they were in 1989 and live births have plummeted.

The participation of women in higher education began to fall after unification (though it varied significantly according to subject). In 1990, it was 7 per cent less than in 1989 though the absolute number of female students rose, as did that of men. The reduction of job security in the Mittelbau hit women especially badly because child-bearing and family responsibilities made them averse to risk. The subjects most likely to be terminated were in the Humanities or in the Social Sciences where there were many women staff. Therefore, women suffered disproportionately from job losses, although there was a special funding programme to help them to obtain the high-level qualifications they needed to get ahead.[7] West German social policies discouraged women from working, and the application of these policies to the East quickly forced women into dependency status (Young, 1993). In the upper echelons of academe, women had been just about as badly underrepresented in the GDR as they were in the FRG, and it was not until the middle of the 1980s that the SED began to construe the gender imbalance in top university positions as a 'problem'; consequently the same low percentage of female professors (about 5 per cent) prevailed in the New Bundesländer as in the Old (Klemm et al., 1992:144, 147).

Conclusion

Dieter Simon, the outspoken former Chair of the Wissenschaftsrat, was very critical of the reform of East German higher education. At the summer school of the union Gewerkschaft für Erziehung und Wissenschaft in Sylt (1995), he made statements such as: 'The ruins of Western academe were the exemplar and the costly model for the upturn in the East…. The West had no conceptual framework for the restructuring. And those in the East who were influential thought back to their own youth – but that was in the

---

7. HSP III: Bund-Länder-Kommission, Drs 96.27, Hochschulprogramm III: Gemeinsames Hochschulprogramm III (HSP III), Bonn, 9.9.1996.

1920s' (Simon, 1995). He believed that mediocrity had triumphed and that there had been a renaissance of the Ivory Tower and of the old-style Ordinarius with chain of office and gown; some of these, he added, were jumped-up post-doctoral Fellows who had been waiting for years for Chairs in the West – in vain! Kiel (1996:168) took a similar view, arguing that although sacrifices had to be made to ensure the freedom of teaching and learning in the East, there was also a great reassertion of professorial dominance and privilege.

The Wissenschaftsrat is not short of criticisms about the German higher education system, and has already formulated them in an extremely trenchant manner (WR, 6.7.1990; WR, 22.1.1993). There is no doubt that these criticisms will inform the debate on the revision of the Federal Framework Law for Higher Education, and change, when it comes, will be applied to West as well as to East Germany. There would have been no point after the Wende in creating two different systems within the one country. To do so would have been to disadvantage the Easterners even more seriously than they were already. The East German students have a number of positive things going for them: a mentality which drives them to finish their courses rapidly, a group consciousness which leads to mutual support and help, and relatively small universities with reasonable staff-student ratios – so far. The first two factors are attitudinal, therefore 'soft' rather than structural, and potentially susceptible to elimination by an overindividualistic culture. If the surveys cited above are accurate (Schnitzer, 1995; Aulerich and Stein, 1997), the young people who were just leaving school at the time of the Wende seem to have ridden the storm very successfully and to have preserved the hope and optimism which should be their birthright. The great successes of the reform of higher education must surely be the increase in access; the abolition of political grounds as criteria for entry into higher education; the increased freedom to choose whatever subject discipline one wishes; and the newly established Fachhochschulen. It is very important that all the good features of East German higher education should be preserved. After all, the Easterners need any competitive edge they can get, and East German universities can be attractive to Westerners too, but only if they build on their strengths.

An adequate number of permanent academic positions is necessary to support the NBL staff-student ratios in higher education, and there is room for debate about what the level of these academic positions should be. It is a pity that it is out of keeping with the West German tradition to have a substantial layer of *permanent* or *long-contract* staff like the lecturers/senior lecturers who form the vast majority of university staff in the UK and whose presence contributes a great deal to pastoral care and satisfying intellectual experience for students. These features of British universities help to make them internationally attractive in a way that Rüttgers (n.d.) fears German universities are not. Surely not every permanent member of staff needs to be qualified at post-doctoral level, have dozens of publications to his or her name and be aged about forty before starting out on his or her career proper. The Mittelbau in the GDR no doubt needed to be shaken up for ideological reasons, but in GDR days it helped to provide a supportive environment for students. The type of Mittelbau tradition in West Germany where people spend the best years of their lives trying to achieve their post-doctoral qualification – only to find that there is no university post for them and they have to leave the institution – strikes some foreigners as wasteful at best and exploitative at worst. Since these people contribute to research, the productiveness of German academe owes much to those who work in poor conditions of service. A new-style Mittelbau with serious teaching responsibilities and a good percentage of secure posts would be worth considering for both East and West.

Where the higher education reforms are less than successful is in teacher training, which is already severely under fire in the West. An official of the Conference of Rectors in Higher Education (Hochschulrektorenkonferenz (HRK)) in a personal interview with the author produced the following critique:

> Teacher education at the universities is not sound in its present form. I think quite different learning conditions need to exist: teacher education is a more or less chance product of accumulated academic disciplines and subdisciplines; there is no overarching conception, and pedagogy plays such a subordinate role that it cannot function and has no chance of being implemented…. If you ask experienced school practitioners what they think of what the HEIs have to offer in the First Phase of teacher education, you find that they hold it in very low esteem. They tell the trainees that they can forget everything they have learned because it is totally irrelevant to school. No one in higher education is interested in what the schools need: that is the point. Comparative education and the history of education are not going to make people into better classroom teachers. Academics are interested in research, and pedagogy has such a minor role that they are not interested in it. Even professors of Education want to be proper scholars and the students are shunted around between the subjects and Education and have no focal point. (Interview conducted in Bonn, 15.3.1995)

A survey by Jung (1997), who is head of a Teacher Training Centre in Bonn, shows that West German trainee teachers rated the Second Phase on the whole very positively. Kretzer (1997) in the same volume reveals that the First Phase is much less valued than the Second, and is alarmed to find that his trainees have had to wait for so long to get launched on their training that most are well into their thirties, and only 5 per cent are below twenty-five. Ulich (1997) in a wide-ranging review of various published surveys finds that many students are frustrated and angry that their university teacher education has been such a waste of time (p. 54); the academic and the practical just do not come together, and they are ill-prepared for practical work in schools – particularly the grammar schools. They need more school experience and more teaching practice during the First Phase, and they need a form of teacher education which will equip them to deal with the world of today: with drugs, racism and xenophobia, to name but three of the uglier manifestations of modern classroom life.

The sort of union of theory and practice which these trainees desire can hardly be provided by the existing traditional university professors working on the existing structures. The doubtful success of the Potsdam Model testifies to this assertion. Professors make a major contribution in interpreting the world both to participants and to policy-makers in Education, but truly to unite theory and practice for schoolteachers, it is necessary to *do* as well as to think – necessary, in other words, to have firsthand experience of the kind of chalkface, classroom reality for which they are preparing their trainees. This is probably neither a reasonable nor a realistic demand to place on academics qualified to the highest international standards who are almost forty by the time they have completed their Habilitation. It would be almost impossible for them reach such standards if they all also had to be qualified and experienced schoolteachers, as British staff in Education are required to be (and even in this case, there are still complaints in the UK about failure to unite theory and practice). It might be better to employ university professors of Education as academics without responsibility for initial teacher training but with the task of doing research, government consultancy, and dealing with in-service and post-graduate education. Other patterns could be explored for the initial stages of training. If the law were to be changed to ensure that graduates suffered no detriment in terms of salary and conditions of service, then it could be a wise move to locate teacher training in the Fachhochschulen which specialise in applying theory to practice. In such a politically controversial move, it would be essential to guard against a deterioration of finance and status for teachers in all school types.

Chapter 7

IN RETROSPECT

The question must now be posed: What was gained and what was lost in the domain of education as a result of education reforms implemented with huge effort and financial outlay after the Wende?

The restructuring of East German education was a speedy response to a situation of great urgency. If more time had been available, then it would have been possible to adopt a gradualist approach. The East German people had been kept in isolation; they lacked international knowledge and experience of how things were done elsewhere. However, once the blinkers were removed they showed a steep learning curve and a passionate interest in educational matters, especially during the period from 1989–90 before their options were limited by exogenous law. An endogenous education reform wave had already begun prior to the Unification Treaty. The East Germans themselves had taken steps to liberalise their curriculum and syllabuses, and to introduce values education for a pluralistic, not a monistic, society – a values education, moreover, which did not altogether exclude religious knowledge. They also wanted the Dual System of vocational education and grammar schools – until they began to see the effects of a divided post-primary school system. It is not sound to say that these institutions were foisted on East Germans since they were already moving in the direction of change. The ideal would surely have been to allow East German opinion to mature and define itself, so that the people could reform their education system out of their inner convictions and extended experience – an experience which could only have been refined through contact with the wider world. That this was not done was largely due to the factor of speed in the reunification process, and to the conviction in some quarters that 'West was Best'.

Chapter 1 of this book addresses itself to the question of whether unification really had to be introduced so quickly, and the answer is an unequivocal

'Yes'. Such speed was not originally what Chancellor Kohl wanted, but it became a situational political imperative. The union of the two Germanys was in essence a merger, though on a mighty scale, and the experience of mergers both in commerce and in education shows that with very few exceptions, speed is essential to success. Overcaution resulting in a hesitant pace allows oppositional forces to mobilise and to defeat the resolve of the would-be unifiers (see Pritchard, 1993). The fact that speed became a primary consideration influenced the entire style of the restructuring, resulting in the wholesale import (some called it 'imposition') of Western institutions. West Germany achieved unification constitutionally by relying on Article 23 rather than Article 146, which meant that there was no negotiated move to enshrine the most positive features of the East German ethos in a new overarching consensus. The circumstances of unification, the bankruptcy of the GDR, the discreditation of its M-L ideology and the fact that the amalgamation had to be accomplished with speed made it more difficult for East Germans to internalise and 'own' the Western world-view. In such circumstances, it is all the more tempting for teachers in times of tension, puzzlement or disenchantment with the reforms to revert to methodologies and materials of earlier times, even if these are considered 'authoritarian'. At present, no empirical evidence exists to show exactly on what scale this is happening.

The GDR unified school was too stultified, too dreary and too restrictive in access to university-preparatory courses in the EOS. There was a widespread belief that the most able pupils were held back. Yet when it became possible to do a comparative study of achievement in East and West German schools, the BIJU research (1994) could find no empirical evidence that this was in fact so, and subject-specific surveys in Geography (Niemz and Stoltmann, 1992) and History (Borries and Lehmann, 1992) showed the superiority of the East German pupils on most measures. These studies have been frequently quoted because they were carried out just after the fall of the Wall and can never again be meaningfully replicated. Change was, however, necessary. The Easterners themselves thought so, as did the West Germans. The reform of the school structure was certainly successful in broadening access to higher education. This was achieved by breaking up the unified school structure into Gymnasien and other less academic school types. Justice was done to the more able, but at the cost of widening the gap between them and the less able with all the motivational, behavioural and emotional problems at the lower end of the scale which the differentiated school system implies. Although there are pathways for transferability between one school type and another, only a small percentage of pupils are in a position to make use of them. The infrastructure which had existed for bringing the less able pupils up to standard has been dismantled: classes are larger, there are fewer lessons per week, teachers no longer pay compulsory visits to pupils' homes, and techniques like shaming a parent at his or her workplace because a child is performing inadequately are – fortunately! – no longer used. The average and below-average East German children can no longer receive the same degree of help which they had received in GDR times, and which had resulted in a much smaller dispersion of marks in the major subjects tested in the BIJU study (1994; 1996). As a result, pupils are left to find their own level to a greater extent than had been the case in the GDR; if some of them are failing, then it is very difficult to 'save' them from that failure and its consequences. The substitution of 'freedom' for 'equality' can be expected to result in a greater polarisation of achievement than was the case in East Germany.

The issue of school structure is a highly emotive one in most countries because it goes to the heart of intellectual and social inequality. It involves the whole process of social reproduction in complex stratified societies. There is no perfect solution, but what one must seek to do in the interests of justice is to ensure as far as possible that recruitment to the higher stratum is from as broad a substratum as possible, and that able people are not disbarred from upward mobility by their social origins. The grammar schools often tend to be the institutions attended by the middle and upper echelons of society, that is those pupils whose parents are expert at articulating and defending their interests. Once created, it is very difficult (though not impossible) to dismantle grammar schools. In England, 86 per cent of pupils are educated in comprehensive schools, whereas Northern Ireland (NI) still has a divided, selective system. In Northern Ireland, the existence of grammar schools and secondary schools has polarised achievement: in *Regional Trends* (1988; 1990; 1991) statistical evidence exists that NI pupils are the among the best and the worst in their scores in public examinations. More of them score top-notch marks in Advanced Level Examinations than anywhere else in the United Kingdom, but at the lower end of the spectrum more NI pupils leave school without a qualification of any sort. Although it will never in future be methodologically possible to do a before-and-after comparison of achievement in the ex-GDR and the NBL, it seems highly likely that the same development could take place there as in Northern Ireland: a polarisation of achievement. Once an elite educational sector is established, other school types are viewed as second best. Their pupils tend to acquire a negative self-image and some of them see themselves as failures for the rest of their lives. The hybrid school types in the New Bundesländer are an achievement in that they are an assertion of distinctiveness, but they exist in the shadow of the Gymnasien whose academic prestige they can never rival. A unified school system up to age fifteen or sixteen, with internal differentiation and a reconceptualisation of examination structure at the end of compulsory education, would likely enable more NBL pupils to maximise their potential. It would also help circumvent the problems caused by the merging or closing of schools due to the East German demographic decline. The Easterners themselves, as shown in the IFS study of 1995 (Rolff et al., 1996), now endorse a unified school system more strongly than a divided one. Perhaps they take the view that in the reform of school structure, increased freedom was necessarily achieved at the expense of equality.

In everyday classroom lessons, there has been a considerable increase in freedom and an improvement has taken place in the quality of life. The atmosphere of fear has gone, as has the grind of being forced to cover almost impossibly large syllabuses. Teachers, pupils and parents all have legal rights to express opinions and to contribute to decision-making. There is choice in the matter of textbooks and a much richer variety of educational materials and resources is available. However, a peculiarity of the 'new' system is that it is run by the 'old' teachers. Most of those who were teachers in the GDR school system are still teachers in the new system and bring their earlier experience and their preconditioning with them. In subjects like Geography, they use this experience to compensate for what they perceive as deficits in school texts or syllabuses. Their different professional training and socialisation makes them still inclined to go for subject coverage rather than social learning, and with the skills which they have at their disposal, they can effectively subvert or undermine some of the new pedagogies if these fail to command their confidence. Yet the traditional GDR skills of sound subject teaching and good syllabus coverage are a great strength in any educational system, and should be valued in the New Bundesländer just as they were in the GDR. There must be real doubt as to whether pupils' self-expression – important as it is – should take precedence over more cognitive operations. Of course the education system must encourage creativity, but to reach its supreme potential, creativity needs to be combined with knowledge. Neither feeling nor form by itself is enough, and the dilemma of what relative weight should be accorded to each is at the heart of progressive education everywhere. It is significant that as a matter of bipartisan political policy in Great Britain, there is now a systematic attempt to compensate for some of the deficits caused by overconcentration on 'progressivism'. As a result, there will be a National Curriculum for trainee primary school teachers in order to ensure that they know how to teach the mechanics of reading and writing rather than just 'creative expression'. It is essential to achieve the optimum balance between the two in East Germany – and not just in basic literacy. If NBL teachers can conjoin their competence in subject teaching with increased flexibility, they will have an extremely powerful combination.

Glaessner (1992:123) is strong on the assumed authoritarian dimension of the East German psyche and sees this as dysfunctional in the economic sense.

> Not only did the political, social and economic reality of the old system produce rigid authoritarian patterns of thought and behaviour; its failure to modernise also meant that the social qualifications vital to a modern society such as flexibility, innovation, performance and mobility could only be inadequately developed.

There is truth in what he says. Nevertheless, contemporary history indicates that Glaessner's postulate of 'authoritarianism' is overstated. In a way, the Peaceful Revolution which led to the fall of the Wall showed that even forty years of political brainwashing had not been completely successful. A sufficient spirit of independence endured to enable the East Germans to shake off the shackles of dictatorship when the time was ripe. This happened despite the fact that many well-educated GDR dissidents had already fled to the West, with the result that the GDR never built a movement like Solidarity in Poland. The Peaceful Revolution took place despite a GDR education system which harmonised with its social and political system, a form of *Gleichschaltung*, unlike the situation in most Western countries where educational, social and political institutions are all in tension with each other and send conflicting messages to the individual. In the end, the GDR education system failed to indoctrinate its pupils and citizens completely. It was unable to convert hearts and minds permanently, and ensure that the East German people were indeed 'all-round socialist personalities'.

By the 1980s, the GDR had become much more pluralistic than the SED would have wished to recognise. In a modern society, there is really no escape from pluralism, and the problem for educators is deciding which values to inculcate, and how to carry out the process through 'education' rather than 'indoctrination'. The restructuring of education in East Germany was intended to promote a free democratic order in society, and it addressed the issue of values and democratisation both indirectly and directly. Indirect approaches were made though pupil and parent representation in the school committee structure, new curricula, syllabuses and textbooks, and teacher training – both in-service and initial. The new facility to travel and the support given by the partnered Old and New Bundesländer all opened up options and helped the Easterners to implement their choices. After 1990, however, those choices were very much constrained by the restrictions imposed by the new legal structures. Direct approaches to values education were made through subjects like Geography and Ethics. The LER initiative of Brandenburg represented a particularly imaginative and courageous attempt to provide values education in a society where Christianity is accepted only by a minority. The question of the Churches' rights will be clarified by the Constitutional Court but even if the judgement is favourable to the Churches, LER will remain unscathed. The government in Brandenburg has every intention of continuing with it.

In the realm of higher education, there has been much success in introducing academic freedom and in broadening access. There are no signs yet that East German students are lapsing into the drawn-out study patterns of their Western counterparts. They seem to have a different ethos, and to be motivated to complete their courses quickly. Higher education has become a greater economic burden for individuals and their families, but it would be unsound to argue that this increased expense means that freedom has been asserted at the cost of social equality. The fact is that in GDR times, access was already dependent on a strong syndrome of social self-recruitment, and education begat education: highly educated families and of course highly placed Party officials contrived to send their children to university, and the real workers and peasants tended to be left behind. The post-Wende situation cannot therefore be said to represent a deterioration of access in social terms when compared with the GDR. Where a distinct disadvantage has occurred, however, is in the position of women. As has been pointed out, East German women lecturers suffered disproportionately from job loss, and there was a decline in the higher education participation of female students in the years after the Wende.

Where the reforms could be judged less than successful is in the academic staff structure at universities. There is no doubt but that Western professorial dominance has been transferred to the East, in terms of both career hierarchy and the numbers of Western professors in certain ideologically sensitive faculties. The former university staff structure in East Germany would have been fertile ground for reform along British lines, resulting in a small number of professors alongside a numerically much larger cohort of tenured or long-contract, well-qualified lecturers. Admittedly, this runs contrary to Germanic tradition and is probably not politically feasible. Such a structure would, however, solve many of the problems that plague West German higher education. The lecturers would have an incentive to maximise research productivity in order to attain Chairs, which would militate against the complaisance of the West German type of professor who, once appointed, feels that he or she has 'made it' and uses academic freedom as an excuse for unproductiveness. The lecturer system could also be used to provide an improved staff-student ratio and increased academic contact, thereby helping to counteract the soullessness of many large West German universities. To date, East German universities are much smaller than those in the West and do not (yet) manifest the impersonality that can leave many students in the Old Bundesländer feeling lonely and unsupported.

One of the most positive features of East German education was the link between theory and practice which was manifested at all levels and is elusive in the West. Vocational Training with Associated Abitur (Berufsbildung mit Abitur) was an excellent institution and it is a pity it has been abolished. Similarly, the GDR model of One-Phase Teacher Education and Training had many advantages; it could certainly have been stripped of ideology and adapted to make a high-quality instrument for the New Bundesländer. The West German Two-Phase Model has been the subject of widespread dissatisfaction and serious criticism. Its extension to the New Bundesländer can only be explained by the need for speed and the desire to minimise newly trained East German teachers' problems in being recognised in the Old Bundesländer – also perhaps by the 'West is Best' syndrome.

Just after the Wende, Count Otto von Lambsdorff, in a surge of welcome and enthusiasm, said: 'Geld gibt es bei uns genug' (We have no shortage of money) (*Der Spiegel,* 13.11.1989:28). He could have had little concept at that stage of the enormous sums which unification was actually going to cost, and the way in which the West German economy would be dragged down by its commitment to the East. The whole country's economic deterioration affected the success of the Dual System in that many employers were either unable or unwilling to train apprentices. Unemployment is now endemic and structural in the NBL, despite public finance initiatives to mitigate it. A strong training system needs a solid economy, and this condition is not yet present in East Germany. Many scholars (e.g. Branson, 1991) have pointed out that the relationship between capitalism and democracy entrains decreased welfare and increased individual responsibility. If, however, capitalism operates in an inhumane way that makes large numbers of people feel worthless and excluded from society, then democracy can be jeopardised. Large sums of money are being spent in an effort to ensure that this does not happen. In the circumstances, a promising stratagem may be to try out new models of vocational training and new patterns of finance. This could be regarded as a far-sighted attempt to plan for the millennium rather than the retreat from perfection which some observers fear.

It must be admitted that some of the formal educational structures exported from West to East are poorly adapted to the NBL education ecology. A highly differentiated secondary school system is not very suitable for New Bundesländer where the birth rate has declined so steeply. The Dual System does not work well when employers are plagued by fear of bankruptcy. The higher education staff structure is ill designed to provide the close staff-student support which once prevailed and, although the problem has not arisen yet, may even contribute to extended years of study. The two-phase teacher training model bestowed on East Germany had attracted heavy criticism in the West prior to its 'export' to the East. Yet despite all criticisms of structure, one is left with the impression that the greatest successes in East German educational reform are at the grass-roots level in the liberalisation of the classroom and of student life. Few teachers want to return to the old regime, and van Buer et al. (1995) find their levels of satisfaction undiminished. It is heartening that research into how students feel psychologically (e.g. Aulerich and Stein, 1997) shows them to be upbeat and hopeful about their life chances. Other empirical studies of students and apprentices show evidence of their high morale and the belief in a positive future for themselves and their families (Buck-Bechler, Jahn and Lewin, 1995; Beer at al., 1995). The majority are keen to work and anxious to stay in East Germany. These findings are grounds for optimism, and indeed it is vital to have confidence in the future of Germany's young people, East and West.

The question of equality has been treated above, particularly in relation to school structure and access to higher education. What remains is to consider differential interpretations of freedom in relation to the meaning of existence. Easterners and Westerners have different traditional concepts of freedom. For the Marxist-Leninist, freedom is a socialised concept anchored in the individual's class position. It is determined by his or her relationship to the means of production, and is conceived as the freedom of *a Collective* of people endeavouring to realise socialism in accord with the objective laws of the historical process, as uniquely understood and interpreted in Marxism-Leninism (see Krejci, 1976:126–30). Easterners have not been brought up to believe in freedom only for themselves and their own interests. In *Wozu lebe ich?* (Kosing, 1983), the notion of everyone achieving happiness by 'doing their own thing' is rejected because no one lives outside society. All individuals depend on the economic, social, political and ideological relationships in society and on its developmental stage (ibid.:8). The meaning of life can be conceived only insofar as people are members of society (seen as 'socialist', of course, in the 1980s). The idea that human beings can only be the recipients of meaning, not its creators, is explicitly rejected in Marxist-Leninist philosophy. Meaning and fulfilment arise from active attempts to contribute to society:

> A life which in its essential content goes beyond the individual and contributes to the realisation of progressive social goals is a meaningful, fulfilled life. On the other hand, a life which essentially is not geared to any social goals beyond the limited self is a senseless waste and is without meaning. (ibid.:10–11)

This is very much an immanent, secular concept of the meaning of existence, and by no means an unworthy one. It is invigorating, and has a certain nobility about it compared with the egoism of purely individual freedom. After the Wende, young East German people were challenged to invent their own definitions of meaning and freedom. The most obvious concept of freedom is Bertrand Russell's (1935) statement that freedom in general may be defined as the absence of obstacles to the realisation of desires. Initially, many East German youths wanted to follow private interests, preferably without being restricted by the demands of others, and this led to many discipline difficulties in schools. It took time for them to discover that freedom was not to be identified with the absence of obstacles to the satisfaction of *any* desire; what was important was the freedom to engage in – and receive satisfaction from – forms of activity possessing especial moral and social significance (Partridge, 1967:223). In addition, East German people wanted freedom to *have* material possessions, and here again they came up against restrictions in freedom because for many of them the resources to acquire goods were not available. The possession of the means or power to realise preferred objectives is part of what it means to be free, so the problem of freedom coincides with the quite different one of how satisfactions are to be maximised (ibid.:222). Despite enormous public expenditure and attempts to erect a new youth infrastructure in the NBL, absence of restraint combined with unsatisfied material desire made many young people think – at least temporarily – that 'freedom' was a cheat. Among the more sophisticated, there was the suspicion that covert manipulation of choice – an incursion into freedom – had not ceased though it was done differently in the NBL than in the GDR. The Geography teachers in Mai and Burpee's 1996 study, for example, felt that an ideological conditioning of a type unfamiliar to them constituted a 'hidden curriculum' of the new syllabuses. These issues are subtle and not easy to tease out, but they are very germane to the democratisation of the New Bundesländer. Eastern and Western concepts of freedom represent two different world-views which can complement and balance each other (though they are too often perceived as antagonistic). During the forty years of division, each Germany ascribed to the other traditions and characteristics which it had repressed at home; the united Germany is confronted with the task of coming to terms with what had been repressed. Because the two traditions can be mutually enriching, it would be a very great pity if the experience of East Germany were to be lost or disregarded. Fortunately, there is an extensive – and growing – literature on the subject to which the present volume represents a further contribution.

APPENDIX I

Articles on Education and Higher Education and Research from the Unification Treaty

Article 37

Education

1. School, vocational or higher education certificates or degrees obtained or officially recognised in the German Democratic Republic shall continue to be valid in the territory specified in Article 3 of this Treaty. Examinations passed or certificates obtained in the territory specified in Article 3 or in the other Länder of the Federal Republic of Germany, including Berlin (West), shall be considered equal and shall convey the same rights if they are of equal value. Their equivalence shall be established by the appropriate competent agency on application. Legal provisions of the Federation and the European Communities regarding the equivalence of examinations and certificates, and special provisions set out in this Treaty take priority. In all cases this shall not affect the right to use academic professional titles and degrees obtained or officially recognised or conferred.

2. The usual recognition procedure operated by the Standing Committee of Federal Ministers of Education (KMK) shall apply to teacher training qualifications. The said Committee shall make appropriate transitional arrangements.

3. Examination certificates issued under the training and the skilled workers' training schemes as well as final examinations and apprentices' final examinations in recognised trained occupations shall be considered equal.

4. The regulations necessary for the reorganisation of the school system in the territory specified in Article 3 of this Treaty shall be adopted by the Länder named in Article 1. The necessary regulations for the recognition of examinations under educational law shall be agreed by the Standing Committee of Federal Ministers of Education. In both cases

they shall be based on the Hamburg Agreement and the other relevant agreements reached by the said Committee.

5. Students who move to another institution of higher education before completing their studies shall have their study and examination record up to that point recognised according to the principles laid down in Section 7 of the General Regulations on Degree Examination Procedures or within the terms of the rules governing admission to state examinations.

6. The entitlement to study at an institution of higher education based on leaving certificates issued by Engineering and Specialist Colleges (Fachschulen) of the German Democratic Republic shall be valid in accordance with the resolution of 10 May 1990 of the Conference of Ministers of Education and Cultural Affairs and its Annex B. Further principles and procedures for the recognition of Specialist College and higher education certificates for the purpose of school and higher education studies based on them shall be developed within the framework of the Conference of Ministers of Education and Cultural Affairs.

Article 38

Higher Education and Research

1. In the united Germany science and research shall continue to constitute important foundations of the state and society. The need to renew science and research in the territory specified in Article 3 of this Treaty while preserving efficient institutions shall be taken into account by an expert report on publicly maintained institutions prepared by the Higher Education Council (Wissenschaftsrat) and to be completed by 31 December 1991, with individual results to be implemented step by step before that date. The following provisions are intended to make possible the preparation of this evaluation and ensure the incorporation of higher education and research in the territory specified in Article 3 of this Treaty into the joint research structure of the Federal Republic of Germany.

2. Upon the accession taking effect, the Academy of Sciences of the German Democratic Republic shall be separated as a learned society from the research institutes and other institutions. The decision as to how the learned society of the Academy of Sciences of the German Democratic Republic is to be continued shall be taken under Land law. For the time being the research institutes and other institutions shall continue to exist up to 31 December 1991 as institutions of the Länder in the territory specified in Article 3 of this Treaty insofar as they have not been previously dissolved or transformed. Transitional arrangements shall be made for the financing of these institutes and institutions up to

31 December 1991; the requisite funds shall be provided in 1991 by the Federation and the Länder named in Article 1 of this Treaty.

3. The employment contracts of the staff employed at the research institutes and other institutions of the Academy of Sciences of the German Democratic Republic shall continue to exist up to 31 December 1991 as limited employment contracts with the Länder to which these institutes and institutions are transferred. The right to cancel these employment contracts with or without notice under the conditions listed in Annex 1 to this Treaty shall remain unaffected.

4. Paragraphs 1 to 3 above shall apply *mutatis mutandis* to the Academy of Architecture and the Academy of Agricultural Sciences of the German Democratic Republic and to the academic institutions subordinate to the Ministry of Food, Agriculture and Forestry.

5. The Federal Government shall begin negotiations with the Länder with a view to adapting or renewing the Bund-Länder agreements under Article 91b of the Basic Law in such a way that educational planning and the promotion of academic research institutions and projects deemed of supraregional importance are extended to the territory specified in Article 3 of this Treaty.

6. The Federal Government shall seek to ensure that the proven methods and programmes of research promotion in the Federal Republic of Germany are applied as soon as possible to the entire federal territory and that the academics and academic institutions in the territory specified in Article 3 of this Treaty are given access to current research promotion schemes. Furthermore, certain schemes for promoting research and development which have expired in the territory of the Federal Republic of Germany shall be reopened for the territory specified in Article 3 of this Treaty; this shall not include fiscal measures.

7. Upon the accession of the German Democratic Republic taking effect, the Research Council of the German Democratic Republic shall be dissolved.

APPENDIX II

A Questionnaire Used to Evaluate Teachers for Political Soundness

Declaration of Activities before 1990

1.1 Have you ever officially or unofficially, as part of your main employment or otherwise, worked for the Ministry of State Security/Office for National Security of the former DDR? ☐ Yes ☐ No
If yes: In what way, where and from when to when? For what reason did the activity cease?

1.2 Have you ever worked for the Ministry of State Security/Office for National Security of the former GDR, occasionally, or on an unpaid basis, through indirect contacts, by way of a duty as travelling cadre, or through contacts to whom you were responsible as a co-worker of local state organs, as leader, or by reason of societal functions? ☐ Yes ☐ No
If yes: In what way, where and from when to when? For what reason did the contacts cease?

1.3 If you answered 'No' to questions 1.1 and 1.2: Did you have contacts which were intended to lead to an increase in your involvement which you declined? ☐ Yes ☐ No
If yes: When and for what tasks were you meant to assume responsibility?

2. Prior to 9 November 1989, did you exercise mandates or functions in or for political parties or mass organisations of the former GDR (for example FDGB, FDJ, GST, DFD, DSF)? In this period did you assume any other prominent position in the former GDR? ☐ Yes ☐ No
If yes: Which functions, mandates, positions? When? Where?

3. Prior to 9 November 1989, were you active in a firm of the former GDR or in one outside the former GDR in a leadership capacity?
☐ Yes ☐ No
If yes: In what firm? What activity? Where? When?

4. Prior to 9 November 1989 did you spend time outside the territory of the former GDR in a professional or social capacity? ☐ Yes ☐ No
   If yes: In what capacity? When? Where?

5. Have you taken a qualification outside the territory of the former GDR? ☐ Yes ☐ No
   If yes: Which one(s)? When? Where?

6. Have you been through a course of education/training other than general or vocational education (for example party political schools,[1] among others)? ☐ Yes ☐ No

If the space for your explanations to questions 1 to 6 on this form is not sufficient, please add another sheet.

✄ ✄ ✄

I am aware that the Land of Saxony has the right to withdraw designation of a civil service category or in certain circumstances to terminate employment without notice if the previous data are incomplete or untrue.

   Moreover I declare my consent to the consultation and use of personal data about me in

- the documents of the Central Registration of the Land Justice Administration in Salzgitter (formerly entrusted with the registration of criminal violations of human rights in the ex-GDR),
- the documents of the former Ministry of State Security/Office for National Security of the former GDR, for the purpose of proving according to paragraph 9, section 2, number 3 of the law of the Volkskammer of the former GDR about the security and use of personal data of the former Ministry of State Security/Office for National Security of August 24 1990 (GB1 and GDR part 1 number 58, page 1419).

So long as I am in public service I am agreed that my personal files/ cadre files may be referred to.

Place/Date   Signature

---

1. The Stasi had its own central training institution, the Law College in Potsdam.

GLOSSARY

Abgrenzung	Demarcation (political, ecclesiastical)
Abitur	Leaving certificate for university matriculation.
ABM	Arbeitsbeschaffungsmaßnahme: Job promotion support programme. Compare British 'ACE' scheme.
ABS	Außerbetriebliche Ausbildungsstätte: An out-of-firm Training Centre accepting apprentices for the whole three years of their apprenticeship. Can overlap in function with ÜBS.
ADW	Akademie der Wissenschaften: Academy of Sciences.
APW	Akademie der Pädagogischen Wissenschaften: Academy of Educational Sciences.
BAföG	Bundesausbildungsförderungsgesetz: Student support loan system.
BMBW	Bundesministerium für Bildung und Wissenschaft: Federal Ministry for Education and Higher Education, merged with other Ministries in 1994 to become BMFT/BWFT.
BMFT/BWFT	Bundesministerium für Bildung, Wissenschaft, Forschung und Technologie (also abbreviated as BWFT): Federal Ministry of Education, Higher Education, Research and Technology.
EV	Einigungsvertrag: Unification Treaty.
FHS	Fachhochschule: Higher education institution similar in mission to the former British polytechnics.
Gesamtschule	Comprehensive school.
GG	Grundgesetz: Basic Law, in effect the Constitution of the Federal Republic of Germany.
Gymnasium	Grammar school; the most academic post-primary school type.
Habilitation	Post-doctoral thesis.
HEP	Hochschulerneuerungsprogramm: Higher Education Renewal Programme.

HS	Hauptschule: 'Main School', the least academic type of post-primary school.
HSP	Hochschulsonderprogramm: Higher Education Special Programme.
IAB	Institut für Arbeitsmarkt- und Berufsforschung der Bundesanstalt für Arbeit: Institute for Labour Market and Vocational Research of the Federal Labour Institute.
KMK	Kultusministerkonferenz: Standing Committee of Federal Ministers of Education.
MBJS	Ministerium für Bildung, Jugend und Sport: Ministry for Education, Youth and Sport.
MfS	Ministerium für Staatssicherheit: Ministry for State Security (Stasi).
Ministerium für Volksbildung	Literally, 'Ministry for the People's Education', usually rendered in the present text simply as 'Ministry of Education'.
PH	Pädagogische Hochschule: College of Education, in effect a type of university specialising in teacher training.
Promotion	Doctoral thesis.
Realschule	Post-primary school type; less academic than the Gymnasium, and more academic than the Hauptschule.
Rechtsstaat	State based on the rule of law.
SED	Sozialistische Einheitspartei Deutschlands: Socialist Unity Party.
SPD	Sozialdemokratische Partei Deutschlands: Social Democratic Party. Left of centre.
THA	Treuhand: Body charged with instituting a market economy and privatisating property in the New Bundesländer.
ÜBS	Überbetriebliche Ausbildungsstätte: An out-of-firm Training Centre where apprentices supplement their in-firm training for part of their apprenticeship. Can overlap with ABS.
Wende	The 'Change' or 'Turnabout' which occurred in 1989 after the fall of the Berlin Wall in East Germany. 'Wende' and 'Change' are used in free variation in the text.
WIP	Wissenschaftler-Integrations-Programm: Programme for the Integration of Academics.
WR	Wissenschaftsrat: Higher Education Council.

REFERENCES

Ahonen, Sirkka. 'A Transformation of History: The Official Representations of History in East Germany and Estonia, 1986–1991', *Culture and Psychology*, Vol. 3, No. 1, 1997:41–62.

Albert, Kati. 'Warum kommen Student(inn)en aus Westdeutschland und aus West-Berlin an die ostberliner Humboldt-Universität?', *hochschule ost*, Vol. 5, Nos 5–6, 1995:95–104.

ALLBUS. See Zentralarchiv für Empirische Sozialforschung, 1993.

Anweiler, O. 'Grundzüge der Bildungspolitik und der Entwicklung des Bildungswesens seit 1945', in O. Anweiler et al. (eds), 1990:11–33.

Anweiler, O., Fuchs, H.-J., Dorner, Martina, and Petermann, E. (eds). *Bildungspolitik in Deutschland, 1945–1990*. Bonn: Bundeszentrale für politische Bildung, 1992.

Anweiler, O., Mitter, O., Peisert, H., Schäfer, H.-P. and Stratenwerth, W. (eds). *Vergleich von Bildung und Erziehung in der Bundesrepublik Deutschland und in der Deutschen Demokratischen Republik*. Cologne: Verlag Wissenschaft und Politik, 1990.

Arbeitsgruppe 'Studienreform in Deutschland aus der Perspektive der neuen Länder', *hochschule ost*, Vol. 5, Nos. 5–6, 1995:78–83.

Arnold, R. and Lipsmeier, R. (eds). *Handbuch der Berufsbildung*. Opladen: Leske and Budrich, 1995.

Aulerich, Gudrun and Stein, Ruth Heidi. 'Wende gut, alles gut? Oder: Sage mir woher Du kommst? Studierende in Dresden und Dortmund sechs Jahre nach der Wende', *hochschule ost*, Vol. 6, No. 1, 1997:124–44.

Autsch, B. 'Ausgangsbedingungen bei der Umstellung des DDR-Berufsbildungssystems aus der Sicht rechtlicher und organisatorischer Rahmenbedingungen', in U. Degen, G. Walden and K. Berger (eds), 1995:15–28.

Bainton, R.H. *Here I Stand*. New York: Mentor, 1955.

Bandura, A. (ed.). *Self-Efficacy in Changing Societies*. New York: Cambridge University Press, 1995.

Bardeleben, R. von, Beicht, Ursula, and Feher, K. 'Cost and Benefit of In-House Professional and Vocational Training.' Berlin and Bonn: Bundesinstitut für Berufsbildung, 1994.

Note: Multiple references for a single author are normally presented in alphabetical order of publication titles rather than chronologically by date.

Basic Law. See GG – Grundgesetz.

Baske, S. 'Die Erweiterterte Oberschule in der DDR und Arbeitslehre', in O. Anweiler et al. (eds), 1990:210–217.

Bastian, J. and Fuhrmann, E. 'Projektunterricht in der Sekundarstufe: Grundlagen und Handlungsperspektiven im Dialog zwischen neuen und alten Bundesländern', in R. Oberliesen (ed.), 1992:169–83.

Bauer, K.O. and Burkard, C. 'Der Lehrer – ein pädagogischer Profi?', in H.-G. Rolff et al., 1992:193–226.

Baumbach, J., Holldack, E. and Klemm, K. 'Demographische Perspektiven, regionale Schulentwicklung und schulrechtliche Rahmenbedingen in Mecklenburg-Vorpommern.' Berlin, Essen: Gutachten im Auftrag der Hans-Böckler-Stiftung, 1994.

BB EK – Brandenburg Evangelische Kirche. Fortschreibung des Gemeinsamen Protokolls vom 9. Juli 1992. Potsdam, 6.7.1993.

————. 'Gemeinsames Protokoll über die Besprechung zwischen Vertretern der Landesregierung von Brandenburg und der Evangelischen Kirche in Berlin-Brandunburg am 09. Juli 1992 in Potsdam zur Durchführung des Evangelischen Religionsunterrichts und zur Mitwirkung der Evangelischen Kirche im Modellversuch "Lernbereich Lebensgestaltung- Ethik- Religion im Schuljahr 1992/93".' Potsdam, 9.7.1992.

BB MBJS – Brandenburg Ministerium für Bildung, Jugend und Sport. 'Abschlußbericht zum Modellversuch "Lernbereich Lebensgestaltung- Ethik-Religion".' Potsdam: MBJS, 1.2.1996.

————. 'Allgemeine Ansprüche an die Unterrichtsgestaltung in den Schulen des Landes Brandenburg (Eckwerte).' Potsdam: MBJS, 30.4.1994.

————. Brandenburgisches Schulgesetz, 12.4.1996.

————. 'Hinweise zum Unterricht im Modellversuch: Lernbereich Lebensgestaltung- Ethik- Religion, Sekundarstufe 1.' Potsdam, 1994.

————. 'Modellrechnungen zur Entwicklung der Schülerzahlen, des Lehrkräftebedarfs und Lehrkräftebestands Land Brandenburg.' Potsdam, 13.6.1995.

————. 'Unterrichtsvorgaben: Lebensgestaltung- Ethik- Religionskunde, Sekundarstufe 1.' Potsdam, 25.6.1996.

————. 'Vereinbarung zwischen der Evangelischen Kirche in Berlin-Brandenburg und dem Ministerium für Bildung, Jugend und Sport über die Durchführung des Evangelischen Religionsunterrichts im Land Brandenburg gemäß para. 9, Abs. 2 und 3 des Brandenburgischen Schulgesetzes.' Potsdam: BB MBJS, 11.2.1997.

Beer, Dagmar, Granato, M. and Schweikert, K. 'In der Mitte der Ausbildung: Auszubildende in den neuen Bundesländern.' Berlin and Bonn: Bundesinstitut für Berufsbildung, 1995.

Beer-Kern, Dagmar. 'Auszubildende und unversorgte Jugendliche: Ausbildungssituation und Fremdenfeindlichkeit', in R. Jansen (ed.), 1995:145–68.

Berger, K. 'Struktur der betrieblichen Ausbildung in Ostdeutschland', in U. Degen, G. Walden and K. Berger (eds), 1995:29–39.

Berndt, Inge. 'Gesellschaftskunde statt Staatsbürgerkunde – ein Etikettenwechsel?', *Pädagogik und Schule in Ost und West*, No. 4, 1990:224–29.

Bertram, B. 'Zur Entwicklung der sozialen Geschlechtverhältnisse in den neuen Bundesländern', *Aus Politik und Zeitgeschichte*, B6, 1993:27–52.

BFSFJ – Bundesministerium für Familie, Senioren, Frauen und Jugend. *Neunter Jugendbericht: Bericht über die Situation der Kinder und Jugendlichen und die Entwicklung der Jugendhilfe in den neuen Bundesländern.* Bonn: BFSFJ, 1994.

Biehl, P., Bizer, C., Degen, R., Mette, N., Rickers, F. and Schweitzer, F. (eds). *Jahrbuch der Religionspädagogik (JRP)*. Neukirchener, Band 11, 1995:17–35.

BIJU – Bildungsverläufe und psychosoziale Entwicklung im Jugendalter.
   1. 'Zwischenbilanz für die Schulen', 1994;
   2. 'Bericht für die Schulen', 1996. Berlin: Max-Planck-Institut für Bildungsforschung.

BLK – Bund-Länder-Kommission für Bildungsplanung und Forschungsförderung. *Entwicklung der Berufsausbildung in den neuen Ländern.* Heft 31. Bonn: BLK, 1993a.

————. *Entwicklungen und vordringliche Maßnahmen in den Tageseinrichtungen für Kinder/Elementarbereich in den neuen Ländern.* Heft 30. Bonn: BLK, 1993b.

————. *Informationen zur Förderung von Frauen im Rahmen des Hochschulerneuerungsprogramms (HEP).* Bonn: BLK, 1993c.

BMBW – Bundesministerium für Bildung und Wissenschaft. 'Abschlußbericht über die Schulbuchaktion zum Schuljahr 1990/91 für die Schulen im Gebiet der ehemaligen GDR.' Bonn, 21.1.1991.

BMBW BBB: *Berufsbildungsberichte.* Bonn: Bundesminister für Bildung und Wissenschaft. Years 1990; 1991; 1992; 1993; 1994; 1995.

Böhm, J., Brune, J., Flörchinger, H., Helbing, Antje and Pinther, A. (eds). *DeutschStunden: Was Jugendliche von der Einheit denken.* Berlin: Argon, 1993.

Borries, B. von and Lehmann, R.H. 'Comparing Empirically Historical Awareness in East and West Germany', paper presented at the Annual Meeting of the American Educational Research Association, 21 April 1992. ERIC search number: ED 357 982.

Bourdieu. P. *Reproduction in Education, Society and Culture.* London and Beverly Hills: Sage, 1977.

Branson, Margaret Stimmann. 'The Education of Citizens in a Market Economy and Its Relationship to a Free Society', Paper delivered to the International Conference on Western Democracy and Eastern Europe: Political, Economic and Social Changes, East Berlin, 14–18 October, 1991.

Brendgen, M., Little, T.D. and Krappmann, L. 'Peer Rejection and Friendship Quality: A View from Both Friends' Perspectives.' Berlin: Max-Planck-Institut für Bildungsforschung, 1996.

Brentjes, S. '"Demokratische Erneuerung" der Leipziger Universität in der Wahrnehmung ihrer Angehörigen', *hochschule ost*, Vol. 6, No. 2, 1997:33–54.

Brinkmann, C. 'Arbeitsmarktentwicklung und Arbeitsmarktpolitik in den neuen Bundesländern: Ergebnisse von Befragungen und Modellrechnungen', in R. Jansen (ed.), 1995:7–32.

Buck-Bechler, Gertraude. '*Das Hochschulwesen der DDR Ende der 80er Jahre*', in R. Mayntz (ed.), 1994a: 11–31.

Buck-Bechler, Gertraude, Jahn, Heidrun and Lewin, D. *Studienentscheidung und Studienengagement in ausgewählten neuen Bundesländern.* Berlin-Karlshorst: Projektgruppe Hochschulforschung, February 1995.

———. 'Studienrealität aus der Sicht der Studierenden', in Gertraude Buck-Bechler et al. (eds), 1997:513–21.

Buck-Bechler, Gertraude, Schaefer, H.-D. and Wagemann, C.-H. (eds). *Hochschulen in den neuen Ländern der Bundesrepublik Deutschland.* Weinheim: Beltz/Deutscher Studien Verlag, 1997.

Buer, J. van, Squarra, D., Ebermann-Richter, P. and Kirchner, C. 'Pädagogische Freiräume, berufliche Zufriedenheit und berufliche Belastung', *Zeitschrift für Pädagogik,* Vol. 41, No. 4, 1995:555–77.

Burkhardt, Anke and Scherer, Dorit. 'Wissenschaftliches Personal und Wissenschaftlicher Nachwuchs', in Gertraude Buck-Bechler et al. (eds), 1997:283–420. Chapters 4 and 5.

Bütow, Birgit. 'Jugend im politischen Umbruch', in U. Hoffmann-Lange (ed.), 1995:85–108.

Büttner, W., Fesser, G., Kaulisch, B., Schröder, W. and Voigt, G. *Geschichte, Klasse 8.* Berlin: Volk und Wissen, 1988.

Butz, P. and Boehnke, K. 'Auswirkungen von ökonomischem Druck auf die psychosoziale Befindlichkeit von Jugendlichen', *Zeitschrift für Pädagogik,* Vol. 43, No. 1, 1997:79–92.

BWFT – Bundesministerium für Bildung, Wissenschaft, Forschung und Technologie. 'Stärkung der Wissenschafts- und Forschungslandschaft in den neuen Ländern und im geeinten Deutschland.' Bonn: BMFT, 1993.

Casey, B. 'Apprentice Training in Germany: The Experiences of the 1980s', in D. Phillips (ed.), 1992:89–111.

Cole, A. 'Looking On: France and the New Germany', *German Politics,* Vol. 2, No. 3, 1993:358–76.

Comenius Institut – Arbeitsstelle Berlin. 'Christenlehre in veränderter Situation: Arbeit mit Kindern Ostdeutschlands.' Berlin: Comenius Institut, 15 December 1992.

Cordell, K. 'The Church: Coming to Terms with Change', in Eva Kolinsky (ed.), 1995:123–34.

Damm-Rüger, Sigrid. 'Frauenerwerbtätigkeit und Frauenbildung in den alten und neuen Bundesländern – bisherige Entwicklung und Perspektiven', *Berufsbildung in Wissenschaft und Praxis,* Vol. 22, No. 2, 1993:3–7.

Davids, Sabine. 'Junge Erwachsene ohne anerkannte Berufsausbildung in den alten und neuen Bundesländern', *Berufsbildung im Wissenschaft und Praxis,* Vol. 22, No. 2, 1993:11–17.

Decher, Sabine. 'Ein Jahr Religionsunterricht in Sachsen-Anhalt – gemeinsam auf Spurensuche, oder: wie selbstverständlich ist die Chance des konfessionellen RU an der staatlichen Schule?', *Schönberger Hefte* 2, 1995:27–35.

Degen, R. 'Evangelischer Religionsunterricht in Ostdeutschland: Zahlen – Interpretationen – Konsequenzen.' Berlin: Comenius-Institut, 3.4.1995.

———. 'Gemeindepädagogische Perspektiven im ostdeutschen Kontext', in P. Biehl, C. Bizer, R. Degen, N. Mette, F. Rickers and F. Schweitzer (eds), *Jahrbuch der Religionspädagogik (JRP),* Neukirchener, Band 11, 1995:17–35.

Degen, U. 'Zur Qualifikation des Ausbildungspersonals in Betrieben und Berufs-schulen der neuen Bundesländer', *Berufsbildung*, Vol. 47, No. 21, 1993:18–19.

Degen, U. and Walden, G. 'Situation, Organisation und Gestaltung der betrieblichen Berufsausbildung in den neuen Ländern: Ausgewählte Ergebnisse einer schriftlichen Befragung 1993/94', in R. Jansen (ed.), 1995:69–110.

Degen, U., Walden, G. and Berger, K. (eds). *Berufsausbildung in den neuen Bundesländern: Daten, Analysen, Perspektiven*. Bundesinstitut für Berufsbildung: Der Generalsekretär, 1995.

Dennis, M. 'Family Policy and Family Function in the German Democratic Republic', Unpublished manuscript, University of Wolverhampton, 1997.

Deutscher Bundestag. 'Katholische Kirche', in 'Rolle und Selbstverständnis der Kirchen in den verschiedenen Phasen der SED-Diktatur', in *Materalien der Enquête-Kommission 'Aufarbeitung von Geschichte und Folgen der SED-Diktatur in Deutschland'*. Bonn: Deutscher Bundestag, Nomos and Suhrkamp Verläge, Band VI/2, 1995.

Deutsches Jugendinstitut (ed.). *Schüler an der Schwelle zur deutschen Einheit*. Opladen: Leske and Budrich, 1992.

Dietrich, T. *Die Pädagogik Peter Petersens: Der Jena-Plan-Beispiel einer humanen Schule*. Bad Heilbrunn: Klinkhardt, 1995.

Döbert, H. *Curricula in der Schule*. Cologne, Weimar, Wien: Böhlau, 1995.

———. *Das Bildungswesen der DDR in Stichworten: Inhaltliche und administrative Sachverhalte und ihre Rechtgrundlagen*. Berlin: Luchterhand, 1995.

———. 'Momente einer Zwischenbilanz – Schule in Ostdeutschland vom äußeren zum inneren Wandel', *Zeitschrift für Bildungsverwaltung*, Vol. 9, No. 1, 1994:25–38.

Döbert, H. and Rudolf, R. with G. Seidel. *Lehrerberuf – Schule – Unterricht: Einstellungen, Meinungen und Urteile ostdeutscher Lehrerinnen und Lehrer: Ergebnisse einer empirischen Untersuchung in Berlin-Ost, Brandenburg und Sachsen*. Frankfurt am Main: Deutsches Institut für Internationale Pädagogische Forschung, 1995.

Dohle, Karen. 'Soziale Beziehungen zwischen Familie und Schule als Entscheidungshilfe für die Schulwahl', *Pädagogik und Schulalltag*, Vol. 52, No. 1, 1997:118–25.

Dudek, P. and Tenorth, H.-E. (eds). *Zeitschrift für Pädagogik*. No. 30. Beiheft, Weinheim: Beltz, 1993.

Eichler, W. and Uhlig, Christa. 'Die Akademie der Pädagogischen Wissenschaften der DDR', in P. Dudek and H.-E. Tenorth (eds), 1993:115–26.

EKD – Evangelische Kirche in Deutschland. *Kirchenzugehörigkeit in Deutschland – Was hat sich verändert' Evangelische und katholische Kirche im Vergleich*. Statische Beilage Nr. 89 zum Amtsblatt der EKD, Heft 10 vom 15. Oktober 1994. Hanover: EKD, 15 October 1994.

———. 'Rahmenplan für die kirchliche Arbeit mit Kindern und Jugendlichen.' Bund der Evangelischen Kirchen: Evangelische Verlagsanstalt (n.d., estimated 1977/78).

EkiBB – Evangelische Kirche in Berlin-Brandenburg. 'Abschlußbericht zum Modellversuch "Lernbereich Lebensgestaltung- Ethik- Religion".' 9.6.1995.

————. Brochure translated into English as 'Evangelical Church in Berlin-Brandenburg: Developments, Tasks, Concepts'. Berlin, July, 1994.

————. *Religionsunterricht und LER im Land Brandenburg. Dokumentation, Stand 30. November 1995.* Berlin, 1995.

Ewert, K. 'Einphasige Lehrerbildung an der Universität Oldenburg – Darstellungen, Anmerkungen, Einschätzung, Vorschläge', in K. Ewert et al. (eds), 1981:97–260.

Ewert, K., Furck, C.-L. and Ohaus, W. and W. (eds). *Gutachten über den Modellversuch 'Einphasige Lehrerbildung an der Universität Oldenburg' und Vorschläge für die zweiphasige Lehrerbildung.* Oldenburg: Universität Oldenburg, 1981.

Fischer, Dietlind, Jacobi, Juliane and Koch-Priewe, Barbara (eds). *Schulentwicklung geht von Frauen aus: Zur Beteiligung von Lehrerinnen an Schulreformen aus professions-geschichtlicher, biographischer, religionspädagogischer und fortbildungsdidaktischer Perspektive.* Weinheim: Deutscher Studien Verlag, 1996.

Fishman, S. and Martin, L. *Estranged Twins: Education and Society in the Two Germanies.* New York: Praeger, 1987.

Flämig, C. et al. (eds). *Handbuch des Wissenschaftrechts, Band 1.* Berlin: Springer, 1996.

Flickermann, D., Weishaupt, H. and Zedler, P. 'Kleine Grundschulen in Deutschland: Ruckblick und Ausblick', in D. Flickermann, H. Weishaupt and P. Zedler (eds), 1998:7–34.

Flickermann, D., Weishaupt, H. and Zedler, P. *Kleine Grundschulen in Europa: Berichte aus elf europäischen Landern.* Weinheim: Beltz, 1998.

Flockton, C.H. 'Economic Reconstruction in the New Bundesländer', Paper delivered to the Association for the Study of German Politics. London: 6–7 May 1994.

————. 'The Federal German Economy in the Early 1990s', *German Politics,* Vol. 2, No. 2, 1993:311–27.

Fourteenth Social Survey: *Das soziale Bild der Studentenschaft in der Bundesrepublik Deutschland: 14. Erhebung des Deutschen Studentenwerks.* Bonn: Der Bundesminister für Bildung, Wissenschaft, Forschung und Technologie (BWFT), 1995. Carried out by Hochschul-Informations-System, Hanover, under the leadership of Dr. K. Schnitzer.

Friedrich, W. 'Mentalitätswandlungen der Jugend in der DDR', *Aus Politik und Zeitgeschichte,* B16–17, 1990:25–37.

Fritsch, R. and Rommel, E. 'Die Praxis der Hochschulen bei der sozialen Zuordnung der Studienbewerber und Aspekte der sozialen Herkunft von Hochschuldirekt- und Fernstudenten.' Berlin: Zentralinstitut für Hochschulbildung, 1987.

Fuchs, H.-W. and Reuter, L.R. with Smoczynski, D. 'Chronikbildungs- und wissenschaftspolitischer Entwicklungen und Ereignisse in Ostdeutschland 1989 bis 1996.' Hamburg: Universität der Bundeswehr, 1997.

Fulbrook, Mary. *Germany 1918–1990: The Divided Nation.* London: Fontana, 1991.

Garton Ash, T. *In Europe's Name.* London: Jonathan Cape, 1993.

GBl. der DDR 1970, Teil II.

GBl. I, Nr. 6, (1965)

GG – *Grundgesetz für die Bundesrepublik Deutschland.* Bonn: Bundeszentrale für politische Bildung, *Stand.* October, 1990.

Glaessner, G-G. *The Unification Process in Germany: From Dictatorship to Democracy.* London: Pinter, 1992.

Goeckel, R.F. *The Lutheran Church and the East German State: Political Conflict and Change under Ulbricht and Honecker.* Ithaca and London: Cornell University Press, 1990.

Goetz, K.H. and Cullen, P.J. 'The Basic Law after Unification: Continued Centrality or Declining Force?', *German Politics,* Vol. 3, No. 3, 1994:5–46.

Goldberger, B. 'Why Europe Should Not Fear the Germans', *German Politics,* Vol. 2, No. 2, 1993:288–310.

Graddol, D. and Thomas, S. (eds). *Language in a Changing Europe.* Clevedon: BAAL and Multilingual Matters, 1995.

Graham, S. and Barker, G.P. 'The Down Side of Help: An Attributional-Developmental Analysis of Helping Behaviour as a Low-Ability Cue', *Journal of Educational Psychology,* Vol. 82, 1990:7–14.

Grass, G. *Two States – One Nation: The Case against German Reunification.* London: Secker and Warburg, 1990.

Grund- und Strukturdaten 1994/95 and 1995/96. Bonn: Bundesministerium für Bildung, Wissenschaft, Forschung und Technologie, December, 1995 and 1996.

Grundmann, S., Luft, H., Reinhold, O., Schmollack, J., Schönefeld, R., Steinbach, H. and Tschacher, G. *Staatsbürgerkunde, Klasse 10.* Berlin: Volk und Wissen, 1989.

Gruner, Petra, 'Nun dachte ich, jetzt fängt's neu an, nun soll's sozial werden …', *Zeitschrift für Pädagogik,* Vol. 41, No. 6, 1995:943–57.

———. *Angepaßt oder mündig? Briefe an Christa Wolf im Herbst 1989.* Berlin: Volk und Wissen, 1990.

Haedayet, W.-F. 'Offener Unterricht – Pädagogischer Mythos oder unterrichtspraktischer Antwort auf eine veränderte soziale Wirklichkeit?', *Pädagogik und Schulalltag,* Vol. 50, No. 3, 1995:314–23.

Hager, Carol J. 'Environmentalism and Democracy in the Two Germanies', *German Politics,* Vol. 1, No. 1, 1992:95–108.

Hall, K.-H. 'Die Hochschulgesetzgebung der neuen Länder als Rahmenbedingung der Neustrukturierung', in R. Mayntz (ed.), 1994a:165–90.

'Hamburger Abkommen' zur Vereinheitlichung auf dem Gebiet des Schulwesens, in E. Jobst (ed.), 1991:124–30.

Händle, Christa. 'Automisierung oder neue Bürokratisierung in der Schulentwicklung?', in M. Hempel (ed.), 1996a:47–60.

———. 'Doppelqualifikation von LehrerInnen in Ost und West', in Astrid Kaiser (ed.), 1996b:115–60.

———. 'Formelle und informelle Bildung von Lehrerinnen für berufliche Aufgaben', in Dietlind Fischer et al. (ed.), 1996c:97–112.

———. 'Gudrun K.: Kulturelles Kapital einer Lehrerin mit Ostbiographie', *Neue Sammlung,* Vol. 36, No. 4, 1996:607–26.

———. 'Wir sind nun mal die Verlierer …?: Paradoxien in der Fort- und Weiterbildung von LehrerInnen in Berlin', in A. Meier and Ursula Rabe-Kleberg, 1993:117–35.

Hanisch, H. and Pollack, D. 'Der Religionsunterricht im Freistaat Sachsen: eine empirische Untersuchung zur Akzeptanz eines neuen Unterrichtsfaches', *Zeitschrift für Evangelische Ethik*, No. 39, 1995:243–48.

Hartmer, M. 'Die Abwicklung der Übernahme: Die neuen Länder auf der Suche nach einem Konzept für die personelle Erneuerung', *Mitteilungen des Hochschulverbands*, 1/1991:4–6.

Hempel, Marlies (ed.). *Geschlecht und Schule*. Potsdam: Frauen-Prisma, 1996.

Henkys, R. *Die evangelischen Kirchen in der DDR: Beiträge zu einer Bestandaufnahme*. Munich, 1982.

Hepp, R.D. and Kergel, Rita Sabine. 'Verortungen: Diskurse im Spannungsfeld des Arbeitslosigkeitsprozesses', *Berliner Debatte*, 1/1995:19–31.

Hill, A.D. (ed.). *International Perspectives on Geographic Education*. Boulder: Center for Geographic Education, University of Colorado at Boulder, 1992.

Himmelstein, K. and Keim, W. (eds). *Erziehungswissenschaft im deutsch-deutschen Vereinigungsprozeß, Jahrbuch für Pädagogik 1992*. Frankfurt am Main: Peter Lang, 1992.

Hoffmann, A. and Chalupsky, J. 'Zwischen Apathie und Aufbruchseuphorie: Lehrerinnen der DDR in der Übergangszeit. Ergebnisse einer empirischer Untersuchung', *Pädagogik und Schule in Ost und West*, No. 2, 1991:114–9.

Hoffmann-Lange, Ursula (ed.). *Jugend und Demokratie in Deutschland: DJI-Jugendsurvey 1*. Opladen: Leske and Budrich, 1995.

Hofmann, J., Soder, H. with Tiedtke, M., Heuer, Jutta and Bartczak, Ines (eds). *Diskussionspapiere der Enquête-Kommission 'Zukünftige Bildungspolitik-Bildung 2000' des 11. Deutschen Bundestages: Inhaltsanalytische Untersuchung von im Zeitraum Oktober 1989 bis März 1990 außerhalb institutionalisierter Strukturen entstandenen bildungskonzeptionellen Vorstellungen*. Bonn: Vorsitzender des Ausschusses für Bildung und Wissenschaft des Deutschen Bundestages Bundeshaus, 1991.

Honecker, M. *Unser sozialistisches Bildungssystem – Wandlungen, Erfolge, neue Horizonte. IX. Pädagogischer Kongreß der DDR. 13. bis 15. Juni 1989*. Berlin: Dietz, 1989.

Hörig, K. E. and Schomann, T. 'Die Entwicklung der studentischen Mitwirkung in Ostdeutschland', *hochschule ost*, Vol. 6, No. 1, 1997:145–52.

Hörner, W. *Bildung und Wissenschaft in der DDR: Ausgangslage und Reform bis Mitte 1990*. Bonn: Bundesminister für Bildung und Wissenschaft, 1990a.

———. 'Polytechnischer Unterricht in der DDR und Arbeitslehre in der BRD', in O. Anweiler et al. (eds), 1990b:218–32.

Horst, Ines. 'Lehrerbildung im Urteil ost- und westdeutscher Studierender', *Pädagogik und Schulalltag*, Vol. 49, No. 1, 1994:119–25.

Huber, P.M. 'Personelle Kontinuität an den Hochschulen der neuen Länder?' Jena, Unpublished paper, 7pp.

Huber, W. 'Religion und Ethik in der Schule.' Unpublished paper (n.d.).

———. 'Wenn der Staat selbst die Wertevermittlung in die Hand nimmt', *Frankfurter Rundschau*, 26.1.1996:18.

Hughes Hallett, A.J. and Ma, Y. 'East Germany, West Germany, and their Mezzogiorno: A Parable for European Economic Integration', *The Economic Journal*, 103, 1993:416–428.

Hughes Hallett, A.J., Ma, Y. and Melitz, J. 'Unification and the Policy Predicament in Germany, *Economic Modelling*, Vol. 13, 1996:519–44.

Hurrelmann, K. 'Plädoyer für eine Schulreform, in der Gymnasien und Gesamtschulen die Basisformen bilden: Zwei-Wege-Modell', in Johann Jakobs Stiftung (ed.), 1992:39–62.

———. 'Politik für Kinder und Jugendliche in den beiden deutschen Staaten', *Pädagogik und Schule in Ost und West*, Vol. 2, No. 2, 1990:79–85.

———. 'Zwei Schulen für das eine Deutschland', in *Die Zeit*, No. 45, 1991.

IAB – Institut für Arbeitsmarkt- und Berufsforschung. Kurzbericht. 'Die Entwicklung der Ausbildungsleistungen von Treuhand- und ex-Treuhandunternehmen', No. 5/27.5.1993.

IPOS – Institut für praxisorientierte Sozialforschung, 'Jugendliche und junge Erwachsene in Deutschland', Mannheim, 1993.

Jahn, Heidrun. 'Die Strukturierung der ostdeutschen Hochschullandschaft', in *Gewerkschaft Erziehung und Wissenschaft, Materialien und Dokumente Hochschule und Forschung*. Frankfurt am Main: Gewerkschaft für Erziehung und Wissenschaft, 1997. Pre-publication copy.

———. 'Entwicklung der Fachhochschulen im tertiären Bereich: Innovative Ansätze in den neuen Bundesländern und Berlin', *Das Hochschulwesen*, Vol. 41, No. 6, 1993:257–63.

———. 'The Fachhochschule – A Response to the Challenges in East Germany?', in *Changes in Higher Education in Central European Countries*. Warsaw: IfiS, 1994.

Jahnke, T. 'Forschen und Lehren – Nach guter Lehre forschen: Das Potsdamer Modell der Lehrerbildung', *hochschule ost*, Vol. 5, No. 1, 1996:17–27.

Jahre, T. 'Bildungsreform in Sachsen?', *Pädagogik und Schulalltag*, Vol. 51, No. 2, 1996:167–73.

Jobst, E. *Das neue deutsche Recht für Schule, Berufsausbildung und Hochschule*. Bad Honnef: K.H. Bock, 1991.

Johann Jakobs Stiftung (ed.). *Jugend, Bildung und Arbeit*. Zürich, 1992.

Johnson, N. 'The Federal Constitutional Court: Facing up to the Strains of Law and Politics in the New Germany', *German Politics*, Vol. 3, No. 3, 1994:131–48.

Joppke, C. 'Why Leipzig? "Exit" and "Voice" in the East German Revolution', *German Politics*, Vol. 2, No. 3, 1993:392–414.

Jugendweihe – Zeitschrift für Mitarbeiter und Helfer, 8 November 1989.

Jung, B. *Evangelisches Schulzentrum Leipzig: Versuch einer Standortbestimmung*. Leipzig: Unimedia, 1996.

Jung, M. 'Wie wirksam, wie unwirksam ist unsere Lehrerbildung? Daten – Fakten – Desiderate', SEMINAR: Lehrerbildung und Schule, Qualität der Lehrer/innen-Ausbildung, Bundesarbeitskreis der Seminar- und Fachleiter/innen (BAK). Rinteln: Merkur, No. 1, 1997:7–34.

Kaiser, A. (ed.). *Frauenstärke ändern Schule*. Bielefeld: Kleine, 1996.

Kaschuba, W., Scholze, T. and Scholze-Irrlitz, Leonore (eds). *Alltagskultur im Umbruch*. Weimar, Cologne, Wien: Böhlau, 1996.

Kell, A. (Hrsg.) *Erziehungswissenschaft im Aufbruch*. Weinheim: Deutscher Studienverlag, 1994.

————. 'Berufliche Schulen in der Spannung von Bildung und Beruf', (Gekürzter Vortrag anläßlich der Namengebung HERWIG-BLANKERTZ-SCHULE für die beruflichen Schulen des Landkreises Kassel in Hofgeismar/Wolfshagen am 22. September 1995), *Zeitschrift für Berufs- und Wirtschaftspädagogik*, Vol. 92, No. 1, 1996.

————. 'Rahmenbedingungen der Berufsbildung', in R. Arnold and A. Lipsmeier (eds), 1995:369–97.

Kelsen, H. 'The International Status of Germany to be Established Immediately upon Termination of the War', *American Journal of International Law*, 38, 1944.

Kiel, S. '"Hochschulerneuerung" an ostdeutschen Hochschulen aus dem Blickwinkel heutiger Verantwortungsträger: Versuch eines Vergleichs und einer kritischen Sichtung', *hochschule ost*, Vol. 5, No. 2, 1996:155–70.

Klapper, J. 'German Unification and the Teaching of Modern Languages: The Methodological Legacy of the GDR', *Comparative Education*, Vol. 28, No. 3, 1992:235–47.

Klein-Allermann, Elke, Kracke, Bärbel, Noack, P. and Hofer, M. 'Micro- and Macrosocial Conditions of Adolescents' Aggressiveness and Antiforeigner Attitudes', *New Directions for Child Development*, No. 70, 1995.

Klemm, K. and Pfeiffer, H. 'Die Berufsschule: Der vergessene Teil des Dualen Systems', in H.-G. Rolff et al. (eds), 1990: 81–104.

Klemm, K., Böttcher, W. and Weegen, M. *Bildungsplanung in den neuen Bundesländern*. Weinheim and Munich: Juventa, 1992.

Klingberg, L. 'Ostliches und Westliches in der deutschen Didaktik-Landschaft: Anmerkungen zum deutsch-deutschen Didaktiker-Dialog', *Pädagogik und Schulalltag*, Vol. 51, No. 4, 1996:503–8.

Klinzing, K. 'Der ostdeutsche akademische Mittelbau auf dem Weg ins vereinigte Deutschland', *hochschule ost*, Vol. 3, No. 4, 1993:61–80.

Kloas, P.W. 'Go West? Eine Studie zu den beruflichen Plänen junger Erwachsener in den neuen Bundesländern', *Berufsbildung im Wissenschaft und Praxis*, Vol. 22, No. 2, 1993:8–10.

Kluge, B. 'Verwirklichte Jenaplan-Pädagogik in Thüringen', *Pädagogik und Schulalltag*, Vol. 50, No. 3, 1995:347–61.

Köhler, R. 'Erfahrungen des Kampfes der revolutionären Arbeiterbewegung für die Brechung des Bildungsmonopols der Ausbeuterklassen stehen im Zentrum der Hochschulgeschichtsforschung der DDR', in *Zentralinstitut für Hochschulbildung (ZHB)*, 1989:6–11.

Kolinsky, Eva (ed.). *Between Hope and Fear: Everyday Life in Post-Unification East Germany. A Case Study of Leipzig*. Keele: Keele University Press, 1995.

————. *Women in Contemporary Germany: Life Work and Politics*. Oxford: Berg, 1989.

Kosing, A. *Wozu lebe ich?* Berlin: Akademie für Gesellschaftswissenschaften beim ZK der SED: Dietz, 1983.

Kossakowski, A. 'Abwicklung der Akademie der Pädagogischen Wissenschaften', in K. Himmelstein and W. Keim (eds), 1992:87–101.

Krappmann, L. 'Reicht der Situationsansatz?', *Neue Sammlung*, Vol. 35, No. 4, 1995:109–24.

Krejci, J. *Social Structure in Divided Germany*. London: Croom Helm, 1976.

Krekel-Eiben, Elisabeth M. and Ulrich, J.G. 'Berufschancen von Jugendlichen in den neuen Bundesländern', *Aus Politik und Zeitgeschichte*, Vol. 43, B19, 1993:13–19.

Kretzer, H. 'Erste und Zweite Phase der Lehrerbildung in der Wahrnehmung von Studienreferendaren und Lehramtsanwärtern', SEMINAR: Lehrerbildung und Schule, Qualität der Lehrer/innen-Ausbildung, Bundesarbeitskreis der Seminar- und Fachleiter/innen (BAK), Rinteln: Merkur, No. 1, 1997:35–50.

Kroymann, Irmgard and Lübke, S.O. *Berufliche Bildung in den neuen Bundesländern*. Cologne: Bund-Verlag, 1992.

Krüger, H.-H. 'Aufwachsen zwischen Staat und Markt: Veränderungen des Kinderlebens im Ost-West-Vergleich', *Zeitschrift für Pädagogik*, Beiheft 35. Weinheim und Basel: Beltz, 1996.

Krull, W. 'Im Osten wie im Westen – Nichts Neues?: Zu den Empfehlungen des Wissenschaftsrats für die Neuordnung der Hochschulen auf dem Gebiet der ehemaligen DDR', in Renate Mayntz (ed.), 1994a:205–25.

Kühn, Heidemarie, Mädchenbildung in der DDR?, *Zeitschrift für Pädagogik*, Vol. 41, No. 1, 1995:91–98.

Kuthe, M. and Schwerd, E. 'Das Forschungsprojekt "Schulstrukturwandel in Thüringen"', in H. Weishaupt, and P. Zedler (eds), 1993:33–48.

Laabs, H.J. *Pädagogisches Wörterbuch*. Berlin: Volk und Wissen, 1987.

Lammel, H.-J. 'Erfahrungen und Errungenschaften des Kampfes der deutschen revolutionären Arbeiterbewegung um die Brechung des Bildungsprivilegs an den Hochschulen', in *Zentralinstitut für Hochschulbildung (ZHB)*, 1989:12–37.

Lange, G. *Katholische Kirche im sozialistischen Staat DDR*. Berlin: Bischöfliches Ordinariat, March 1993.

Leonhardy, U. 'To be Continued: The Constitutional Reform Comissions from a Länder Perspective', *German Politics*, Vol. 3, No. 3, 1994:75–98.

Leschinsky, A. and Schnabel, K. 'Ein Modellversuch am Kreuzweg', *Zeitschrift für Pädagogik*, Vol. 42, No. 1, 1996:31–55.

Leschinsky, A. *Vorleben oder Nachdenken?* Frankfurt am Main: Diesterweg, 1996.

Lewin, K. and Heublein, U. 'Zwischen NC und der Suche nach guten Studienbedingungen: Studienanfänger zwischen Ost- und Westdeutschland', *hochschule ost*, Vol. 4, No. 4, 1995:71–90.

Liscka, I. 'Zugang zum grundständigen Studium', in Gertraude Buck-Bechler, H.-D. Schaefer, and C.-H. Wagemann (eds), 1997:251–62.

Little, T.D., Oettingen Gabriele, Stetsenko, Anna and Baltes, P.B. 'Children's Action-Control Beliefs about School Performance: How do American Children Compare with German and Russian Children?', *Journal of Personality and Social Psychology*, Vol. 69, No. 4, 1995:686–700.

Lost, C. 'Der pädagogische-totalitäre Anspruch in der DDR', *Zeitschrift für Pädagogik*, Beiheft 30, 1993:139–48.

———. 'Die Kommission für deutsche Erziehungs- und Schulgeschichte 1990 – Personen, Probleme, Bilanzen', in K. Himmelstein and W. Keim (eds), 1992:119–33.

Lynn, R. *Educational Achievement in Japan: Lessons for the West*. Basingstoke: Macmillan, 1988.

Maaz, H.-J. *Der Gefühlsstau*. Munich: Knaur, 1992.

Mai, U. and Burpee, P. 'Experiencing the New Geography in East Germany', *McGill Journal of Education*, Vol. 31, No. 1, 1996:25–35.

Maier, Petra and Wenske, C. 'Personelle "Erneuerung" der Hochschulen in Mecklenburg-Vorpommern', in H. Schramm (ed.), 1993:31–34.

Marsh, D. *Germany and Europe*. London: Heinemann, 1994.

Maser, W. *Genossen beten nicht. Kirchenkampf des Kommunismus*. Cologne, 1963.

Mauthe, Anne and Pfeiffer, H. 'Schülerinnen und Schüler gestalten mit – Entwicklungen schulischer Partizipation und Vorstellung eines Modellversuchs', in H.-G. Rolff et al. (eds), 1996:221–259.

Mayntz, Renate (ed.). *Aufbruch und Reform von oben: Ostdeutsche Universitäten im Transformationsprozeß*. Frankfurt am Main: Campus, 1994a.

Mayntz, Renate. *Deutsche Forschung im Einigungsprozeß: Die Transformation der Akademie der Wissenschaften der DDR 1989 bis 1992*. Frankfurt am Main: Campus, 1994b.

Meier, A. and Rabe-Kleberg, Ursula (eds). *Weiterbildung, Lebenslauf, sozialer Wandel*. Neuwied and Berlin: Luchterhand, 1993.

Melzer, W. and Stenke, Dorit. 'Schulentwicklung und Schulforschung in den ostdeutschen Bundesländern', in H.-G. Rolff et al. (eds), 1996:307–38.

Merkens, H., Classen, Gabriele and Bergs-Winkels, Dagmar. 'Familiale und schulische Einflüsse auf die Konstitutierung des Selbst in der Jugendarbeit', *Zeitschrift für Pädagogik*, Vol. 43, No. 1, 1997:93–112.

Mertens, D. 'Das Konzept der Schlüsselqualifikation als Flexibilisierungsinstrument', in E. Nuissl et al. (eds), 1988:33–46.

Mertens, L. 'Studentinnen in der DDR – erst gefördert, dann vom Staat benachteiligt', *hochschule ost*, Vol. 5, No. 3, 1996:102–13.

Micropaedia, 15th Edition of the Encyclopaedia Britannica, Vol. 2, Chicago: University of Chicago Press, 1992:138.

Moeller, M.L. and Maaz, H.-J. *Die Einigkeit beginnt zu zweit: Eine deutsch-deutsches Zwiegespräch*. Berlin: Rowohlt, 1991.

Mohrmann, Ute 'Festhalten am Brauch: Jugendweihe vor und nach der "Wende"', in W. Kaschuba et al. (eds), 1996:197–213.

Motschmann, S. plus 20 Co-workers. *Heimatkunde*. Berlin: Volk und Wissen, 1985.

MPI – Max Planck Institut für Bildungsforschung. *Das Bildungswesen in der Bundesrepublik: Strukturen und Entwicklungen im Überblick*. Reinbek bei Hamburg: Rowohlt, 1994.

Münch, J. 'Probleme der Lehrlingsausbildung in der Bundesrepublik Deutschland', in O. Anweiler et al. (eds), 1990:316–25.

Nature, 'Deutsche Akademiker finden Karriereboom im Osten', in *hochschule ost*, Jul./Aug. 1994: 45–46.

Nickel, Hildegard Maria 'Frauen in der DDR', *Aus Politik und Zeitgeschichte*, B16–17, 1990:39–45.

Niemz, G. *Das neue Bild des Geographieunterrichts: Frankfurter Beiträge zur Didaktik der Geographie, Band 11*. Frankfurt am Main: Institut für Didaktik der Geographie, 1989.

————. 'Trends in German Geography Education for the Turn of the Millennium', *International Journal of Social Education*, Vol. 10, No. 2, 1996:42–52.

Niemz, G. and Stoltman, J.P. 'Inter Geo II: The Development and Field Trials of an International Geography Test', in A.D. Hill (ed.), 1992:3–29.

Ninth Youth Report. See BFSFJ, 1994.

Nipkow, K.E. 'Der pädagogische Umgang mit dem weltanschaulich-religiösen Pluralismus auf dem Prüfstein', *Zeitschrift für Pädagogik*, Vol. 42, No. 1, 1996:57–70.

Noack, A. 'Die evangelische Studentengemeinde in der DDR im Blickfeld des MfS', *hochschule ost*, Vol. 5, No. 1, 1996:81–94.

Noack, P., Hofer, M. and Youniss, J. (eds). *Psychological Responses to Social Change*. Berlin: de Gruyter, 1995.

Nuissl, E., Siebert, H. and Weinberg, J. *Literatur und Forschungsreport Weiterbildung*. Münster, 1988.

Oberliesen, R. *Schule Ost – Schule West: Ein deutsch-deutscher Reformdialog*. Hamburg: Bergmann and Helbig, 1992.

Oesterreich, D. 'Jugend in der Krise', *Aus Politik und Zeitgeschichte*, Vol. 43, B19, 1993:21–31.

Oettingen Gabriele, Little, T.D., Lindenberger, U. and Baltes, P.B. 'Causality, Agency and Control Beliefs in East versus West Berlin Children: A Natural Experiment on the Role of Context', *Journal of Personality and Social Psychology*, Vol. 66, No. 3, 1994:579–95.

Oettingen, G. 'Cross-cultural Perspectives on Self-Efficacy', in A. Bandura (ed.), 1995:149–76.

Offe, C. 'German Reunification as a "Natural Experiment"', *German Politics*, Vol. 1, No. 1, 1992:1–12.

Olbertz, J.H. 'Es schreibt sich besser auf unbeschriebenen Blättern ...' *Das Hochschulwesen*, Vol. 44, No. 1, 1996:28–37.

Oswald, H. and Krappmann, L. 'Social Life of Children in a Former Bipartite City', in P. Noack, M. Hofer and J. Youniss (eds), 1995:163–85.

Otto, H. 'Vom Regen in die Traufe: Bei der Übernahme der Lehrerausbildung aus dem Westen haben die neuen Länder auf ein krisenhaftes Auslaufmodell gesetzt', *hochschule ost*, Vol. 5, No. 2, 1996:172–8.

Partridge, P.H. 'Freedom', in *The Enclyclopaedia of Philosophy, Vols 3 and 4, Epictetus to Logic*. New York: Collier and Macmillan, 1967.

Pasternak, P. Editorial, *hochschule ost*, Vol. 6, No. 1, 1997:1.

Peters, Angelika. 'Ist Brandenburg verpflichtet, Religion im Stundenplan zu verankern?', *Frankfurter Rundschau*, 15.2.1996.

Peto, W. *Berlin: Die Mauer – Aufbau, Zerfall, Abriß: Ungewohnte Perspektiven einer nicht mehr vorhandenen Grenze*. Frankfurt am Main: pmi Verlag, 1997.

Phillips, D. (ed.). *Lessons of Cross-Cultural Comparison in Education*. Wallingford: Triangle, 1992.

Phillips, D. and Kaser, M. (eds). *Education and Economic Change in Eastern Europe and the Former Soviet Union*. Wallingford: Triangle, 1992.

Phillips, D. 'Transitions and Traditions: Educational Developments in the New Germany in their Historical Context', in D. Phillips and M. Kaser (eds), 1992:7–14.

Plath, M. and Weishaupt, H. 'Die Regelschule in Thüringen: Innenansichten von drei Schulen', *Die Deutsche Schule*, Vol. 87, No. 3, 1995:363–77.

PLIB – Pädagogisches Landesinstitut Brandenburg. *Der Brandenburger Modellversuch zum Lernbereich 'Lebensgestaltung-Ethik-Religion' (LER) Abschlußbericht der Projektgruppe, parts 1 and 2*. Prepared by C. Lange, P. Kriesel and G. Eggers. Ludwigsfelde, April 1995.

Potsdam – University of. 'Die zweite Stufe des Potsdamer Modells', Potsdam, 17.5.95.

Prins, G. (ed.). *Spring in Winter: The 1989 Revolutions*. Manchester and New York: Manchester University Press, 1990.

Pritchard, R.M.O. 'German Classrooms Observed: A Foreigner's Perspective', *Oxford Review of Education*, Vol. 18, No. 3, 1992:213–25.

———. 'Mergers and Linkages in British Higher Education', *Higher Education Quarterly*, Vol. 47, No. 2, 1993:79–102.

———. *The End of Elitism? The Democratisation of the West German University System*. Oxford and New York: Berg, 1990.

———. 'The German Dual System', *Comparative Education*, Vol. 28, No. 1, 1992:131–43.

———. 'The Struggle to Democratise German Teacher Education', *Oxford Review of Education*, Vol. 19, No. 3, 1993:355–71.

Protze, N. 'Umweltprobleme in den neuen Bundesländern als Thema im Geographieunterricht', *Geographie und Schule*, Vol. 6, 1994:33–35.

Prützel-Thomas, Monika. 'The Property Question Revisited: The Restitution Myth', *German Politics*, Vol. 4, No. 3, 1995:112–27.

Railton, N.M. 'Youth and the Church in East Germany.' Unpublished Ph.D. thesis, University of Dundee, 1986.

Ramm, T. 'Die Bildungsverfassungen', in O. Anweiler et al. (eds), 1990:34–56.

Rase-Schefler, Kerstin. 'West-Lehrerin im Ost-Gymnasium', in E. Rösner et al., 1996:100–2.

Regional Trends 23, Government Statistical Service, London. London: HMSO, 1988, 1990, 1991 (3 separate volumes).

Reich, J. 'Reflections on Becoming an East German Dissident', in G. Prins (ed.), 1990:65–98.

Reiche, S. 'Hochschulaufbau in Brandenburg', *hochschule ost*, Vol. 6, No. 1, 1997:86–100.

Renck, L. 'Eine Sozialwirklichkeit, die keine Volkskirche kennt', *Deutsche Lehrerzeitung Special* 49/50, 12 December 1996:22.

Ress, G. 'The Constitution and the Maastricht Treaty: Between Cooperation and Conflict', *German Politics*, Vol. 3, No. 3, 1994: 47–74.

Rippl, Susanne and Boehnke, K. 'Authoritarianism: Adolescents from East and West Germany and the United States Compared', *New Directions for Child Development*, No. 70, 1995:57–70.

Roeder, P.M. 'Der föderalisierte Bildungsrat', *Zeitschrift für Pädagogik*, Vol. 43, No. 1, 1997:131–48.

Rolff, H.-G., Bauer, K.-O., Klemm, K. and Pfeiffer, H. (eds). *Jahrbuch der Schulentwicklung Band 6: Daten, Beispiele und Perspektiven*. Weinheim und München: Juventa, Institut für Schulentwicklungsforschung, 1990.

————. *Jahrbuch der Schulentwicklung Band 7: Daten, Beispiele und Perspektiven.* Weinheim und München: Juventa, Institut für Schulentwicklungsforschung, 1992.

Rolff, H.-G., Bauer, K.-O., Klemm, K., Pfeiffer, H. and Schulz-Zander, R. (eds). *Jahrbuch der Schulentwicklung Band 8: Daten, Beispiele und Perspektiven.* Weinheim und München: Juventa, Institut für Schulentwicklungsforschung, 1994.

Rolff, H.-G., Bauer, K.-O., Klemm, K. and Pfeiffer, H. (eds). *Jahrbuch der Schulentwicklung Band 9: Daten, Beispiele und Perspektiven.* Weinheim und München: Juventa, Institut für Schulentwicklungsforschung, 1996.

Rosenholtz, S.J. and Rosenholtz, S.H. 'Classroom Organisation and the Perception of Ability', *Sociology of Education*, Vol. 54, 1981:132–40.

Roskin, M.G. *The Rebirth of East Europe.* Englewood Cliffs, N.J.: Prentice Hall, 1994 (first publ. 1991).

Rösner, E., Böttcher, W. and Brandt. H. (eds). *Lehreralltag-Alltagslehrer: Authentische Berichte aus der Schulwirklichkeit.* Weinheim und Basel: Beltz, 1996.

Rotenhan, E. von. *Krise und Chance der Fachhochschule.* Munich: Kaiser, 1980.

Rühle, J. and Holzweißig, G. *13. August 1991: Die Mauer von Berlin.* Cologne: Deutschland Archiv, 1991.

Russell, B. *Sceptical Essays.* London: Allen and Unwin, 1977 (first publ. 1935).

Rust, V.D. 'Transformation of History Instruction in East German Schools', *Compare*, Vol. 23, No. 1, 1993:205–17.

Rust, V.D. and Rust, Diane. *The Unification of German Education.* New York: Garland, 1995.

Rüttgers, J. 'Hochschulen für das 21. Jahrhundert.' Bonn: Bundesminister für Bildung, Wissenschaft, Forschung und Technologie, n.d.

Schäfer, H.-P. 'Berufsorientierung und Berufsberatung', in O. Anweiler et al. (eds), 1990a:299–306.

————. 'Das System der Berufsbildung in der DDR', in O. Anweiler et al. (eds), 1990b:312–5.

————. 'Definition und Entwicklung der Berufsbildung in der DDR', in O. Anweiler et al. (eds), 1990c:282–4.

————. 'Probleme der Lehrlingausbildung in der DDR', in O. Anweiler et al. (eds), 1990d:316–25.

————. 'Vollzeitschulische Ausbildungsgänge (Fachschulen) in der DDR', in O. Anweiler et al. (eds), 1990e:340–6.

Schäuble, W. *Der Vertrag: Wie ich über die deutsche Einheit verhandelte.* Stuttgart: Deutsche-Verlags-Gesellschaft, 1991.

Scheilke, Chr. Th. 'Religion in der Schule einer pluralen Gesellschaft: Zusammenfassung des Votums bei der Anhörung vom Bündnis 90/Die Grünen 'Zur Zukunft des Religionsunterrichts' am 14. Mai 1996 im Berliner Abgeordnetenhaus.' Münster: Comenius-Institut, 1996.

Schell, M. and Kalinka, W. *Stasi und kein Ende.* Bürgerkomitee Leipzig: Forum Verlag Leipzig, 1991.

Schiedermair, H. 'Deutsches Hochschulwesen der Gegenwart – eine Bestandaufnahme', in C. Flämig et al., 1996:37–120.

Schmidt, G. 'Lehrerbildung und Lehrerschaft in der DDR', in O. Anweiler et al., 1990:526–38.

Schmidt, H. 'Die Integrationskraft der dualen Berufsbildung muß sich bewahren', *Berufsbildung im Wissenschaft und Praxis*, Vol. 22, No. 2, 1993:1–2.

Schmitz, M. *Wendestreß: Die psychosozialen Kosten der deutschen Einheit.* Berlin: Rowohlt, 1995.

Schnabel, K. 'Ausländerfeindlichkeit bei Jugendlichen in Deutschland: eine Synopse empirischer Befunde seit 1990', *Zeitschrift für Pädagogik*, Vol. 39, No. 5, 1993:799–822.

Schnabel, K., Baumert, J. and Roeder, P.M. 'Zum Wandel des Schulsystems in den neuen Bundesländern', *Neue Sammlung*, Vol. 36, No. 4, 1996:531–44.

Schneider, M.C. 'Chancengleichheit oder Kaderauslese?', *Zeitschrift für Pädagogik*, Vol. 41, No. 6, 1995:959–83.

Schneider, N.F. *Familie und private Lebensführung in West- und Ostdeutschland.* Stuttgart: Ferdinand Enke Verlag, 1994.

Schnitzer, K. 1995. See Fourteenth Social Survey.

Schober, Karen. 'Der schwierige Übergang zum Dualen System: Berufsbildung in den neuen Bundesländern.' Nürnberg: Institut für Arbeitsmarkt- und Berufsforschung (IAB) der Bundesanstalt für Arbeit, No. 3, 1994.

———. 'Junge Frauen beim Übergang vom Bildungs- ins Beschäftigungssystem: Die Lage in den neuen Bundesländern', in *Arbeitsmarkt für Frauen 2000 – Ein Schritt vor oder ein Schritt zurück?* Nürnberg: Institut für Arbeitsmarkt- und Berufsforschung (IAB) der Bundesanstalt für Arbeit, 1994:523–66.

———. 'Von der Lehrstellenbilanz zum Lehrstellenmarkt – Auswirkungen der "Wende" auf das Ausbildungsverhalten von Jugendlichen und Betrieben und auf die Strukturen beruflicher Erstausbildung', in R. Jansen (ed.), 1995:33–68.

Schober, Karen and Rauch, Angela. 'Gute Noten trotz schwieriger Arbeitsmarktlage.' Nürnberg: Institut für Arbeitsmarkt- und Berufsforschung (IAB) der Bundesanstalt für Arbeit, 13.7.1995.

Schramm, Hilde (ed.). *Hochschule im Umbruch: Zwischenbilanz Ost: Orientierungen und Expertenwissen zum Handeln.* Berlin, Gewerkschaft für Erziehung und Wissenschaft: BasisDruck, 1993.

Schreier, G. 'Reforming Teacher Training and the School System', *World Affairs*, Vol. 154, No. 1, 1991:36–40.

Schurer, B. 'Lehr- und lernmethodische Neuorientierungen', in O. Anweiler et al. (eds), 1990:357–62.

Schwarz, Gabriele. 'Ostdeutsche Ausbilder bewähren sich im Dualen System', *Berufsbildung*, Vol. 47, No. 21, 1993:20–21.

Schwerin, E. 'Die Bildungsreform in der DDR als gesamtgesellschaftlicher Prozeß', *Pädagogik und Schule in Ost und West*, Vol. 2, No. 2, 1990:68–75.

Simon, D. 'Hochschulerneuerung Ost mit Amtskettchen und Talaren', in Deutsche Presse-Agentur: Dienst für Kulturpolitik, 11.09.1995.

Skinner, E.A., Chapman, M. and Baltes, P.B. 'Children's Beliefs about Control, Means-Ends and Agency: Developmental Differences During Middle Childhood', *International Journal of Behavioral Development*, Vol. 11, 1988a:369–88.

———. 'Control, Means-Ends and Agency Beliefs: A New Conceptualisation and Its Measurement During Childhood, *Journal of Personality and Social Psychology*, Vol. 54, 1988b:117–33.

————. 'The Control, Agency and Means-Ends Beliefs Interview', *Materialien aus der Bildungsforschung, Nr. 31.* Berlin: Max-Planck-Institut, 1988c.

Skrypietz, I. 'Militant Right-Wing Extremism in Germany, *German Politics*, Vol. 3, No. 1, 1994:133–40.

Sommer, Ute, 'Freiraum geben, denn Kinder können einander viel lehren', *Märkische Allgemeine Zeitung*, 26.04.1995:6.

Southern, D. 'Restitution or Compensation: The Property Question', *German Politics*, Vol. 2, No. 3, 1993:436–49.

————. 'The Constitutional Framework of the New Germany', *German Politics*, Vol. 1, No. 1, 1992:31–49.

Spiegel, 13 November 1989; 9 March 1990:134–135.

Stafette: Monatsschrift der evangelischen Jugend, Weißensee, 1947–Jan. 1953.

Starck, C. 'The Constitutionalisation Process of the New Länder: A Source of Inspiration for the Basic Law', *German Politics*, Vol. 3, No. 3, 1994:118–30.

Steedman, Hilary. 'The Economics of Youth Training in Germany', *The Economic Journal*, No. 103, 1993:1279–91.

Steinert, W. 'Wahl zwischen gleichberechtigten Alternativen: Der Weg zu verantwortlicher Werteerziehung und Bildung in der Schule', *Deutsche Lehrerzeitung Special*, 49/50, 12 December 1996:21.

Stenke, D., Stump, A. and Melzer, W. *Die Mittelschule im Transformationsprozeß des sächsichen Bildungswesens.* Dresden: Technische Universität, Projektgruppe Schulevaluation, 1995. Unpublished manuscript.

Stevenson, P. 'Communicative Conflict in the "New" Germany: Adaptation and Change in Public Discourse', in D. Graddol and S. Thomas (eds), 1995:104–11.

Straube, P.-P. 'The Influence of the State Security Agency of the GDR on Higher Education', in *European Education: A Journal of Translations*, Spring 1996:72–83.

Szabo, S.F. *The Diplomacy of German Unification.* New York: St. Martin's Press, 1992.

Teichler, U. 'Zur Rolle der Hochschulstrukturkommissionen der Länder im Transformationsprozeß', in Renate Mayntz (ed.), 1994a:227–58.

Tosch, F. 'Projektorientiertes Lernen an Regelschulen im Land Brandenburg', *Pädagogik und Schulalltag*, Vol. 51, No. 4, 1996:520–38.

Treml, A.K. 'Ethik als Unterrichtsfach in den verschiedenen Bundesländern: eine Zwischenbilanz', in A.K. Treml (ed.). *Ethik macht Schule: Moralische Kommunikation in Schule und Unterricht.* Ethik und Unterricht Sonderheft. Frankfurt am Main: Diesterweg, 1994:18–29.

Tüffers, H. '"Abgewickelt" – und was nun? Zur Rechtslage der betroffenen Hochschullehrer', *Mitteilungen des Hochschulverbandes*, 1/1991:20–22.

————. 'Hochschullehrer bisherigen Rechts', *Forschung und Lehre*, 9/1995:505.

Uhle, A. 'Das brandenburgische Lehrfach "Lebensgestaltung- Ethik- Religionskunde" – ein verfassungskonformes Substitut für den Religionsunterricht?' *Kirche und Recht*, 1/1996:15–27.

Uhlendorff, H., Krappmann, L. and Oswald, H. 'Familie in Ost- und West-Berlin: Erziehungseinstellungen und Kinderfreundschaften', *Zeitschrift für Pädagogik*, Vol. 43, No. 1, 1997:35–53.

Ulich, K. 'Lehrer/Innen-Ausbildung im Urteil der Betroffenen: Ergebnisse und Folgerungen', SEMINAR: Lehrerbildung und Schule, Qualität der Lehrer/innen-Ausbildung, Bundesarbeitskreis der Seminar- und Fachleiter/innen (BAK), Rinteln: Merkur, No. 1, 1997:51–64.

Ulrich, J.G. and Westhoff, G. 'Ausbildung und berufliche Integration von jungen Fachkräften in den neuen Bundesländern: Ergebnisse einer Befragung von Ausbildungsabsolventen mit Lehrbeginn 1989/90', in R. Jansen (ed.), 1995:111–44.

Vom Sinn unseres Lebens. Berlin: Zentraler Ausschuß für Jugendweihe in der Deutschen Demokratischen Republik, 1983.

Waterkamp, D. 'Conclusions for Vocational Education in Germany from a Comparison with French and Dutch Vocational Education', Paper for the 39th annual conference of the Comparative and International Education Society, Boston, Mass.: 29 March–2 April 1995.

———. *Handbuch zum Bildungswesen der DDR.* Berlin: Spitz, 1987.

Weidenfeld, W. and Korte, K.-R. (eds). *Handwörterbuch zur deutschen Einheit.* Frankfurt am Main and New York: Campus, 1992.

Weiler, H.N., Mintrop, H.A. and Fuhrmann, Elisabeth. *Educational Change and Social Transformation.* London: Falmer, 1996.

Weishaupt, H. and Zedler, P. 'Aspecte der aktuellen Schulentwicklung in den neuen Ländern', in H.-G. Rolff et al. (eds), 1994:395–429.

Weishaupt, H. and Zedler, P. (eds). *Schulstrukturwandel in Thüringen: Ergebnisse einer Befragung von Schulen, Eltern und Lehrern in der Stadt Erfurt.* Erfurt: Pädagogische Hochschule, 1993.

Weltall, Erde, Mensch: Ein Sammelwerk zur Entwicklungsgeschichte von Natur und Gesellschaft. Berlin: Verlag Neues Leben, 1954.

Westle, Bettina. 'Nationale Identität und Nationalismus', in Ursula Hoffmann-Lange (ed.), 1995:195–243.

Wild, Elke and Wild, K.P. 'Familiale Sozialisation und schulische Lernmotivation', *Zeitschrift für Pädagogik,* Vol. 43, No. 1, 1997:55–77.

Winkler, G. (ed.). *Frauenreport '90.* Berlin: Verlag Die Wirtschaft, 1990.

Wolski-Prenger, F. 'Arbeitslosenarbeit in den neuen Bundesländern: Eine Bilanz nach drei Jahren Massenarbeitslosigkeit', *Aus Politik und Zeitgeschichte,* B35, 27 August 1993:41–47.

WR – Wissenschaftsrat. *Empfehlungen zur Lehrerbildung in den neuen Ländern.* Cologne: Wissenschaftsrat, 1991.

———. 'Perspektiven für Wissenschaft und Forschung auf dem Weg zur deutschen Einheit: 12 Empfehlungen.' Cologne: Wissenschaftsrat, 6.7.1990.

———. '10 Thesen zur Hochschulpolitik.' Cologne: Wissenschaftsrat, 22.1.1993.

Young, B. 'Nothing but Gloom: Women and Academia in the New Germany', *German Politics,* Vol. 2, No. 1, 1993:62–77.

Zedler, P. 'Bildungspolitische Erklärung zu Brennpunkten der Schulentwicklung in der Bundesrepublik Deutschland: Struktur, Probleme, Disparitäten, Grundbildung in der Sekundarstufe 1.' *Erziehungswissenschaft,* Vol. 3, No. 5, 1992:43–50.

Zentralarchiv für Empirische Sozialforschung an der Universität zu Köln. *Allgemeine Bevölkerungsumfrage der Sozialwissenschaften, ALLBUS 1992. Codebuch.* Cologne: ZA, 1993.

Zentralinstitut für Hochschulbildung (ZHB). *Brechung des Bildungsprivilegs der Ausbeuterklassen an der Hochschule: Erfahrungen und Probleme in Geschichte und Gegenwart.* Berlin: ZHB, 1989.

INDEX